Anonymous

A Treatise on the Coins of the Realm

In a letter to the king

Anonymous

A Treatise on the Coins of the Realm
In a letter to the king

ISBN/EAN: 9783743407541

Manufactured in Europe, USA, Canada, Australia, Japa

Cover: Foto ©ninafisch / pixelio.de

Manufactured and distributed by brebook publishing software (www.brebook.com)

Anonymous

A Treatise on the Coins of the Realm

TREATISE

ON THE

COINS OF THE REALM;

IN A

LETTER TO THE KING.

BY

CHARLES 1ST EARL OF LIVERPOOL.

LONDON:
EFFINGHAM WILSON, ROYAL EXCHANGE.

1880.

LONDON:
REPRINTED AT THE BANK OF ENGLAND;
JOHN COE, SUPERINTENDENT.

BANK OF ENGLAND,
10th *December*, 1879.

SIR,

THE discussions which have lately taken place on International Currency, and the appeals which disputants on both sides have made to the 1st Lord Liverpool's Letter to the King on Coins, have brought to light the fact that the work has been for some time virtually out of print.

We have considered that we should be rendering a service to the public by using some of the means at our disposal to republish this valuable treatise which deals exhaustively not only with metallic circulation, but also with the abuses of which the issue of Paper-Money is susceptible.

We trust that you will signify your approval of this measure by permitting us to inscribe this new edition to you in your double capacity of Chancellor of the Exchequer, and Master of Her Majesty's Mint.

We remain,

Your obedient faithful Servants,

J. W. BIRCH,
H. R. GRENFELL,
} *Governors.*

THE RIGHT HONORABLE
SIR STAFFORD NORTHCOTE, BART., M.P.

INTRODUCTION.

SIR CHARLES JENKINSON, 1st EARL OF LIVERPOOL, lived before the time when political success was deemed to be "an ill-requited slavery mocked with the name of power."

In the early part of the reign of George III. fortune as well as fame rewarded the successful candidate of official life. Neither Civil Grand Crosses of the Bath, Stars of India, or those of St. Michael and St. George, were invented; but wealth could be accumulated in politics and in the Church, as well as at the Bar.

Among the numerous claimants for Royal favour none seem to have more richly deserved it than the writer of "The Letter to the King on Coins," and few men seem to have been more eager to take advantage of every opening which presented itself to obtain it.

He was born on the 10th May, 1727.

In 1756 he published a Dissertation on "The Establishment of a Constitutional Force in England

Independent of the Standing Army," and soon after a "Discourse on the Conduct of the Government of Great Britain with respect to Neutral Nations during the Present War." No doubt these works would show great merit. But his advancement was not due to them, but to an election song during the Oxfordshire Election Petition, which disturbed the whole County of Oxford, and occupied Parliament for weeks after all public business had been completed. His friend, Sir Edward Turner, was declared duly elected, and that gentleman left no stone unturned to force Mr. Jenkinson on the notice of the Earl of Bute.

The number of his places after this date was so great that it is very difficult to verify them.

We find that, after filling several subordinate offices under Government, he became in 1772 Vice-Treasurer of Ireland; that he purchased from Mr. Fox the place of Clerk of the Pells in Ireland in 1775, and that he was raised to the post of Secretary at War in 1778.

On the fall of Lord North he set to work to compile a collection of Treaties; and in 1786, at the instance of Mr. Pitt, he was made Chancellor of the Duchy of Lancaster, President of the Board of Trade, and raised to the peerage with the title of Lord Hawkesbury.

On the decease of his relative, Sir Banks Jenkinson, he procured the lucrative place of Collector of the Customs inwards.

In 1796, he was made Earl of Liverpool. In 1799 and 1800, his son, Lord Hawkesbury, afterwards Prime Minister and 2nd Earl, was Master of the Mint. In the notices published on the death of the 1st Earl, he is stated to have been Master of the Mint, but we can find no trace of it in the records of that office.

On the 7th February, 1798, in consequence of an address from the House of Commons, the then existing Committee of Council on Coins was dissolved, and a new Committee appointed—called the Select Committee to take into consideration the Coins of the United Kingdom, and Lord Liverpool was a member of both.

It appears from the "Letter," that he proposed to the Committee "the mode in which he thought they should proceed, and the principles on which they should act," but obstructions were raised, which prevented the completion of the proposed measures. These obstructions, which were said to be due to the opposition of the Chief Justice of the Common Pleas, probably also stopped the production of the Report.

Lord Liverpool was shortly afterwards seized with illness, which confined him to his couch for more than four years, so that the "Letter to the King" was not published till 1805. He died on the 17th December, 1808, full of years and honors.

In reprinting this work, suggestions have been made to us to continue the history of Currency and Coinage down to the present day on the same plan, but it was felt that the history of the Coinage would be more properly undertaken by the authorities of the Mint; and that the great changes which, since 1805, have been made in the laws affecting the Paper Currency had already been made the subject of histories and treatises too numerous to mention.

It will be sufficient to say that the present Mint regulations are in exact conformity with Lord Liverpool's suggestions, and that the existing laws limiting the issue of Bank Notes were devised to remedy the evils to which he called public attention in his remarks on Paper Currency, so that, after years of legislative labour, his wishes are well-nigh fulfilled, that "every branch of the circulating medium should be founded on solid, wise, and *Honest* principles."

J. W. B.
H. R. G.

BANK OF ENGLAND,
    10th *December*, 1879.

TABLE OF CONTENTS.

CHAPTER		PAGE
I.	An account of the state of the Coins in 1760, and in subsequent years	1
II.	Definition of Money or Coin, and of the Metals of which it is made	9
III.	Imperfections to which, as a standard Measure or equivalent, Coins are subject	11
IV.	The necessity of making such Coins as are the principal measure of property of one Metal; and the propriety of making Coins of different Metals for the convenience of traffic	15
V.	Of the authority by which Coins are made current	21
VI.	Of the English standard of Silver and Gold	29
VII.	Of the Tower or Moneyer's Pound, and the Pound Troy	34
VIII.	Of the several ways in which Coins may be debased	37
IX.	Of debasements in the Pound in tale	39
X.	Of the first Gold Coins made in England	44
XI.	Of relative values of Gold to Silver	49
XII.	Of the great inconvenience and expence arising from the fluctuations of the relative values of Gold to Silver	63
XIII.	Of the alterations and debasements of the Coins by lowering the standard or fineness of the Metal	97
XIV.	Of profits made by exchanging Silver Coins for Gold Coins.	102

CONTENTS.

CHAPTER		PAGE
XV.	Of the reformation in the Monetary System, begun in the reign of Edward VI. and finished in that of Queen Elizabeth...	105
XVI.	Of apparent motives for the alterations and debasements made in the Coins at successive periods.......	115
XVII.	Of the principles of Coinage, and reasons for adopting or confirming them..	128
XVIII.	Variations of the value of Silver and Gold Bullion ...	166
XIX.	Precautions necessary for regulating the principles of Coinage	170
XX.	Objections stated and considered	182
XXI.	Of the Gold Coins previous to the year 1774, and of those now in circulation	194
XXII.	Of the art of Assaying, and the deficiency from standard fineness in different Reigns	202
XXIII.	Of the Silver Coins, and the deficiency of those in circulation at different periods............................	206
XXIV.	An account of several ways of calling in deficient Coins	211
XXV.	Of Spanish Dollars now in circulation.......................	216
XXVI.	Of the Copper Coins, and the relative expence of coining Gold, Silver, and Copper	218
XXVII.	Considerations on the state of the Mint....................	225
XXVIII.	Of the necessity of regulations to prevent the diminution of the weight of Coins, and of the ancient office of King's Exchanger	231
XXIX.	Of Paper currency, so far as Coins are affected by it...	245
XXX.	Conclusion	257
APPENDIX.	Containing an account of relative values of Gold to Silver among the ancient Persians, Grecians, and Romans	265

A TREATISE

ON THE

COINS OF THE REALM;

IN A

LETTER TO THE KING.

CHAPTER I.

An Account of the state of the Coins in 1760, and in subsequent years.

SIRE,

It is a part of Your Royal Functions to attend to the state of the Coins of Your Realm, and to cause every defect to be removed, which mistaken policy has introduced, or the waste of time may have wrought in them.—It is also, I well know, Your Majesty's earnest wish and inclination, on this and on every other occasion, to consult the convenience, and provide for the interests of your People.—For these reasons I have thought it my duty to address to Your Majesty a Treatise, which has for its object, to explain and elucidate the true principles of Coinage; to point out the errors committed in this respect under the authority of Your Royal Predecessors, and to suggest the best methods of preventing such evils for the future.

CHAP. 1.

AT Your Majesty's accession to the Throne in 1760, the Coins of Your Realm were in an imperfect state;—those made of Silver, in particular.—The Crown Pieces had almost wholly disappeared; though of these, there had been coined, at the general Recoinage in the reign of King William, and occasionally afterwards, a number that amounted in value to 1,553,047*l.** Great numbers of the Half Crowns had in like manner disappeared; and the number that remained was by no means adequate to the purposes for which they were intended; though, of these, there had been coined, during the before-mentioned period, a number that amounted in value to 2,329,570*l.*—Such of the Half Crowns as remained in circulation were, in a certain degree, defaced and impaired.—The Silver Coins, which were then principally current, consisted of Shillings and Sixpences. The number of Shillings, that had been coined during the same period, amounted in value to 3,232,680*l.*—The number of Sixpences and pieces of smaller denomination, so coined, amounted in value to 960,795*l.*—The Shillings had, at this time, lost almost every mark of impression, whether of head, or of reverse, or of inscription, or of graining at the edges. The Sixpences were in a worse state. I do not know of any account that was taken of their deficiency in weight at this period; but, from experiments that have since been made, I think I may assert, that the deficiency of the Shillings, even then, amounted to $\frac{1}{6}$ of their

---

* According to an estimate made by the Officers of the Mint from the accounts in their possession.

original weight; and that of the Sixpences to at least a Fourth.*

The causes of the very impaired and deficient state of these Silver Coins were, that the heavy pieces had in general been melted down or exported, and the remainder diminished by wear or by filing. A considerable profit was derived from this last practice: and very little Silver Bullion had been brought to the Mint to be coined; for the value of Silver Bullion, as estimated at Your Majesty's Mint, was lower, compared with that of Gold, than the prices at which these metals respectively sold in the market. It appears, that from the year 1717 (when Sir Isaac Newton made his report on the relative value of Gold and Silver, as estimated at the Mint, and as sold at the market) to the year 1760, the quantity of Silver, which had been brought to the Mint to be coined, amounted in value only to 584,575l. 14s. 11½d.; a very small supply indeed, for so long a period as 43 years, of that species of Coin which is most in currency, and consequently is most exposed to deficiency by wear, and to loss by other contingencies.

Though the Gold Coin was in a less imperfect state at Your Majesty's accession to the Throne, it was, even then, on the decline: and this decline increased so rapidly, that, in the year 1773, the deficiency in weight, of the Gold Coins then in circulation, was become very considerable;

* In the years 1787 and 1798, experiments were made by the Officers of the Mint, to shew the deficiency of weight, at those times, of the several sorts of Silver Coins. The results of these experiments will be stated hereafter.

so that, as soon as any new Gold Coin was brought from the Mint, these perfect pieces were exchanged, or bought up, for the old deficient Coins, and immediately melted down or exported. Indeed, the general deficiency of the Gold Coins in circulation was so notorious, that it was estimated in all our exchanges with foreign countries; and all payments to such countries were enhanced in proportion to the deficiency of these Coins: and such was, at that time, the state of the currency of this country, that there was very little of good or perfect Coin of any metal circulating in it. The evil was so great, that Government found it necessary to take this difficult subject into their immediate consideration, and to endeavour to apply a remedy to it. On this occasion I addressed a Letter to a Noble Lord, who was then Chancellor of Your Majesty's Exchequer, suggesting what appeared to me the proper remedy for this evil. I proposed, that, with a view to the general reform of the Coins of the Realm, all the deficient Gold Coin should, in the first place, be called in and recoined;—that a compensation should be made to the holders of this deficient Gold Coin, under certain limits and restrictions;—and that, after this operation had been completed, the currency of the Gold Coin should, in future, be regulated by weight as well as by tale, (which was conformable to the ancient laws of this kingdom,) and that the several pieces should not be legal tender, if they were diminished, by wearing or otherwise, below a certain weight, to be determined by Your Majesty's Proclamation. Your Majesty was pleased to approve of this advice, and to propose to Your Parliament, on the 13th day of January, 1774, the calling in and recoining all the deficient Gold Coins; and the Chancellor of Your Exchequer opened the whole of this plan to the House of Commons, who approved of the measure, which was carried into immediate execution, without any complaint, and with great success. The defects, which had previously existed in this species of Coin, were thereby removed; and the regulation, then established, of weighing the Gold Coin, has been the means of preserving it at nearly the state of perfection to which it was then brought. I need not enter into any further detail of the regulations at that time established; as they will appear in the Acts passed, and in the Proclamations issued on that occasion. It is fortunate, that, by this recoinage, the Gold Coin was brought to such a state of perfection, and that so little is now left to be performed for its farther improvement; especially at a time when we are under the necessity of entering on the more difficult task of remedying the deficiencies in the Coins made of other metals.

A difficulty then existed, and continues to exist, which must necessarily be removed, before any plan can be adopted for the improvement of the Silver Coin. I have already observed, that Gold and Silver, in reference to each other, are estimated at Your Majesty's Mint at a different value or price, than these metals are generally sold for at the market. As long as this difference subsists, both these metals will not be brought, in a sufficient quantity, to the Mint, to be coined: that metal only will be brought, which is estimated at the lowest value with reference to the other; and Coins of both metals cannot be sent into circulation at the same time, without exposing the public to a traffic of one sort of Coin against the other; by which the traders in money would make a considerable profit, to the great detriment of Your Majesty's subjects. And this mischievous practice, and the frauds committed in carrying it on, are the more to be apprehended in this country, where the Mint is free;—that is, where every one has a right to bring Gold or Silver to the Mint, to be converted into Coin; not at the charge of the person who so brings it, but of the public: for, since the 18th Charles II. ch. 3. the charge of coining Gold and Silver has been born by the public; and, contrary to the practice of most other countries, no seigneurage has been taken. To prevent this evil, it is necessary to determine, whether there must not be a standard, or superior Coin, made of one metal only; and whether the Coins made of other metals must not be made, and take their value, with reference to this standard Coin, and become subservient to it;—and, in such case, of what metal this standard Coin, to which the preeminence and preference are to be given, should be made. These are delicate and very difficult questions, which require great consideration. Many persons, of acknowledged abilities and great authority, have entertained different opinions on this subject. I will not at present farther disclose my sentiments upon it, as a considerable portion of what I intend to write will be employed in the discussion of these questions; and I wish that the opinion which I have formed should appear to be the result of the reasons I shall offer, and of the facts which I shall state:—conscious, that any opinion I may deliver cannot derive any weight from my single judgment, in opposition to the respectable authorities from which I am forced, on this occasion, to differ.

No farther measure was adopted for the improvement of the Coins of the realm, and particularly of the Silver Coin, though so very defective, for more than twenty years; when, in consequence of an Address of the House of Commons, recommending a new Copper Coinage, Your Majesty was pleased, by Your Order in Council of the 7th Feb. 1798, to appoint a Committee, who were to take into consideration the state of the Coins of this kingdom, and the present establishment and constitution of Your Majesty's Mint; and to propose such improvements, in both these respects, as might appear to them to be necessary. Your Majesty was also pleased to insert my name among those members of Your Privy Council who were to form this Committee. Having had some experience in a business of this nature, and having occasionally reflected upon it, I ventured to open to the Committee, at their first meeting, the mode in which I thought they should proceed in the execution of Your Majesty's commands; and I suggested the principles, which, in my opinion, ought to be adopted for the further improvement of the Coins of this realm. The Committee made some progress in their enquiries on this extensive and difficult subject; and, in conformity with the wishes of the House of Commons, they established the principles, on which the Copper Coin should in future be made ;— and a certain quantity of Coins, made according to these

CHAP. 1. principles, was sent into circulation, very much to the satisfaction of Your Majesty's subjects:—but obstructions were raised, which prevented the completion of this measure.—At this period, I was seized with a violent disease, which has now confined me to my house, and generally to my couch, for more than four years;—unable to hold a pen, or to turn over the leaves of a book, from which I might derive information. At intervals, however, when I have of late providentially obtained some respite from pain and extreme weakness, I have endeavoured to revise so much as I had before occasionally written;—to arrange other materials previously collected;—and to reduce the whole to a form not unfit for perusal. A Treatise, written on so abstruse and complicated a subject, by one exposed to great infirmities, must contain some repetitions, slight inaccuracies, and other imperfections. Arrived as I now am on the verge of life, I hasten to present what I have thus written, though not exempt from errors, to Your Majesty, as my last service,—if it shall deserve that name;—in grateful remembrance of the generous protection, which Your Majesty has never ceased to afford me, and of the many and great favours, which You have graciously conferred upon me.

CHAPTER II.

Definition of Money or Coin, and of the Metals of which it is made.

THE Money or Coin of a country is the standard measure, by which the value of all things, bought and sold, is regulated and ascertained;—and it is itself, at the same time, the value, or equivalent, for which goods are exchanged, and in which contracts are generally made payable.—In this last respect, Money, as a measure, differs from all others; and to the combination of the two qualities before defined, which constitute the essence of Money, the principal difficulties, that attend it, in speculation and practice, both as a measure and an equivalent, are to be ascribed. These two qualities can never be brought perfectly to unite and agree; for if Money were a measure alone, and made like all other measures of a material of little or no value, it would not answer the purpose of an equivalent. And if it is made, in order to answer the purpose of an equivalent, of a material of value, subject to frequent variations, according to the price at which such material sells at the market, it fails on that account in the quality of a standard or measure, and will not continue to be perfectly uniform and at all times the same.

<small>This definition of Money, though not always so accurately expressed, is given by all authors, from Aristotle to the present time; and there is no need, therefore, of any particular quotation.</small>

CHAP. 2.   In all civilized nations, Money has been made either of Gold, or Silver, or Copper, frequently of all three, and sometimes of a metal composed of Silver and Copper, in certain proportions, commonly called Billon. It has been found by long experience, and by the concurrent opinion of civilized nations in all ages, that these metals, and particularly Gold and Silver, are the fittest materials, of which Money can be made. Gold and Silver are perfectly homogeneous in themselves, for no physical difference can be found in any pound of pure Gold, or of pure Silver, whether the production of Europe, Asia, Africa, or America. They are divisible with the greatest accuracy into exact proportions or parts. From their value they are not too bulky for the common purposes of exchange; and in all these respects they serve better than any other material, as an equivalent. And lastly they are less consumable or subject to decay, than most other commodities.

Certain portions of these metals, with an impression struck upon them, by order of the Sovereign, as a guarantee of their purity and weight, serve as Coin.

CHAPTER III.

Imperfections to which, as a standard Measure or equivalent, Coins are subject.

COINS made of Gold, or Silver, or of any other metal, whether considered as a measure or equivalent, are however subject to the following imperfections.

As each of these metals varies in its value with respect to the commodities, for which it is exchanged, so it will vary for the same reason also in its value, in successive periods, even with respect to itself; and this variation is occasioned by the greater or less quantity that may happen to be, at different times, in the market, or in circulation. Any given quantity or weight of Gold or Silver is at present of much less value, than the same quantity or weight before the discovery of the mines of America. And if any commodity is either manufactured or produced at present, in exactly the same quantity as it was in the reign of Henry VII. when these mines were first discovered, and the demand for this commodity should be equal, a pound of Gold or Silver will not purchase as much of it now, as it would have purchased in the former period. Coins are on that account an imperfect measure, though they are made of one metal only.

But if Coins are made of two of these metals, a second imperfection is then introduced; for any two of these metals, in successive periods, vary in value with respect to each other. The value of fine Gold, compared with that of fine Silver, was rated, in the 43d of Elizabeth, at less than 11 to 1, at the English Mint. But when Guineas were first coined in 1663, the value of fine Gold, compared with that of fine Silver, was rated in the English Mint at $14\frac{331}{682}$ to 1. Guineas were then coined as 20 Shilling Pieces, and declared by the Mint indenture to be current as such. They have since been made current by Proclamation as 21 Shilling Pieces. The relative value therefore of fine Gold to fine Silver, in the Coins of this kingdom, is now as $15\frac{2859}{13640}$ to 1. And in the Mints of several foreign countries, the value of Gold, compared with that of Silver, is rated still higher. These metals will also occasionally vary in their value, even at the same time, in different countries; and Exchange Brokers, and many Bankers, are induced, on this account, to carry on a traffic in these metals, and in the Coins made of them, to their own profit, and to the loss of others.

If the Sovereign takes upon himself to determine the rate or value, at which Coins made of different metals shall at the same time pass in currency, a third imperfection is introduced into the system; for it is not possible that he should be able to pursue, with sufficient accuracy, the various fluctuations and changes, that may in a short time happen, in the relative values of these different metals. Their prices at the market will therefore frequently differ from the rate, at which he has valued them in his Coins; and when Coins made of

different metals are equally legal tender, there will of
course be two measures of property, differing occasionally
from each other. A profit will always in such case be
made by those who traffic in Coins, by exchanging that
Coin, which has the least intrinsic value, for that which
has the greatest. The debtor will find it his interest to
make his payments in the Coin made of that metal, which
is overvalued at the Mint; and such Coins, as are made
of the metal undervalued at the Mint, will always be
melted down and exported.

Another imperfection arises from the gradual wear of
the Coins made of either of these metals; for though the
materials, of which they are made, are less subject to
diminution, by daily and common use, than almost any
other commodity, they are still subject to it in a certain
degree, from friction, and sometimes from other causes.
If this diminution is considerable, the Money Jobber will
avail himself of the inequality, to which pieces of Coin of
the same denomination are, in this respect, subject; he
will collect and convert into Bullion the most weighty of
them, and make a profit thereby; and those Coins only,
which are less perfect, will be left in general circulation.

Of the four imperfections before stated, the first,
which arises from the variation in the price or value of
any one metal, in successive periods, with respect to
itself, is so inherent in the very subject, that it does not
admit of a remedy. It produces however less inconvenience than either of the other three. It chiefly affects
leases, contracts, and grants of long continuance. The
three other imperfections may in some degree be remedied.

CHAP. 3. I shall endeavour, in this Letter, humbly to submit to Your Majesty such principles of Coinage, as will tend in a great measure to remedy the second and third of these imperfections: and if Your Majesty shall be pleased, after full consideration, to approve of these principles, it will be the duty of Your Majesty's servants to propose such measures as shall make all the Coins of this kingdom correspond in future with these principles; and also to advise Your Majesty to establish such regulations as shall remedy, as far as possible, the fourth and last of the imperfections before stated.—Of this last point however I shall treat more at large in a subsequent part of this Letter.

CHAPTER IV.

The necessity of making such Coins as are the principal measure of property of one Metal; and the propriety of making Coins of different Metals for the convenience of traffic.

THE Money or Coin, which is to be the principal measure of property, ought to be made of one metal only. Such is the opinion of Sir William Petty, Mr. Locke, Mr. Harris, and of all the eminent writers on Coin. Sir William Petty says, that *one* of the metals is the only fit matter for Money. Mr. Locke calls this sort of Money the Money of Account, or the Measure of Commerce or Contracts; and he adds, "that two metals, such as Gold "and Silver, cannot be the measure of commerce both "together in any country." Mr. Harris, in his Essay on Money and Coins, delivers it as his opinion, that only one metal can be the Money, or standard measure of property and commerce in any country; and he calls this sort of Money *the Standard of Money.* These three authors assign their reasons in support of a principle in which they all concur; their reasons are, in substance, the same; and are so convincing, that the truth of this principle can no longer be controverted. I shall be obliged to have recourse to the reasons they have offered in support of their opinion, in a future part of this Letter;

_{Sir Wm. Petty's Political Anatomy of Ireland, ch. 10.}

_{See Mr. Locke's further considerations on raising the value of Money, Folio edition, 1759. vol. ii. p. 75, 76.}

_{See Mr. Harris's Essay on Money and Coins, Part I. ch. 2. sect. 7.}

so that it is not necessary to detain Your Majesty by stating them at present. The truth of this principle in fact results from the nature and uses of Money, as before described.—The before mentioned writers have assigned different names to this superior sort of Money, or Coins, by which the Coins made of other metals are to be regulated, and to which they are to be subservient. The Coins, which are to be the principal measure of property, must of course be legal tender without limitation. I shall call this superior sort of Money, or Coins, the principal Measure of Property, or Standard Coin: and having clearly defined my idea, I conceive I have a right to make use of these terms in the sense which I have given to them.

Certain, however, as the principle is, that the Money or Coins of any country, which are to be the principal measure of property, can be made of one metal only; the convenience of traffic necessarily requires, that in rich and commercial countries, there should be Coins made of several metals, adapted to the several sorts of purchases or exchanges, for which they are intended. Coins made of Gold alone, or of Silver alone, in such countries, will not answer all the purposes of traffic. Coins of Gold are not well adapted for the retail trade, in which sort of traffic the greatest number of the subjects of every country are principally concerned; and Coins of Silver are too bulky for larger payments, and are, in that respect, inconvenient.—It is necessary therefore, that in commercial countries there should be Coins made of different metals. And if the Coins, which are the principal measure of property and instrument of commerce, can only be made of one of these metals; the inferior Coins, made of other metals, must be legal tender only in a limited degree, as the Sovereign shall direct; and so far only they are the measure of property: and if they are accepted in payment for a larger sum, with the consent of the receiver, (as may sometimes be the case,) they may then be said to be the representatives of the Coins which are the principal measure of property,* and their value must be made to correspond with it, as accurately as the nature of the subject will admit. It is by adopting this rule, or principle, that the second and third of the imperfections before stated will be avoided, or at least the ill effects resulting from them will be diminished as much as possible. This is the highest state of perfection, to which any system of Coinage can, in my opinion, be brought; and it is sufficiently perfect to answer all the purposes of exchange, and commercial intercourse. But it must be confessed, that, notwithstanding all the endeavours of men of the greatest talents, and most acute understandings, such is the nature of this business, that absolute perfection and complete accuracy, in practice at least, cannot be attained.

* Such has been from the beginning the state of our legal Copper Coins, and it continues to be so at present: and such has also been the state of our present deficient Silver Coins, considered as Coins, from the passing of the Act of 14 Geo. III. ch. 42. All this will be further explained hereafter. So that this principle has already been approved by the Legislature, though it has not been carried to its proper extent.

Mr. Locke, who thought that Silver Coins were the only Money of account or measure of property, was of opinion, that Coins of Gold might be left to take their rate or value according to the relative price of Gold to Silver at the market;—and he was led to form this opinion, from observing, that in his time, Guineas, and other Gold Coins, had taken their relative value in this manner, and passed in currency accordingly. But finding afterwards that these Gold Coins had risen in their value, compared with the defective Silver Coins then in circulation, to an extravagant rate, he so far changed his former opinion, as to acknowledge "that "Gold Coin may safely have a price as well as stamp "set upon them by public authority, so that the value "be set under the market price."—And the Legislature of this kingdom acted in conformity to this opinion, when, in the reign of King William, they limited the value of Guineas by two different Acts, so that they should not pass in currency *above* a certain value therein described. They left them however to be exchanged at any rate *under* the limited value; and as the Gold Coin had risen to an extravagant value, while the Recoinage of the Silver Coins was under consideration, it actually happened, that when this Recoinage was completed, Guineas fell in their rate or value below the value limited in these Acts, without any interposition of public authority. But Mr. Harris differed in this respect from the opinion of Mr. Locke. He thought that the regulation of the value of Coins, that is, the nominal value at which they were to be legal

Chap. 4.

See Mr. Locke's Treatise above mentioned.

See Mr. Harris's Essay above mentioned. Note, p. 64.

tender, was a subject of too much importance to be entrusted, at any time, to private judgment: and it is certain, that there has generally been a clause in the Mint indentures of Your Majesty, and all Your predecessors, declaring at what nominal rate or value the Coins therein directed to be made, should be current. It is indeed hardly possible, that the people in general, particularly those of an inferior class, should be able to exercise any true judgment on the intrinsic or relative value of the metals, of which any Coins are composed; and if they were to attempt to exercise such judgment, they would be exposed to perpetual frauds and impositions from Money Jobbers and others, who understand this business better than themselves. The practice of all governments in every age has coincided with the opinion of Mr. Harris; and experience has evinced the necessity of fixing, by public authority, the rate or value of Coins of every denomination, permitted to be current as lawful Money, or legal tender.

The Coins of every kingdom or state are the measure of property and commerce, within every such kingdom or state, according to the nominal value declared, and authorised by the Sovereign, so far as they are made legal tender.

In exchanges with foreign countries, and in payments made to them, the intrinsic value of the metal, of which the Coin is made, is the only measure of property and commerce; because the authority of Sovereigns cannot extend to regulate payments made in foreign countries, where they have no power or jurisdiction.

CHAP. 4. It follows, from what has just been said, that it is necessary in this place to state, by what authority, and in what manner, Coins are made current at a certain rate or value, and become in that respect legal tender, particularly within these Your Majesty's dominions.

CHAPTER V.

Of the authority by which Coins are made current.

THERE is no doubt, that the Sovereigns of most of the kingdoms and states of Europe have enjoyed and exercised, from time immemorial, the right of declaring at what rate or value the Coins of every denomination, permitted to be current in their respective dominions, shall pass, and become, in that respect, lawful Coins, or legal tender. In this Your Majesty's kingdom, Your royal Predecessors have always enjoyed and exercised this right. Sir Matthew Hale reckons this right *inter Jura Majestatis*, and says, that it is an unquestionable prerogative of the Crown; and he treats with great ability of the nature and extent of this prerogative. In very ancient times, some of the powerful and rebellious Barons appear to have assumed this right contrary to law, "which," as Sir Matthew Hale observes, "occa-"sioned great confusion and corruption in Money and "Commerce;" and he adds, that Henry II. coming to the crown, reformed this usurpation and abuse:—in the articles of peace between Stephen and Henry, there was one, which required, that the Silver Coin* should be one and the same throughout the kingdom. In times less

See Sir Matthew Hale's Pleas of the Crown, vol. i. ch. 17. and Sir John Davis's Case of mixed Monies.

See Hoveden *sub anno* 1149. Sir M. Hale, p.199. and Wilkins's Laws of Henry II. p. 320.

Mat. Paris, p.159.

---

* There was at this time probably no Gold Coin in currency; at least, none that was made at the English Mint.

ancient, the Monarchs of this kingdom have occasionally conferred this right by special charters on divers ecclesiastical corporations, such as the Archbishops of Canterbury and York, the Bishop of Durham, &c., and on some of the most dignified Abbots. But Sir Matthew Hale adds, " that they had only the profit of Coinage " and the residence of some moneyers at their cities, &c.— " and that they had not the power of instituting either " the alloy, the denomination, or the stamp." The stamps were usually sent to them by the Treasurer and Barons of the Exchequer, by the King's command, under his Great Seal; and the Masters of these Mints, or the chief officers employed therein, were sworn to the King for the just execution of their offices. It appears, from the Coins made in these Mints, which have been preserved, that they were in general of the smaller denominations; and it is probable that the right of coining, which was given to them by these charters, was restrained to pieces of this description: but the practice of devolving this right of coining Gold and Silver to the corporations before mentioned, has never been exercised since the reign of Edward VI.

The Kings of this realm had frequently Mints of their own, not only in London, but in Southwark, Calais, Bristol, Hull, Dublin, and many other cities and towns of England and Ireland; but these were all Royal Mints, and under the immediate management and direction of the King's officers.

The right of setting a rate, or nominal value, on Coins authorised to be current, has been exercised by the Kings of this realm in two ways:

Marginal notes: See a Charter of King John allowing this privilege to Hubert, Archbishop of Canterbury. Will. Leg. Johannis, p. 355.

First. By their Mint indentures, in which a clause is inserted, declaring, at what rate or nominal value the Coins, therein ordered to be made, shall be current.

Secondly. By Proclamation.

Sir M. Hale inclines to think, that proclamations are not absolutely necessary to legitimate any Coin made at the Mint, or to make it current; but that the Mint indenture, or general usage, is in this respect sufficient evidence, except in the following cases:

First. To legitimate or make current base Coin, or such as is below the standard of sterling. He observes, that a proclamation is in this case necessary, in order to dispense with the provisions of the statute of 25 Ed. III. ch. 13. and the 9 Henry V. Session 2. ch. 6.*

Secondly. To raise any Coin already in currency to a higher denomination or extrinsic value.

Thirdly. To decry any Money already current, that is, either to reject it wholly out of circulation, or to make

* Sir William Blackstone is of opinion, that by the statute of 25 Ed. III. ch. 13. the King's prerogative seemeth not to extend to the debasing or enhancing the value of the Coin below or above the sterling value. He acknowledges, however, that Sir Matthew Hale appears to be of another opinion. But if this opinion of Sir William Blackstone is true, the King is also restrained, by the same statute, from diminishing the weight of his Gold or Silver Money. It will be seen, in the subsequent parts of this Letter, whether this interpretation of the statute was ever thought to be well founded. The Gold of all the Gold Coins now circulating in the kingdom has more alloy in it, and consequently is of a baser standard, than in 25 Ed. III. Blackstone's Commentaries, book i. ch. 7.—What is called in the text the 9 Henry V. is, in Sir Matthew Hale's Pleas of the Crown, said to be the 4th Henry V. ch. 6. which last statute has no relation to this subject: and this mistake is probably owing to the copyists or printers of Sir Matthew Hale's work.

CHAP. 5. it pass at a less rate or value than that, at which it has hitherto been current. In conformity to this rule, a proclamation was issued on the 17th day of December, 1717, reducing the value of Guineas from 21*s.* 6*d.* to 21*s.*: and there are many other instances of the same kind in preceding periods.

Fourthly. To make foreign Coin current at a determined rate or value.

The reasons, which make proclamations necessary in the two last instances, are so evident, that there is no occasion to state them.

In consequence of the great confusion introduced into the system of our Coins by the frequent debasements and alterations, that were made in them during the latter part of the reign of Henry VIII. and the reign of Edward VI. a new practice was introduced in the first year of Edward VI. of notifying to the public the rate or value of some of our Silver Coins, by placing on the face of them figures, denoting at what rate, or value, they should be taken in payment. The variety of Silver Coins, then in circulation, of the same denominations, though of different intrinsic values, made it highly convenient that the people should in this manner be apprised of the rate, or value, at which the Sovereign intended that they should be current. This practice continued in use in some of the subsequent reigns, but not in that of Elizabeth (none of whose Coins have any such figure upon them): and the same practice of placing figures on some of our Gold Coins, to denote the nominal value at which they should be current, was first introduced in the beginning of the reign of James I. But this manner of ascertaining the nominal value of our Coins has been discontinued for about a century past, except in small Silver Coins, under the value of a Sixpence, which still have figures denoting the rate, at which they are to pass, on the reverse of them. It may yet be doubted, whether this method of ascertaining the nominal value of Coins would, in the sense of Sir Matthew Hale, legitimate these Coins, especially as he wrote when this practice still subsisted, and makes no mention of it. It is, however, certainly a proof of the intention of the Sovereign in this respect, and might be left to the decision of a jury in any litigated question.

This great prerogative, however, which the Kings of this realm have immemorially enjoyed and exercised, of giving currency to the Coins made at their Mint, and sometimes to foreign Coins, at a determinate rate or value, and of enhancing them and debasing them at their pleasure, is of so important and delicate a nature, and the justice and honour of the Sovereign, as well as the interests of his people, are so deeply concerned in it, that it ought to be exercised with the greatest judgment and discretion. It appears from the ancient histories and chronicles of this country, that very serious evils have occasionally resulted from the abuse of it; and Parliament has frequently complained of these abuses, and has sometimes endeavoured, on that account, to restrain this branch of the prerogative: for in the 5th Ed. II. it was provided by the Lords Ordainers, (persons, who at that time were intrusted with the government of the kingdom,)

CHAP. 5. that no change should be made in the Coin of this realm, without the consent of the Barons in Parliament; but this, among other regulations made by these Lords Ordainers, was repealed in a subsequent year of this King's reign. Another attempt was made by the Commons in the 20th Edward III. to restrain this prerogative; but Edward III. frustrated their request, by returning an evasive answer to their petition. The frequent debasements, made by this Monarch in his Coins, induced the Commons, in the 25th year of his reign, to make a further attempt; and they petitioned that the Money of Gold and Silver then current should not be impaired in weight, or alloy. The answer returned to this petition was a promise on the part of the King, " that as soon " as a good way could be found, the Money of Gold " and Silver should be put into its ancient state." In imitation of this Monarch, the Kings of this realm, in succeeding periods, very frequently exercised this prerogative, as will be shewn in the subsequent parts of this Letter; and this prerogative was at length recognized and confirmed by an Act of Parliament passed in the 19th Henry VII. ch. 5. by which it was enacted, that all Gold and Silver Coins "shall be current for the sum " that they were coined for;" and by an Act passed in the 5th and 6th years of Edward VI. ch. 19. by which it was enacted, that " if any person exchanged any coined " Gold, or coined Silver, receiving or paying any more " in value, than the same is, or shall be declared by His " Majesty's Proclamation to be, current for, within His " Majesty's dominions, the same shall be forfeited," and the persons so offending shall be punished in the manner therein directed.*

Such is the history of the law of this kingdom, with reference to the prerogative exercised by Your royal Predecessors in the regulation of their Coins; and such was the extent of this prerogative, as stated by Sir Matthew Hale, when he wrote his History of the Pleas of the Crown. Previous to that period, several statutes were passed, establishing regulations with respect to the royal Mints, and requiring that the Coins issued from them should be of due weight; but not one, that took from the Sovereign the right of giving to the Coins, circulating in his dominions, their denominative value. In what respects the Legislature has thought fit to limit the exercise of this prerogative, since the death of that great lawyer, will be shewn hereafter.

Though this great prerogative is, however, unquestionable, it is certainly adviseable, that in the exercise of it, whenever any great change is intended to be made, the King should avail himself of the wisdom and support of his Parliament. Sir Matthew Hale observes, that it is neither safe, nor honourable, for the King to imbase his Coin below sterling; "if it be at any time done, it is fit " to be done by the assent of Parliament;" and he concludes, that, on such occasions, "*fieri non debuit, factum*

See Sir Matthew Hale's Pleas of the Crown, vol. 1. p. 194. ed. folio.

---

* In a subsequent period, that is, in the 6th and 7th William III. ch. 17. this prerogative is farther confirmed and acknowledged, by enacting additional penalties against those "who shall receive or pay " any unclipped Silver Money, of the Coin of this kingdom, for more " than in tale it was coined for, and ought by law to go for."

CHAP. 5.   *valet.*"—It has happened, that, since the Revolution, the Kings of this realm have occasionally exercised this prerogative, on smaller occasions, without consulting the two Houses of Parliament: yet, on greater occasions, such as a general Recoinage, they have always thought it right to avail themselves of their advice and support.

CHAPTER VI.

Of the English standard of Silver and Gold.

IT will be proper now to give Your Majesty some account, in a short history of the Coins of this realm, of the manner, in which Your royal Predecessors have exercised this great prerogative.—Many writers of acknowledged abilities have treated of the principles of Coinage, and have certainly thrown great light on the subject; but they have founded their systems too much on principles merely speculative, and have not sufficiently adverted to many facts, with which the history of this and many other countries would have furnished them. By these they would have learnt to correct the errors they have sometimes committed, and they would have applied their principles with more certainty, and better success. It cannot be denied, that in all the affairs of life, particularly such as relate to the private concerns of a whole people, experience is the surest guide. In such transactions there are little circumstances, with which the merely speculative man is wholly unacquainted. These can be learnt only from experience; and, if proper attention be not paid to them, they will occasionally defeat the advantages expected to be derived from the wisest system founded on speculation alone. Mr. Locke became sensible, that, by trusting solely to speculation, he had,

CHAP. 6. at least in one instance, been led into an error. To avoid, therefore, errors of this nature, I not only intend to treat of the subject of Coinage in a speculative view, but I shall endeavour to establish the opinions which I may advance, by a discreet reference to facts, and by adverting to many circumstances, which have occurred in the history of the Coins of this kingdom. In pursuing this plan, I shall be obliged to take a larger range, and to lay before Your Majesty some account of the Coins of the realm from an early period, and of the alterations and debasements, that, from time to time, have been made in them, as well as the motives, which induced preceding Monarchs to authorise these alterations and debasements, and the consequences, salutary or mischievous, that resulted from them. I am sensible that I shall thereby be obliged to extend this Letter to a greater length than I could wish. If however I should have the good fortune to place this subject in a clear and satisfactory light, so as to enable Your Majesty to form a more correct and safer judgment on the improvements necessary to be made in the Coins of Your kingdom; I am induced to hope, that You will condescend to pardon the length of this Letter, and not think the time wholly misemployed, which may be necessary for the perusal of it.

To elucidate what I have to offer, I will begin by stating, as correctly as I am able, what was the standard or fineness of the metals, of which these Coins were made, in successive periods.

The true English standard of the Silver, of which our Coins were made, was 11 oz. 2 dwts. fine, and 18 dwts.

alloy. This is called the old standard, or the standard of the old Sterling. It is the more general opinion, that this was the standard of the Silver Coins made in the reign of William I. The principal English writers on Coins, who must be supposed to have assayed the Coins made in those ancient times, and still preserved in the cabinets of those who have collected them, are of this opinion: there are, however, some lawyers and antiquaries, who express doubts on this subject, and infer, from ancient records, that, previous to the reign of Edward I. Silver Coins were occasionally made of a different standard, sometimes better, and sometimes worse. But it is probable, that such of these Coins as were of a more debased standard (if any such ever existed) were made contrary to law, by the rebellious Barons, or by others, who abused the privilege granted to them by their Sovereigns, of having Mints within their respective jurisdictions; for it appears, by an ordinance of Henry II. which he published in his Duchy of Normandy, in the year 1158; and by various other French records, published by Mons. le Blanc, in his Traité Historique des Monnoies de France, that the English Silver Pennies, then called Esterlings, or Sterlings, were estimated by foreign nations, from the year last mentioned, and for more than a century subsequent thereto, to be equal to a pennyweight of Silver, of the fineness or standard before mentioned: and it is certain, that in the 28th year of the reign of Edward I. an indented Trial Piece, of the fineness of 11 oz. 2 dwts. fine, and 18 dwts. alloy, was lodged in the Exchequer. This indented Trial Piece was at

CHAP. 6.

Vide Le Blanc, p. 166.

CHAP. 6. that time said to be of the *old standard*, which clearly proves, that such must have been considered as the standard of our Silver Coins, for a long time before. There is no doubt, that, from the 28th year of Edward I. all our Silver Coins have been made of this standard, except for a short period of sixteen years, from the 34th Henry VIII. to the 2d Elizabeth.

When Gold Coins were first made at the English Mint, the standard of the Gold put into them was of 23 carats $3\frac{1}{2}$ grains fine, and $\frac{1}{2}$ grain of alloy; and it so continued, without any variation, to the 18th Henry VIII. who in that year first introduced a new standard of Gold of 22 carats fine, and 2 carats alloy, of which he made some of his Gold Coins. The first of these standards was called the old standard; the second was called the new standard, or Crown Gold, because Crowns, or pieces of the value of five Shillings, were first coined of this new standard.

Henry VIII. made his Gold Coins of both these standards, under different denominations; and this practice was continued by his Successors to the year 1663, that is, the 15th Charles II. From that period to the present time, the Gold, of which the Coins of this kingdom have been made, has been invariably of the new standard, anciently called Crown Gold; though some of the Coins made of the old standard, previous to that period, continued to be current till the year 1732, when, by proclamation, they were forbidden to be any longer current.

It will enable Your Majesty the better to understand the changes, that have taken place in the Coins of the realm, if I give, in the next place, an account of the weights made use of at the Mint, for the purpose of weighing and regulating these Coins.

CHAPTER VII.

Of the Tower or Moneyer's Pound, and the Pound Troy.

<small>See Martin Folkes's Table of English Silver and Gold Coins, p. 3. Clarke on Coins, p. 15.</small>

THE Pound weight, which was made use of in the Mints of this realm, till the 18th* Henry VIII. for weighing Gold and Silver, was the Tower Pound, or what is called the Moneyer's Pound; it was lighter than the Pound Troy, by three quarters of an ounce Troy. It is certain, that this Tower Pound is the same that had been used by our Saxon ancestors in weighing the precious metals; and nearly the same that was made use of, for the same purpose, in the principal cities of Germany: this Pound was called by French writers the

---

* Mr. Clarke contends, that the Tower Pound was changed for the Troy Pound, in the 12th Henry VII. and he quotes a statute of that year in confirmation of it. This statute, as well as a preceding one, to which it refers, does not appear to me to introduce any new weights, but only to regulate the existing ones, which had been made in a very imperfect manner; and, for that purpose, orders accurate specimens to be sent to every city and great town. I have adhered therefore to Mr. Folkes's decision on this point, (which indeed is of no great importance) as his reasons appear to me to be sufficiently convincing. If the Tower Pound, which had been in use at the Mint for many centuries, and preserved there with great care, had then been changed for the Troy Pound, it should have been expressly said so in the statute, as it is in the verdict relating to the Coinage of the 30th Oct. 18 Henry VIII. which is preserved in the Exchequer.

Rochelle Pound.* Henry VIII. in the 18th year of his reign forbade the use of the Tower Pound in his Mint, and introduced the Troy Pound in its stead, which has continued to be used there ever since.

At the accession of William I. to the throne of England, the Pound in tale of the Silver Coins current in this kingdom was equal to the Pound weight of standard Silver, that is, the Tower Pound before mentioned. The Pound in tale was divided into twenty Shillings, and each Shilling into twelve Pence or Sterlings. The Pound weight was divided into twelve ounces, and each ounce into twenty pennyweights; so that each Penny or Sterling weighed one pennyweight or twenty-four grains. The only Coins made in this early period were Pennies or Sterlings. This simple system of Coinage, by which the Pound in tale was made equal to the Pound in weight, and was divided in the manner before mentioned, is supposed to have been first introduced by Charlemagne into France and his other extensive dominions, towards the end of the eighth century. It might have been introduced from thence into this island in the time of our Saxon ancestors, by the influence of the Norman Princes, who had a considerable connection with this kingdom, before William, Duke of Normandy, took possession of the throne. The system of Coinage, thus described, continued without any alteration in the

---

* It is natural to conclude, that the English Pound and the Rochelle Pound might be the same; for, in ancient times, the city of Rochelle was, for a long period, under the dominion of the English Princes.

CHAP. 7. weight of our Silver Monies till the 28th of Edward I. It is true, that Half Pennies, then frequently called Mailles, as well as Farthings, were introduced by Henry I. Pennies however were still, during the whole of this period, the highest denomination of our Silver Coins.

Edward I. in his 28th year, first debased our Silver Coins.

CHAPTER VIII.

Of the several ways in which Coins may be debased.

BEFORE I proceed to give an account of the successive debasements, made in our Coins, it is proper to observe, that Coins may be debased in three different ways.

First, By diminishing the quantity or weight of the metal of a certain standard, of which any Coin of a given denomination is made.

Secondly, By raising the nominal value of Coins of a given weight, and made of a metal of a certain standard; that is, by making them current, or legal tender, at a higher rate, than that at which they passed before.

Thirdly, By lowering the standard or fineness of the metal, of which Coins of a given weight and denomination are made; that is, by diminishing the quantity of pure metal, and proportionally increasing the quantity of alloy.

I shall be enabled to state in a clearer light the successive debasements made in the Coins of this realm, if I arrange them, in conformity to the different manners of debasing Coins before stated, under the following heads.

First, The alterations and debasements made in the Silver Coins of this realm, by diminishing the quantity or weight of standard Silver put into them. The Silver

CHAP. 8.   Coins have always been debased in this manner, except in the short period of nine years, from the 34th Henry VIII. to the 6th Edward VI.

Secondly, The alterations and debasements made in the Gold Coins of this realm, either by diminishing the quantity or weight of the Gold put into them, or by raising the nominal value of the existing Coins, in order to preserve the relative proportion or value of the Gold Coins with that of the Silver Coins current at successive periods. The Gold Coins of the realm have been debased in both these manners, but more frequently in the latter.

Thirdly, I shall reserve for a distinct head an account of the extraordinary and violent alterations and debasements, that were made in the Coins of this realm, particularly by lowering the standard of the metal put into the Silver Coins, during the short period before mentioned. At the end of that period, a reformation of the Coins of the realm, from the late unexampled debasements, commenced, though it was not completed, and though the old standard of the Silver put into our Coins was not perfectly restored till the 2d Elizabeth. The various and violent proceedings, which took place from the 34th Henry VIII. to the 6th Edward VI. may be considered as a sort of convulsion in the monetary system, and proper therefore for a separate head.

It is necessary, in calculating these debasements, to adhere to one and the same weight; and as the Tower Pound was the longest in use, I shall make my calculations according to the Tower Pound.

CHAPTER IX.

Of debasements in the Pound in tale.

IT has already been stated, that Edward I. in the 28th year of his reign, first debased the Silver Coins of this realm.

In this year he diminished the quantity or weight of Sterling Silver, in the Silver Coins of the several denominations made at his Mint. He coined the Pound weight of Sterling Silver into twenty Shillings and three Pence in tale; so that the Pound Sterling in tale was thereby debased $1\frac{10}{81}$ per cent.

This King first coined Silver Groats of the value of four Pennies, which took the name of Groats from their being larger Coins, than any that had yet been made. The Groats coined by this Prince were but few; and this denomination of Money did not become generally current till the reign of Edward III.

The second debasement of our Silver Coins was in the 18th Edward III. who then coined the Tower Pound of Sterling Silver into twenty-two Shillings and two Pence in tale; and the Pound Sterling in tale was thereby further debased $8\frac{5816}{10773}$ per cent.

The third debasement of our Silver Coins was in the 20th* year of the same King, who then coined

---

* Stow imputes this debasement to the advice of William Edington, Bishop of Winchester, and Treasurer of England. He calls him a person

CHAP. 9. the Tower Pound of Sterling Silver into twenty-two Shillings and six Pence in tale; and the Pound Sterling in tale was thereby further debased $1\frac{403}{1197}$ per cent.

The fourth debasement of our Silver Coins was in the 27th year of this King, who then coined the Tower Pound of Sterling Silver into twenty-five Shillings in tale; and the Pound Sterling in tale was thereby further debased $8\frac{3}{8}$ per cent.

The fifth debasement of our Silver Coins was in the 13th Henry IV. who then coined the Tower Pound of Sterling Silver into thirty Shillings in tale; and the Pound Sterling in tale was thereby further debased $13\frac{1}{3}$ per cent.

The sixth debasement of our Silver Coins was in the 4th of Edward IV. who then coined the Tower Pound of Sterling Silver into thirty-seven Shillings and six Pence in tale; and the Pound Sterling in tale was thereby further debased $13\frac{1}{3}$ per cent.

Henry VII. who made no change in the weight of his Silver Coins, first coined Shillings, which had before been only a Money of Account. Shillings however did not become generally current till the reign of his successor Henry VIII. and they were then commonly called Testons.

The seventh debasement of our Silver Coins was in the 18th year of Henry VIII. who then coined the

" loving the King's commoditie more than the wealth of the realme
" and common people," and adds, that "victuals and merchandise
" became dearer through the whole realme."

Pound Troy of Sterling Silver into forty-five Shillings, or according to the Tower Pound into 42s. 2¼d.; and the Pound Sterling in tale was thereby further debased 5 23/27 per cent.

This King first coined Crown Pieces of Silver of the nominal value of five Shillings; but it is supposed that he made but few of them, and that they did not become generally current till the reign of Queen Mary.

In the reign of Queen Mary Silver Half Crowns were first Coined, and Silver Crowns became generally current.

The eighth debasement, of which I shall take notice under this head, was in the 2d year of Queen Elizabeth. Of the great and extraordinary debasements in the standard of the metal of which our Coins were made, between the 18th Henry VIII. and the 6th Edward VI. as well as of the proceedings for the reformation of the Coin in the last year of the reign of Edward VI. and also during the whole of the reign of Queen Mary to the 2d of Elizabeth, I shall give a separate account hereafter.

Queen Elizabeth, in the second year of her reign, restored the Silver Coins of her realm to the standard of old Sterling, and she coined the Pound Troy of Sterling Silver into sixty Shillings in tale, or according to the Tower Pound into 56s. 3d.; and the Pound Sterling in tale, compared with what it had been in the 18th Henry VIII. was thereby further debased 11 23/27 per cent.

The ninth and last debasement of our Silver Coins was in the 43d Elizabeth, who then coined the Pound

CHAP. 9. Troy of Sterling Silver into sixty-two Shillings, or according to the Tower Pound into 58s. 1½d.; and the Pound Sterling in tale was thereby further debased $1\frac{41}{279}$ per cent.

The total of the debasements from the 1st William I. when the Tower Pound in weight and the Pound in tale were the same, was now $\frac{6100}{93}$ or $65\frac{55}{93}$ per cent.

So that the value of a Pound in tale is now less than it was in the 1st of William I. in the ratio of $\frac{32}{93}$ to 1, or 32 to 93.

It appears, from the history of this country, that other proposals for debasing the Silver Coins of the realm were under consideration, but were never carried into execution. In the year 1561, the 3d Elizabeth, many of the ministers of this Queen advised her Majesty to make a new debasement in these Coins; but the Lord Treasurer Burleigh opposed this measure, and prevented it; and he resisted with spirit every attempt of the like nature, as long as he continued in power. After his decease, Queen Elizabeth was induced, in the 43d year of her reign, to make the ninth and last debasement of the Silver Coins, as before stated.

In 1612, the 9th James I. a proposition was made for debasing the Silver Coins, by coining Silver at 10 oz. 10 dwts. fine, and by cutting the Pound Troy into 64 Shillings. Another proposition was made in the same year for debasing the Silver Coins, by cutting a Pound Troy of standard Silver into 64 Shillings. And in 1619, the 16th James I. directions were actually given to the Attorney General to prepare new indentures, by

See Sir Robert Cotton's posthumous Works, p. 197.

which the Pound Troy of standard Silver should be coined into 66 Shillings; but these directions were soon afterwards recalled; and by the advice of eminent merchants, as well as of the Officers of the Mint, and occasionally of Sir Francis Bacon, afterwards Lord Verulam, all these proposals were rejected.

In 1627, the 2d year of the reign of Charles I. another proposition was made for debasing the Silver Coins, by cutting the Pound Troy of standard Silver into 70 Shillings and 6 Pence. On which occasion, Sir Robert Cotton made the famous speech published in his posthumous Works against the debasement of the Silver Coin, which has been attributed to Sir Thomas Roe. And in 1640, the 15th Charles I. other proposals were made for debasing the Silver Coin, by diminishing the quantity of pure Silver put into these Coins, and proportionally increasing the alloy; but all these propositions were rejected.

The proposition of Mr. Lowndes for debasing the Silver Coins, in his Report to the Lords of the Treasury in 1695, in which he recommends, that the Pound Troy of standard Silver should be coined into 77s. 6d., is well known. It was resisted by Mr. Locke in his Treatise, intituled, "Further Considerations concerning raising "the value of Money." Some of the members of the Government at that time are supposed to have favoured this proposition; but King William and his Parliament rejected it.

CHAPTER X.

Of the first Gold Coins made in England.

I WILL, in the next place, proceed to the second head, under which I have arranged the alterations and debasements made in the Coins of this realm. The alterations, under this head, were practised on our Gold Coins; and in two different ways; sometimes, by diminishing the quantity of Gold put into the current Gold Coins of a given denomination; but more frequently, by raising the nominal value of these Coins, with an evident intention of preserving a proportionate value between them and the Silver Coins intended to be current, according to the relative value of Gold to Silver at the market in each respective period.

It is not necessary on this occasion to say any thing on the question, so much agitated by antiquaries, whether any, and what Coins of Gold were made by the British or Saxon Monarchs of this country, at their Mints. It is probable that, in times of peace and prosperity, some Gold Coins might occasionally have been made by the Monarchs of these two races; but after the kingdom had been wasted and reduced to a state of the greatest poverty by the successive invasions of the Saxons and Danes, there appears to have been an interval of many years, in which no Gold Coins were

made at any Mint in this country. And as far as any CHAP. 10.
discovery has hitherto been made, it is certain, that no
such Coins were struck at the English Mint from the 1st
William I. to the 41st year of Henry III. that is, during
a period of one hundred and ninety-one years.

It was generally believed till the year 1732, that
Edward III. was the first of the English Kings who
coined at their Mints any Gold Coins: but in a manuscript preserved in the Archives of the city of London,
it was then discovered, that Henry III. in the latter part
of his reign, that is, in his 41st year, made what was
called a Penny of fine Gold, weighing two Sterlings, or
the 120th part of the Tower Pound; which Gold Penny
was to pass for twenty Sterlings or Silver Pennies in
tale; and this information has since been confirmed by
the discovery of an original precept, directed to the Mayor
and Sheriffs of the City of London, to enforce the currency of this Gold Money, and by several liberates, in
which these Gold Pennies are mentioned, among the
records in the Tower. These Gold Coins were called
Pennies, because the word Penny, or, in the French
language, *Denier*, was in these early times the common
term for Money in general, of whatever metal it might
be made: and the French King St. Lewis, who was
cotemporary with Henry III. first made a Gold Coin,
which was called *Denier à l'Aignel*, the figure of a lamb
or sheep being impressed upon it. It is probable however, that these Gold Pennies were not coined by
Henry III. in any great number: one only specimen of
his Gold Coins has yet been discovered. It is certain

CHAP. 10.

that the citizens of London made representations against these Gold Coins very soon after they were first issued; and the King put forth a proclamation, declaring that nobody was obliged to take them, and whoever chose to receive them in payment might bring them to his Exchange, and receive there the value, at which each had been made current; but half a Sterling, or the value of half a Silver Penny, was to be deducted, probably to compensate the charge of Coinage. From these circumstances it may be inferred, that these Gold Pennies did not then get into general circulation. There is hitherto no evidence, that the two immediate successors of this King, that is, either Edward I. or Edward II. ever made any Gold Coins at their Mints. It is not indeed surprising, that in these early times no Gold should have been coined at the English Mint. In the reigns of William I. and William II. and during a great part of the reign of Henry I. the King's rents, arising from his demesnes, (which were at that time the principal part of the Royal revenue), though reserved in Money, were answered in cattle, corn, and other provisions, " because Money was " then scarce among the people." The rents of private landholders continued to be paid in kind to a still later period. The commerce of the country, whether foreign or internal, was during this period of no great extent. It is probable therefore, that the quantity even of Silver Money in circulation could not be great; and the largest denomination of it, hitherto in currency, was but a Penny or Sterling, equal in value to something less than three Pennies of our present Money. There could then

See Madox's History of the Exchequer.

See Sir Matthew Hale, p. 199. where he refers to the Black Book in the Exchequer.

of course be little occasion, in the internal traffic of the kingdom, for Coins made of Gold. It is not improbable however that a small quantity of the Gold Coins of foreign countries might be brought into the kingdom, by means of our foreign commerce, and be occasionally current within it. Our ancient records make frequent mention of Byzants; and it is certain, that there were at that time circulating through every part of Europe, and employed in the payment of larger sums, Gold Coins made by the Greek Emperors of Constantinople, called Byzants, or Byzantines. These were made of fine Gold, that is, of 24 carats fine. Antiquaries are not agreed concerning the weight of the Byzants; it is probable however, that each of them originally weighed a *Drachma*, or Dram, that is, the eighth part of an ounce, so that its value was nearly equal to 10 Shillings of our present Money. After the example of the Greek Emperors, other Sovereigns of Europe made Gold Coins, which they called Byzantines, though of a different weight and value; and the several sorts of Byzantines made in different countries were on this account occasionally distinguished, by adding to their original name that of the people, or country, where they were made. In a subsequent period, that is, about the year 1252, another sort of Gold Coin was introduced into circulation among the nations of Europe; they were first coined at Florence, and therefore were called Florences. They were probably made in imitation of the Byzantines; for about this time the Greek Refugees began to fly from Constantinople, and sought an asylum principally in

Chap. 10.

See Du Cange's Glossary and Supplement, article Byzant.

See Du Cange as above.

See Du Cange's Glossary and Supplement, article Florence.

CHAP. 10.

See Le Blanc, p. 154. and Prolegomenes.

Florence. These Florences were made also of fine Gold, and an ounce was coined into eight of them; and they were therefore originally of the same weight and value as the Byzantines. Le Blanc observes, that these Coins, called Florences, were very famous in every part of Europe; and that there was hardly a Sovereign, who did not make them: he even thinks, that this name of Florences was for some time given to every sort of Gold Money, whatever the value or weight of it might be. It is certain, however, that these Florences, or Florins, were by degrees very much depreciated, and that at length Coins of the same name were made of Silver; and Florins of this last description are the Money of Account, in many countries, to this day.

CHAPTER XI.

Of relative values of Gold to Silver.

WHEN Edward III. at the commencement of the 18th year of his reign, began to make Gold Coins at the English Mint, the people of this kingdom, following the example set them in many countries on the continent, frequently called these new Gold Coins, Florences, or Florins: and in the Proclamation for giving them currency, they are said to weigh " *Deux petits Florins de* *Florence de bons Pois.*" They were in fact nearly of that weight, for they weighed 4 dwts. 19¼ grs. They were made of Gold of the old English standard, that is, 23 carats 3½ grains fine, and ½ gr. alloy; 50 of them were coined out of a Tower Pound weight of Gold, making in tale 15*l.* of the Money of that time; and each of them was current for 6*s.* of that money, and was intrinsically worth about 19*s.* of our present Money. At the same time he coined pieces, weighing, some of them, half of that before mentioned, and others a quarter, but all of the same fineness, and in due proportion: and as the Tower Pound of standard Silver was then coined into 22*s.* 2*d.*, the value of a Pound of fine Gold, compared with the value of a Pound of fine Silver, was estimated as $12\frac{14844}{25403}$ to 1. The Gold in these Coins was thought to be overvalued, in proportion to the Silver Coin then

Side notes: See Martin Folkes's Table of English Gold Coins, p. 3, and p. 121, 122. See Rymer, v. 5. p. 403. De Proclamatione super Auro cudendo.

E

CHAP. II.

Rymer, v. 5.
p. 416.

Ibid. p. 424.

Ibid. p. 416.

current, and they were on that account generally refused in payment. For this reason, they were ordered by a Proclamation, dated the 9th July in the same year, to be taken in payment only with the consent of those, to whom they were offered; and by another Proclamation, dated 20th August following, they were ordered to be no longer current. It is probable that they were generally brought to the Mint, and recoined; for none of them have yet been found, except a Quarter Florin.

On the 9th July of the same year, this King issued three new sorts of Gold Money; one to be called the Noble d'Or, or Noble, ordered to be of the weight of 6 dwts. $1\frac{3}{4}$ gr., which was to pass at 6s. 8d., or half a Mark in tale. It was made of Gold of the old standard. At the same time he coined Half Nobles, sometimes called Maille Nobles, and Quarter Nobles, sometimes called Farthing Nobles, in due proportion. The Tower Pound of Gold was to be coined into $39\frac{1}{2}$ of these Nobles, and to pass in tale at 13l. 3s. 4d. of the Money of that time; and as the Tower Pound of Silver was still coined into 22s. 2d., the value of a Pound of fine Gold, compared with the value of a Pound of fine Silver, was now estimated as $11\frac{1175}{25403}$ to 1. This new Gold Coin was not at first acceptable to the people, and it was therefore ordered, that no one should be obliged to take it in payment for any sum less than twenty Shillings. But as it probably became in a short time more acceptable, it was soon afterwards ordered not to be refused in any payment whatsoever. In this manner, Coins of Gold made at the English Mint were at length introduced into general circulation among the people, though with some difficulty. At this time the commerce of the kingdom began greatly to increase; and Edward III. had given security to it, by several naval victories lately obtained, particularly by one, in which he had destroyed the French navy, off the coast of Flanders. In commemoration of this great event, there was placed on the face of these Nobles, the King, standing in the center of a ship, armed, with his sword drawn in his right hand, and his shield in his left; and Gold Coins, with nearly a similar device, continued to be made at the English Mint, for more than two centuries and a half, subsequent to this period.

In the 20th year of this King's reign, when he a second time debased his Silver Money, he reduced the weight of the Nobles to 5 dwts. $8\frac{4}{7}$ grs. and he at the same time coined Half and Quarter Nobles in due proportion. The Nobles were to pass, as before, at 6s. 8d. A Tower Pound of Gold of the old standard was to be coined into 42 Nobles, and was to make in tale 14l. of the Money of that time; and as the Tower Pound of Silver was then coined into 22s. 6d., the value of a Pound of fine Gold, compared with the value of a Pound of fine Silver, was estimated as $11\frac{1637}{2805}$ to 1.

In the 27th year of this King's reign, when he a third time debased his Silver Money, he reduced the weight of the Nobles to 5 dwts. 8 grs. making Half and Quarter Nobles in due proportion. These Nobles were to pass, as before, at 6s. 8d. A Tower Pound of Gold of the old standard was to be coined into 45 Nobles, and was to make in tale 15l. of the Money of that time; and as the

Tower Pound of Silver was then coined into 25s., the value of a Pound of fine Gold, compared with the value of a Pound of fine Silver, was estimated as $11\frac{131}{535}$ to 1.

In the 13th year of Henry IV. when this King debased his Silver Coin, he reduced the weight of the Nobles to 4 dwts. 19¼ grs. making 'Half and Quarter Nobles in due proportion. The Nobles were to pass, as before, at 6s. 8d. A Tower Pound of Gold of the old standard was to be coined into 50 Nobles, and was to make in tale 16l. 13s. 4d. of the money of that time; and as the Tower Pound of Silver was then coined into 30s., the value of a Pound of fine Gold, compared with the value of a Pound of fine Silver, was estimated as $10\frac{109}{573}$ to 1.

From that period, the Kings of this realm, when they debased their Silver Coins, by diminishing the weight of them, introduced a new method of preserving the relative value of Gold to Silver in their Coins, by frequently raising the nominal value of the Gold Coins then in currency, and by obliging their subjects to receive them at this increased value. But as the people were, from long usage, now accustomed to Gold Coins of a certain nominal rate and value, that is, of half a Mark, or 6s. 8d., and to its subdivisions 3s. 4d. and 1s. 8d., the Kings of this realm, when they so raised the nominal value of the existing Gold Coins, generally introduced into circulation new pieces of Gold Coin, of the same nominal values, to which the people had been accustomed, though under different names; and when, in a subsequent period, Gold Coins, of the nominal value of 20 Shillings, and 10

Shillings, were introduced into currency, the same practice was adopted, whenever any alterations were made in such Gold Coins.

In the 4th year of the reign of Edward IV. when this King debased his Silver Coin, he raised the value of the Nobles then in circulation, from 6s. 8d. to 8s. 4d. But he soon afterwards made a new Gold Coin, which he called an Angel, because there was represented an Angel on the face of it. He continued however the figure of a ship; but he placed it on the reverse of this Coin. Each of these Angels was to be current at 6s. 8d., weighing 3 dwts. 13¼ grs. He made Angelets, or Half Angels, in due proportion. A Tower Pound of Gold of the old standard was to be coined into sixty-seven Angels and a half, and was to make in tale 22l. 10s. This King continued however to Coin Nobles, Half Nobles, and Quarter Nobles, precisely of the same weights as those made in the 27th year of Edward III. which were now to pass at 10s.; but they received a new name, and were called Rials, or Rose Nobles. A Tower Pound of Gold of the old standard was to be coined into 45 of these Nobles, and was to make in tale 22l. 10s. of the Money of that time. An Angel and a Half were of the same rate and value as one Rial, or Rose Noble; and as the Tower Pound of Silver was then coined into 37s. 6d., the value of a Pound of fine Gold, compared with the value of a Pound of fine Silver, was estimated, as in the 27th Edward III. in the proportion of $11\frac{131}{935}$ to 1.

Though Henry VII. did not debase either his Gold or Silver Coins, he introduced a new sort of Gold Coin into currency, which was to pass for 20 Shillings, and weighed 10 dwts. 16 grs. which was exactly double the weight of the Rial, or Rose Noble, which then passed at 10 Shillings. It was called a Sovereign, or Double Rial; but very few of them were coined in this reign. On this Sovereign, or Double Rial, the King was represented sitting on his throne in royal robes, and crowned.

In the 18th year of Henry VIII. when the Silver Coin was again debased, this King raised the value of the several Gold Coins then in circulation. He raised the Sovereign, or Double Rial, from 20s. to 22s. 6d.; the Rial, from 10s. to 11s. 3d.; the Angel, from 6s. 8d. to 7s. 6d.: but he at the same time made a new Gold Coin of the old standard, which was to be current at 6s. 8d., weighing 2 dwts. 23 grs. Troy, (which weight was at this time first introduced into the English Mint,) and he called it a George Noble. He coined at the same time Half George Nobles, (which were also called Forty Penny Pieces) in due proportion. A Troy Pound of Gold of the old standard was to be coined into eighty-one of these George Nobles, and was to make in tale 27*l*. of the Money of that time. This King coined also at the same time pieces of Gold Coin of a new standard, that is, 22 carats fine, and 2 alloy; they were called Crowns, and each of these Crowns was to weigh 2 dwts. 9¼ grs. of Gold of this new standard; and was to pass for five Shillings. He made also Half Crowns of Gold of the same standard in due proportion. A Troy Pound of Gold of this new standard was to be coined into 100½ Crowns, and was to make in tale 25*l*. 2s. 6d.

of the Money of that time; and as the Tower Pound of Silver was then coined into 45s. the value of a Pound of fine Gold in Coins of the old standard, compared with the value of a Pound of fine Silver, was estimated as in the 4th Edward IV. in the proportion of $11\frac{121}{955}$ to 1, and the value of a Pound of fine Gold in Coins of the new standard, compared with the value of a Pound of fine Silver, was estimated in the proportion of $11\frac{59}{220}$ to 1.

For reasons already stated, I shall pass over all the proceedings with respect to the Gold Coin, from the 18th Henry VIII. to the 2d Elizabeth. Yet it will be proper to observe, that Edward VI. in the 6th year of his reign, raised the value of the Sovereigns of the old standard to 30 Shillings, the old Rials to 15 Shillings, the Angels to 10 Shillings, and their respective subdivisions in due proportion. He coined also, in the 6th year of his reign, Gold Crowns of the new standard, weighing 1 dwt. $18\frac{1}{4}$ grs. and Half Crowns in proportion. His Father coined, in the 34th year of his reign, Gold Sovereigns of the new standard, which were to pass at twenty Shillings, weighing 8 dwts. 8 grs. These he afterwards reduced to 8 dwts. and they were farther reduced by Edward VI. in the said 6th year of his reign, to 7 dwts. $6\frac{1}{2}$ grs. In this state the Gold Coins continued during all the reign of Queen Mary, and Queen Elizabeth found them in this state at her accession. She made no alteration at this time, either in the weight or the value, at which these Gold Coins were to be current, with respect to the Pound in tale; but, by restoring the Silver to 11 oz. 2 dwts. fine, and 18 dwts. alloy, she altered the value of the

CHAP. II. Gold Coins, compared with those of Silver. According to several indentures, before her 43d year, a Troy Pound of Gold of the old standard was to be coined into twenty-four Sovereigns, and the smaller pieces of Gold Coin of the old standard in due proportion; and was to make in tale 36*l.* of the Money of that time. And the Troy Pound of Crown Gold of the new standard was to be coined into 33 Sovereigns, and the smaller Gold Coins of the new standard in due proportion; and was to make in tale 33*l.* of the Money of that time. And as the Pound of Silver was then coined into 60 Shillings, the value of a Pound of fine Gold in Coins of the old standard, compared with the value of a Pound of fine Silver, was estimated in the proportion of $11\frac{131}{555}$ to 1; and the value of a Pound of fine Gold in Coins of the new standard, compared with the value of a Pound of fine Silver, was estimated as $11\frac{1}{10}$ to 1. In Coins of the old standard therefore, the relative value of Gold to Silver was as in the 18th of Henry VIII. but in Coins of the new standard, the value of Gold, when compared with Silver, was less by $\frac{37}{220}$, than in that period.

In the 43d of Elizabeth, when the Silver Coin was again debased, and put upon the footing on which it stands at present, this Queen diminished the quantity of Gold, which she put into her Coins, both of the old and new standard. She reduced the weight of the Angel of the old standard, which had before weighed 3 dwts. 8 grs. to 3 dwts. 7 grs. and the Half and Quarter Angels in due proportion. The Troy Pound of Gold of this standard was to be coined into 73 Angels, and was to pass in tale at 36l. 10s. of the Money of that time. She reduced the Sovereigns of the new standard, which had before weighed 7 dwts. 6½ grs. to 7 dwts. 4 grs. and the smaller Coins of this new standard in due proportion. The Troy Pound of Gold of this standard was to be coined into 33 Sovereigns and an half, and was to pass in tale at 33l. 10s. of the Money of that time; and as the Pound of Silver was then coined into 62s., the value of a Pound of fine Gold in Coins of the old standard, compared with the value of a Pound of fine Silver, was estimated as $10\frac{5614}{5921}$ to 1; and the value of a Pound of fine Gold in Coins of the new standard, compared with the value of a Pound of fine Silver, was estimated as $10\frac{617}{682}$ to 1.

As from this period no further alteration or debasement has been made in our Silver Coins, I am now only to consider, what alteration was henceforth made in our Gold Coins, in order to bring the value of them in tale to a due proportion with the value in tale of our Silver Coins, according to the relative value of Gold to Silver in each respective period.

It is singular, that to this period, though the Mines of America had long been discovered, and great quantities of the precious metals had in consequence thereof been imported into Europe, the relative prices of these metals do not appear from the Mint indentures to have very much varied from what they had been in former times. It is possible that the increasing luxury of the different countries of Europe, in plate and other articles during this time, might have employed and absorbed a considerable part of the Silver, that had been hitherto imported; and it should be recollected, that the productive Silver Mines of Potosi had not then been discovered above fifty-five years. However, it can hardly be conceived, that some rise in the value of Gold, compared with Silver, had not at that time taken place in the market, though it had not been observed, and though the value of it in our Gold Coins had not been raised in consequence thereof, by those who had the direction of the English Mint. Queen Elizabeth, in her 43d year, estimated the value of Gold to Silver, even in a less proportion than it had ever been, in any period since the 18th Edward III. except in the 13th Henry IV. and except in the nine years from the 34th Henry VIII. to the 6th Edward VI. when no attention appears to have been paid to the relative values of these precious metals, as will be stated hereafter. But from this period, the value of Gold, compared with Silver, appears, even from the Mint indentures, to have risen rapidly; for in the 2d and 3d of James I. this Monarch found it necessary, on that account, to diminish the weight of his Gold Coins. He reduced the weight of the Angel of the old standard from 3 dwts. 7 grs. to 2 dwts. 23 grs. and the other Gold Coins of this standard in due proportion. The Troy Pound of Gold of this standard was to be coined into 81 Angels, and was to pass in tale at 40*l*. 10*s*. of the Money of that time. He reduced the Sovereign, or Piece of 20 Shillings of the new standard, from 7 dwts. 4 grs. to 6 dwts. 10¾ grs. and the smaller Gold Coins of this standard in proportion. The Troy Pound of Gold of this standard was to be coined into 37½ Sovereigns; and was to pass in tale at 37*l*. 4*s*. of the Money of that time: and as the Pound of Silver was then coined into 62*s*., the value of a Pound of fine Gold in Coins of the old standard, compared with the value of a Pound of fine Silver, was estimated as $12\frac{876}{592}$ to 1; and the value of a Pound of fine Gold in Coins of the new standard, compared with the value of a Pound of fine Silver, was estimated as $12\frac{186}{1705}$ to 1. This was a rise in the value of Gold in the old standard of $10\frac{70}{73}$ per cent. and in the new standard of $11\frac{3}{67}$ per cent.

To distinguish the new Sovereigns, or Twenty Shilling Pieces, made by this King, from the old, he changed their name, and called them Unites; and further, to enable his subjects more easily to distinguish the nominal value of this, as well as of the other Gold Coins made by him, he now began to put figures on the face of them, denoting the nominal value, at which they were respectively to be current. The practice of thus ascertaining the nominal value of Coins had hitherto been applied to the Silver Coins only.

This King, in the 9th year of his reign, raised, by proclamation, all Gold Coins hitherto in circulation, two Shillings in the Pound, or 10 per. cent. so that the Rose Rial was to pass for 33 Shillings, and the smaller Coins of this standard in due proportion. The Unite was to pass for 22 Shillings, and the smaller Gold Coins of this standard in due proportion; which, added to the former rise in the 2d and 3d year of his reign, made a total rise, during the short space of seven years, in the value of

CHAP. II. Gold, compared with that of Silver, of $20\frac{7.0}{7.3}$ per cent. in Coins of the old standard, and of $21\frac{3}{67}$ per cent. in Coins of the new standard. The value of a Pound of fine Gold in Coins of the old standard, compared with the value of a Pound of fine Silver, was now estimated as $13\frac{10732}{29065}$ to 1; and the value of a Pound of fine Gold, in Coins of the new standard, compared with the value of a Pound of fine Silver, was estimated as $13\frac{248}{775}$ to 1. This King, in the next year, coined Pieces of Gold of the old standard to pass for 30s., 15s., and 10s., proportionally diminishing their weight.

In the 17th year of this King, he a third time raised the value of Gold in his Coins. The last mentioned Piece of Gold Coin of the old standard, which in the 10th year of his reign weighed 8 dwts. $4\frac{1}{4}$ grs. and was to pass for 30s., was reduced to 8 dwts. 2 grs. and the other Gold Coins of the same standard, in like proportion. He now made 20s. Pieces of the new standard, weighing 5 dwts. $20\frac{1}{2}$ grs. which were called Laurels; and new 10s. Pieces called Double Crowns, and 5s. Pieces called Crowns, diminishing their weight in due proportion; and thereby further raised the value of Gold compared with that of Silver $1\frac{3}{22}$ per cent. in Coins of the old standard, and $\frac{100}{491}$ per cent. in Coins of the new standard. The value of a Pound of fine Gold, in Coins of the old standard, compared with the value of a Pound of fine Silver, was now estimated as $13\frac{2050}{5921}$ to 1; and the value of a Pound of fine Gold, in Coins of the new standard, compared with the value of a Pound of fine Silver, was estimated as $13\frac{118}{341}$ to 1.

No further alteration was made in the weight of the Gold Coins, or in their relative value with respect to the Silver Coins, during the remainder of this King's reign; and no alteration in either of these respects was ever made through the whole of the reign of Charles I. nor during the time of the Commonwealth; but the persons, who during this last period governed the kingdom, changed the devices on the face and reverse, both of our Gold and Silver Coins.

Charles II. at his Restoration, by his first indenture with the Master of the Mint, ordered, that his Coins should be made exactly the same in weight and fineness, as those, that had been made in the time of his Father, Charles I.: but in his 15th year, that is, the 3d year after the Restoration, he reduced the quantity of Gold, which he put into his Coins of the new standard. There is no reason to believe, that any Gold Coins of the old standard were made at the Mint of that King, or in any subsequent reign. The weight of the last Twenty Shilling Piece of the new standard, which was called a Laurel, was 5 dwts. 20½ grs. The weight of the new Piece of the same standard, which was intended in like manner to pass for 20s. was 5 dwts. 9½ grs. This Piece was afterwards called a Guinea. He coined also Pieces, which were to pass for 10 Shillings, and were called Half Guineas. He coined no other Gold Coins of this standard, except a few double Guineas and Five Pound Pieces, all which were made in due proportion. The Troy Pound of Gold, of the new standard, was to be coined into 44½ of these 20s. Pieces or Guineas, which

CHAP. 11. were intended to pass in tale for 44*l*. 10*s*.; and the value of a Pound of fine Gold, compared with the value of a Pound of fine Silver, was then estimated as $14\frac{331}{682}$ to 1; and the value of Gold, compared with that of Silver, was at this time raised $8\frac{22}{41}$ per cent. As upon the accession of James I. to the English Crown, the value of a Pound of fine Gold, compared with the value of a Pound of fine Silver, was estimated as $10\frac{817}{682}$ to 1, the rise in the value of Gold in the space of sixty years was upon the whole $32\frac{50}{87}$ per cent.: and as it can hardly be doubted, that most other articles, as well as Gold, increased in their price, compared with Silver, during the whole of this period, those who were entitled to receipts from ancient feefarm or other rents, as well as annuities, which had subsisted at the commencement of this period, must have lost in effect, by this diminution of the price of Silver, nearly one third of the original value of such rents and annuities.

See Fleetwood's Chronicon Pretiosum, and Sir Geo. Shuckburgh's Tables founded thereon.

CHAPTER XII.

Of the great inconvenience and expence arising from the fluctuations of the relative values of Gold to Silver.

FROM the account thus laid before Your Majesty of the variation in the relative values of Gold and Silver, as estimated in the Mints of this kingdom, from the time when Gold Coins were first made therein, after the accession of William I. it appears, that in the 41st Henry III. fine Gold compared with fine Silver was estimated in the Gold Coins or Pennies made by that King, at a lower value, than in any subsequent period; that is, as $9\frac{57}{101}$ to 1: and that in the beginning of the 18th year of Edward III. when he first made Florences, or Florins, the value of fine Gold, compared with the value of fine Silver, was estimated at a higher rate than in any subsequent period previous to the 9th James I. that is, as $12\frac{14844}{25403}$ to 1. It has already been stated, that the people were dissatisfied with both these valuations, and refused to take either these Gold Pennies or Florins in payment; though it may seem extraordinary, that they should not have been ready to take in payment the Gold Coins made by Henry III. as the Gold in them was valued so very low. On the other hand, the complaints of the people in the 18th Edward III. were

CHAP. 12. probably well founded; for by comparing the value which this King set on the Gold in his Florins, with the value at which it was estimated in the Gold Pennies of Henry III. the rise in the value of Gold at the market during this interval must indeed have been very great, to justify Edward III. in setting so high a value on it in his Florins. In consequence however of these complaints, this King, in a subsequent part of the same year, when he first coined Nobles, reduced the value of Gold, compared with Silver, in these Nobles, to the proportion of $11\frac{1175}{25403}$ to 1, as has been before stated. The people still complained that the value of the Gold in these Nobles was rated too high, and for a short time refused to take them in payment; but soon afterwards they became satisfied with this valuation, and were ready to receive them in all payments whatsoever, so that they became generally current.

It is difficult to explain, on any just principles, the transactions last stated, or the motives which influenced the opinions of the people with respect to these Coins. The most probable conjecture is, that as no Gold Coin had been made at the English Mints for at least 195 years previous to the 41st of Henry III. and probably for a much longer period ; and as the people had during that time carried on but little commercial intercourse with foreign nations, the price of Gold in this kingdom might be very low, because there had been, during the whole of that time, the less use and demand for it. The people might further object to these new Gold Pennies, from a natural aversion to novelty in a business, in which their interests were so deeply concerned: but, with the increasing commerce of the kingdom, this metal might gradually rise in its value before the 18th Edward III. and he might on this account be induced to estimate the value of it in his Florins at the high rate before stated. It is not improbable also, that this great Monarch, who was constantly in want of Money for his foreign wars, and who had, on that account, at three different times debased his Silver Coins, might expect, by over-rating the Gold in Coins of that metal, to increase his revenue. He certainly rated it too high; and for this reason, when he coined Nobles in a subsequent part of the same year, he considerably reduced the value, at which he rated the Gold put into them. The people for a short time thought the Gold in these Nobles was still over-rated; but considerable quantities of it being brought to the Mint to be coined, and these Coins becoming generally current, the price of Gold naturally rose in consequence of this new use and demand for it, and the people then became satisfied with the value at which this King had estimated it in his Nobles.

From the 18th of Edward III. to the 2d of James I. the highest valuation of fine Gold compared with fine Silver was in the 20th Edward III. when it was estimated as $11\frac{1637}{2865}$ to 1. The lowest valuation was in the 13th Henry IV. when it was estimated as $10\frac{129}{573}$ to 1; so that the variation during this long period was 12 per cent. I have not been able to find in the records or chronicles of this kingdom any symptoms of dissatisfaction or complaint, during the whole of this time,

Chap. 12. either as to any excess or defect in the valuation of Gold compared with Silver in the Coins made at the English Mint, except in the short space of about nine years, from the 34th Henry VIII. to the 6th Edward VI. (of which some account will be given under the next head of this Letter;) so that it is probable, that there was no great excess or defect in the relative values of the two precious metals, as estimated at the English Mint, compared with the price of them at the market, during more than two centuries and a half.

It is certain also, that the currency of the country, during those times, consisted chiefly of Silver Coins; and that the number of Gold Coins then in circulation bore but a very small proportion to those of Silver. The people might perhaps on that account be induced to pay less attention to the relative value of the two precious metals in the different sorts of Coin, and to estimate it with less accuracy. Besides, it is possible, that the Mines and other sources, from which these metals are procured, might, in the whole of that period, have afforded a more regular and proportionate supply of each of them, than they have done in later times.

From the 2d James I. inclusive, to the 15th of Charles II. the rise in the value of Gold, compared with Silver, was very great and rapid. It has already been stated, according to the different estimates made of it in the Mints of this kingdom, that this rise amounted in sixty years to $32\frac{59}{67}$ per cent. or nearly one third. The great inconveniences, which the people of this kingdom suffered from the many and sudden changes in the value of these metals, during these sixty years, and the difficulties, to which Government was on that account exposed, are fully proved by many entries in the Books of Your Majesty's Privy Council, and by the chronicles and writings of those times. The ministers who then served the Crown, among whom there were men of great knowledge and talents, and particularly Sir Francis Bacon, the first philosopher of the age, had frequent consultations on this subject, by order of their Sovereign; and they took the advice of merchants, bankers, and other persons, supposed to be best versed in a business of this nature: but they were never able to discover any sufficient remedy for the evil. It is certain, that the rise in the value of Gold made by James I. in the 2d and 3d year of his reign, was rendered necessary by the exportation of the Gold Coin, which had for some time been experienced, and by the very small quantity of it that was then left in circulation. This rise, which was equal to $10\frac{79}{3}$ per cent. in the Gold Coins of the old standard, and to $11\frac{3}{67}$ per cent. in the Gold Coins of the new standard, as before stated, produced a partial and temporary relief; for Stowe, in his Chronicle, observes, that *" and for six years after, here was more " plentie of Golde than ever was before;"* but he confesses, that this plenty of Gold Coin did not continue in circulation for any length of time, and that it afterwards began to be exported. It soon became evident, that the last mentioned rise of the value of Gold in the Coins of this kingdom was not sufficient to make it equal to the relative value of Gold to Silver at the market: King

_{CHAP. 12.}

Stowe's Chronicle, p. 912.

James therefore was under the necessity, in the 9th year of his reign, of farther raising the value of his Gold Coins 10 per cent. The proclamation, by which this second rise was commanded, assigns the reasons, on which it was founded, and the principles, on which this Monarch, by the advice of his Privy Council, proceeded, on that occasion; for it is there expressly said, "that " the Unite or Gold Coin, that passed for 20 Shillings " in England, was valued in foreign countries, and par- " ticularly in Holland, at 22 Shillings;" that is, at 10 per cent. more than the value at which it was current in England; and it was on this account that he raised the value of his Gold Coin then in circulation 10 per cent. Experience however soon proved, that the Government had now erred in the opposite extreme, and that this rise was too great; for it appears, from undoubted testimonies, that, subsequent to it, the Silver Coin began to be exported, in like manner as the Gold Coin had been before. It is observed by Mr. Munn, that "this last raising of Gold " 10 in the hundred did bring in great store thereof, " more than we were accustomed to have in the king- " dom; but that it carried away all, or the most part of " our Silver." And it is acknowledged by a Letter from the Lords of the Privy Council to King James, dated the 30th November 1618, that for the last seven years " Silver had been scarce at the Mint, though Gold " had been plentiful." This fact is confirmed by a Certificate of the Officers of the Mint annexed to the Letter before mentioned, by which it is proved, that in seven years previous to the year 1616 there had been coined no more than 57,689*l.* 9*s.* of Silver; and in the last of these years no more than 216*l.* 4*s.* 6*d.*; but that in the same seven years there had been coined of Gold 1,546,309*l.* 1*s.* 10*d.*; and in the same Certificate it is shewn, that in the last seven years of the reign of Queen Elizabeth, there had been coined of Silver 844,433*l.* 4*s.* 4*d.*, and of Gold no more than 104,280*l.* 12*s.* This want of Silver Coin continued afterwards to increase, and very small quantities of Silver Bullion were brought to the Mint. The Gold Coins, which were then issued from it in great plenty, were immediately clipped, or otherwise diminished in their value. To remove both these evils, by a proclamation issued on the 14th May, in the 10th year of his reign, that is, in the year 1612, entitled, " For the better staying of Treasure within the " Realm, and also for the procuring and inviting of the " same to be brought as well to his kingdom as to his " Mint," King James thought fit " *to set the prices of* " *foreign Gold and Silver in their several species.*"

CHAP. 12.

See this proclamation referred to in the proclamation of the 4th February 1619, quoted hereafter.

By another proclamation issued on the 23d day of March, in the 12th year of his reign, that is, in the year 1614, King James having first declared, *that the Treasure of Gold and Silver brought into the Realm hath bene by sundry Acts of Parliament ordained to be as an immoveable and perpetuall stocke, which should never go forth againe, but should receive a daily increase without diminution, and be conserved as well for the making and maintaining of just and honourable warres, either offensive or defensive, as for adorning the kingdom*

See Collection of Proclamations in the Council-Office, vol. 2.

CHAP. 12.

in time of peace; and having complained, *that great quantities of Gold and Silver are continually carried forth into forraigne parts, not only for supply of Commerce in respect of the excesse of forreigne commodities (which is a thing in itselfe intolerable), but also upon secret and subtill gaines, made at the Mints abroad,* which artifices as he does not approve nor much lesse emulate, but is desirous to frustrate, orders, that the statutes made and in force against the exportation of Gold or Silver in coin, jewells, plate, or vessell, or howsoever, should be strictly carried into execution under the severest penalties.

In a subsequent period the Privy Council were ordered by the King to take this subject into consideration. Sir Francis Bacon, then Lord Chancellor, and Sir Edward Coke frequently attended. There were many consultations in the years 1618 and 1619; and the Officers of the Mint, and the principal Merchants of the city of London, were called on for their advice; but it appears, that these Officers and the Merchants differed greatly in their opinions, with respect to the remedy. When it was found that they could not agree, they were ordered to hold separate meetings, and each of them to make a separate report. The Privy Council, after having heard various propositions offered to them, thought fit to order, that the East India Company and the Goldsmith's Company should make bye-laws, binding themselves not to give a higher price for Silver, than that at which it was received at the Mint: and when these bye-laws were presented to the Board on the 21st

See the Proceedings in the Council Books in the years 1618, 1619, 1620.

January 16 $\frac{19}{20}$, "the Lords found them defective in point " of penalty;" and they add, that this penalty " ought " to have been expressed by a clause to the following " effect, *upon such further penalty as his Majesty shall* " *be pleased to lay upon the Company.*" Another proposition was at that time made, and at first adopted by the Privy Council, for coining the Pound Troy of standard Silver into 66 Shillings ; but upon further consideration the execution of this measure was suspended.

When it is considered that the real cause of this great evil, and the many ill consequences which it produced, was the high price at which Gold had been estimated in the Coins of this realm for some years past, it is matter of astonishment, that King James should, just at that time, that is in his 17th year, again raise the value of the Gold in his Coins, and thereby increase the difficulties to which his subjects were exposed. There is reason however to suspect, that it was intended to keep this measure secret. Mr. Lowndes has published no Mint Indenture of this King of a later date than his 10th year; and it is probable, that he could not find any. Diligent search has been made in the repositories where such Indentures are usually kept, and no Mint Indenture made in the 17th year of James I. can be found. In a manuscript Treatise, which appears to have been written at that time by a person of eminence, King James is advised to keep for some time secret all alterations made in his Coins; but a Mint Indenture of the 21st of James I. has been found, in which this rise in the value of Gold in the Coins is ordered. It was probably

CHAP. 12.

Rushworth's Hist. Collec. part ii. vol. L p. 149, 150.

See Rymer's Fœd. vol. 17. p. 133. and Collection of Proclamations in the Council-Office, vol. 2.

made as early as his 17th year, by some private order, of which no trace can be discovered; and indeed all the writers on Coin agree that it was then made. This rise was however but small; it was $1\frac{3}{22}$ per cent. in the old standard, and $\frac{100}{491}$ per cent. in the Coins of the new standard, as before stated. The necessary consequence was, that a still greater scarcity of Silver Coin ensued, and that a very small quantity of Silver Bullion was brought by the merchants to the Mint during the remainder of this reign, and during the whole, or at least a considerable part of the reign of Charles I. and it is mentioned in Rushworth, in his account of the year 1632, "that there was such plenty of Gold, and such "scarcity of Silver, that the drovers and farmers, who "brought cattle to Smithfield, would ordinarily make "their bargain to be paid in Silver; and that it was "usual to give two pence, and sometimes more, to "change a 20*s*. Piece of full weight."

It appears that, during this period, the Government adopted other measures to remove the great inconveniences, to which the commerce of the kingdom continued to be exposed, from this inequality in the intrinsic value of the Coins made of the two metals. By another proclamation issued on the 4th February 1618, King James confirmed his proclamation of the 14th May 1612; and observing, that *the drawing of Moneys into the Goldsmith's hand, by turning Silver into Gold, upon profit of Exchange, doth make it the more ready to be ingrossed into the merchant's hand for transportation to Mints abroad,* he prohibited the melting down the Gold or Silver Coin of the realm, in order to convert the same into plate. He also prohibited the " excessive use of " Gold and Silver Foliate in every sort of ornament, " except in making armour, or at funerals."

On the 11th June 1622, that is in the 20th year of James I. a third proclamation was issued by this King, acknowledging the scarcity of Gold and Silver, in consequence of the exportation thereof from this kingdom, and complaining that his former proclamations had not been obeyed, "*notwithstanding some remarkable examples of* "*Justice in his High Court of Star Chamber.*" He thereby confirms the foregoing proclamation, and also prohibits the exportation of these metals, not only in *Coin*, but in *Bullion*, and in every other state or condition whatsoever, under the severest penalties. He also prohibits the making any Gold or Silver thread, or the selling of Gold or Silver Bullion to any person, except *to the Officers of his Majesty's Mint and Changes*, unless it " be for making of *Amells**, or repairing old Plate, so " as to make it as good as Sterling ;". and he further prohibits the selling of any fine Silver, or Silver allayed, molten into mass, to any person whatsoever, or by one Goldsmith to another.

By a subsequent proclamation, dated the 10th July 1624, that is in the 22d. year of his reign, King James again acknowledging that his former proclamations had not produced the effect that was expected from them,

See Rymer, vol. 17. p. 376. and Collection of Proclamations in the Council-Office, vol. 2.

See Rymer, vol. 17. p. 605. and Collection of Proclamations in the Council-Office, vol. 2.

---

* An old term for works in enamel, or other fine works in Gold or Silver. See Stat. 4th Hen. VII. ch. 2.

CHAP. 12.

thought fit, in consequence of a complaint of the House of Commons, to revoke a Charter he had granted to the Company of Gold Wire Drawers, who were charged with having contributed to the waste of Gold and Silver. He again prohibits the sale of Silver or Gold, except to the Officers of his Majesty's Mint and Changes, and to the Goldsmiths within the realm, "for the augmentation " and mending of Coin and Plate;" and he requires, " that no refiner sell to any person any manner of Silver " in mass;"—and "that no Goldsmith sell any fine " Silver allayed, or molten into mass, to any person or " persons whatsoever, nor one Goldsmith to another, " except for the making of Amells, or the amending of " Plate to make it as good as Sterling."

Charles I. on the 21st December 1626, that is in the 2d year of his reign, revived the ancient office of King's Exchanger, and granted the same to the Earl of Holland; and in a proclamation dated 25th May following, this King, complaining that the former proclamations of his Father had not been carried into due execution, and that the weightiest and best Moneys were culled out and molten down, so that there was a great scarcity, particularly of Silver Coin, and that such as remained was greatly "enfeebled;" and that the price of Silver at the market being raised above the price, at which it was valued at the Mint, no Silver Bullion was brought to it, because the merchants lost thereby; therefore ordered, *that no person, except the said Earl of Holland, should presume to exchange or buy any manner of Bullion in any species of foreign Coin, or in Ingots, or in any*

Rymer, vol. 18, p. 896.

other form whatsoever. He also confirmed all the before mentioned proclamations of his Father, and issued long instructions for carrying strictly into execution this proclamation, as well as those of his Father.

By a decree in the Star Chamber Court on the 7th February 1636, seven persons, convicted of culling out the most weighty Pieces of the Coin of this realm, and melting them down, and exporting the same, as well as foreign Coin and Bullion, to foreign parts, were fined 8,100*l.*, and committed prisoners to the Fleet till they paid the fines so set upon them. It is asserted, that individuals had by those practices made a profit of 7 or 8,000*l.* per annum. There were several other proceedings for offences of this nature, in the Court of Star Chamber; and some men of great consideration in the commercial world, who were accused of these practices, received the King's pardon.

Rushworth's Historical Collections, vol. 2. p. 350.

But notwithstanding the proclamations before mentioned, and the severities exercised for enforcing the execution of them, it appears, from a writer who lived in those times, that Silver, either in foreign Coin or Bullion, was sold during the whole of this reign at 1*d.*, 2*d.*, 3*d.*, &c. per oz. above the Mint price; and he alledges, that 30,000*l.* in Sixpences, Shillings, and Half Crowns, were melted annually by one single Goldsmith, for six years together, from 1624 to 1630.

Violett's humble Declaration, &c. 4to. 1643. p. 23.

Violett's Proposals to Oliver Cromwell, fol. 1656, p. 89.

In the reign of Charles I. Lord Cottington, by virtue of a commission under the Great Seal, made an advantageous contract with the King of Spain for bringing Silver into England. A great quantity was imported;

See Lenke on Coins, p. 301.

CHAP. 12.

and in consequence of the conditions imposed on the merchants, who were parties to this contract, a considerable proportion of it was brought to the Mint to be coined, from 1630 to 1643. This measure, though of an extraordinary nature, appears to have been the most effectual remedy for affording a supply of Silver Coin, that was adopted in the course of that reign.

On the 18th March 1640, information was given to the House of Commons of the exportation of Coin; and they appointed a Committee to take the same into consideration. Mr. Violett, who during this time wrote many treatises on Coin, was ordered to attend, together with other persons: but it does not appear from their proceedings that they did any thing effectual in this business.

Commons Journals, vol. 5. p. 286.

On the 1st September 1647, the Parliament again took this subject into consideration; they ordered a declaration to be prepared for the security of such merchants as should bring any Bullion into the Tower;

See Scobel's Collection, p. 132.

and the Lords and Commons passed an ordinance, on the 6th September in that year, prohibiting the currency of any clipped or unlawful diminished Silver Coins; but declaring that such diminished Silver Coins might be received in payments for a limited time at 4s. 10d. per oz. Troy, or 4s. 4½d. per oz. Avoirdupoise.

There is an entry in the Journals of the House of Commons, on the 3rd November 1647, permitting the exportation to the East Indies of 6,000l. in foreign Coin and foreign Bullion of Silver; which clearly proves that the Parliament at this time would not suffer even foreign Coin and Bullion, without their permission, to be exported from this country.

The foregoing facts have been stated as proofs of the distresses, which prevailed during those times, in the monetary system of the kingdom, and of the embarrassments, to which the commerce of it was on that account exposed. Many of the remedies then applied are precedents by no means worthy of imitation. Further proofs, if they were necessary, might be adduced from the Records, the Journals, and the Pamphlets then published; but it is proper to observe, that the general histories of those times are, as usual, very deficient in information of this nature.

It happened, however, that the evils resulting from an imperfect estimation of the relative values of the two precious metals, by degrees diminished; for during the whole of this period the price of Gold continued gradually to rise, and at length became so high, as to administer a complete remedy, by preventing the exportation of the Silver Coin. It is impossible, at this distance of time, to say precisely when this event took place; it probably happened about the commencement of the government of the Commonwealth; for it appears, by the best account that can be procured, though it is not official, of the quantity of Money coined at the Mint from the year 1649 to 1658, that much more Silver was then brought to the Mint than Gold. The quantity of Silver coined there during that period is stated by Sir William Davenant at 1,000,000*l.*; the quantity of Gold coined

See Davenant's Discourses, p. 33 to 39.

there during the same period is stated by another writer at no more than 154,000*l.*

However, the price of Gold compared with that of Silver continued still to rise; so that Charles II. was under the necessity, soon after the Restoration, that is in 1663, to raise the value of Gold in his Coins. It has already been stated, that the weight of the 20*s.* Piece, which in the 17th James I. was 5 dwts. 20½ grs. was reduced by Charles II. to 5 dwts. 9½ grs. and this was a rise in the value of Gold of $8\frac{22}{41}$ per cent. This last mentioned Coin, since called a Guinea, was ordered in the Mint Indenture to pass for 20*s.*; but it immediately became current at a higher rate, by general consent, without any authority from Government. Mr. Locke, and other writers, who lived during these times, asserts, that during the reigns of Charles II. and James II. the Guinea passed at from 21*s.* to 22*s.*; and Mr. Locke further adds, "that the Gold Coins varied in their value "according to the current rate;" that is, according to the relative value of Gold to Silver at the market. The subjects of this country paid no attention on this occasion to the rate set upon these Coins in the Mint Indenture. There is indeed an order in the Council Books, directing the Attorney General to prepare a proclamation for making these new Coins current, according to the rate prescribed in the Mint Indenture: but it does not appear that any such proclamation was ever issued, or that any other measure was taken to enforce obedience to the intention of Government, as expressed in the said Indenture.

Those who advised their Sovereign no further to CHAP. 12.
interpose his authority on this occasion, certainly acted
wisely; for if he had obliged the people to receive these
Gold Coins at the low rate before mentioned, they would
certainly all have been melted down and exported, as fast
as they were issued from the Mint; and the additional
value, which the people gave to these Gold Coins, above
the nominal value, at which they were rated in the Mint
Indenture, evidently proves, that the public was then
disposed to measure the value of every thing bought and
sold, by the Silver Coins, as best adapted to the state of
our commerce at that time. These Gold Coins therefore
took their natural or intrinsic value, compared with those
of Silver, and rose in their price in like manner with
every other commodity.

In the reigns of Charles II. and James II. the Silver
Coins, of which the old hammered Money constituted a
considerable part, had been gradually diminished, by
clipping, and other frauds. In the beginning of the The great
reign of King William III. these practices increased William III.
rapidly; and the Silver Coins were in general become
so very defective, that it was found, upon experiments
made by the Officers of the Exchequer, in the year See a Table at
the end of
1695, that they wanted, upon the whole, nearly one half Mr. Lowndes's
Report on the
of their weight. The great evils, to which the people, Silver Coins, in
which these
as well as the Government, were thereby exposed, are experiments are
accurately
fully described by Mr. Lowndes, who was then Secretary stated.
of the Treasury, in a Report made by him on the 12th
September of that year, to the Lords Commissioners of
his Majesty's Treasury. He informs their Lordships,

Chap. 12. "that in consequence of the defective state of the Silver
"Coin, great contentions daily arose among the King's
"subjects, in fairs, markets, shops, and other places
"throughout the kingdom, to the disturbance of the
"public peace;—that many bargains and dealings were
"totally prevented and laid aside, which lessened trade
"in general;—that persons, before they concluded any
"bargain, were necessitated first to settle the price or
"value of the very Money they were to receive for their
"goods; and that they set a price on their goods accord-
"ingly;—that these practices had been one great cause
"of the raising the price, not only of all merchandises,
"but of every article necessary for the sustenance of the
"common people, to their great grievance*;—that the
"receipt and collection of the public taxes, revenues,
"and debts, were extremely retarded, to the damage of
"his Majesty, and to the prejudice of a vigorous prose-
"cution of the war; so that there never were in his
"remembrance so many bonds given and lying unsatisfied
"at the Custom House, or so vast an arrear of excises;
"—that, from the same cause, many complaints were
"daily transmitted from the Commissioners, Receivers,
"and Collectors of the land-tax." And in proof of the
degree to which the receipt of that tax had been affected,
by the defective state of the Coin, Mr. Lowndes referred
the Lords of the Treasury to the account of the sum
brought into the Exchequer in the course of that year,

* Mr. Locke, in his Answer to Mr. Lowndes, confirms this account of Mr. Lowndes, that all sorts of provisions and commodities had risen excessively.

compared with the timely payments of the like tax in preceding years. With respect to the foreign commerce, Mr. Lowndes observes, "that the exchange with the Low " Countries was fallen so very low, that the public lost " about four Shillings in the Pound upon all Monies " remitted thither;—that the exchange to Hamburgh " and the East countries for all naval stores and other " goods was still lower; and to all places in the Medi- " terranean, the exchange was yet more to the prejudice " of this country; and that there were very great losses, " on that account, in remitting Money for the payment " of our fleets and armies:" and he further observes, " that the price of Silver in Bullion was risen to 6s. 5d. " per ounce, and that the Guinea having risen to 30s., " passed in currency at a much higher value than the " price of Silver in Bullion would then justify." * The consequence was, that all the Silver Bullion in the kingdom, that could be collected, instead of being brought to the Mint, was exported in return for Gold Bullion, in which foreigners made their payments to their own advantage, and to the great detriment of the merchants and manufacturers of this country, who had any commercial intercourse with them.

Such was the alarming situation of the kingdom at a period when it was engaged in a foreign war, on the success of which depended the preservation of our liberties, and all the benefits derived from the Revolution.

* Silver Bullion had risen in price 24½ per cent. The Gold Coin in tale had risen about 36⅓ per cent.

CHAP. 12.

Among the various parties, into which the kingdom was at that time divided, there was not one, which did not think that some remedy was absolutely necessary. Many propositions were made. Two of these most attracted the attention of the public; one, offered by Mr. Lowndes, who had long been Secretary of the Treasury; the other, by Mr. John Locke. The conduct of this difficult business fell to the lot of Mr. Charles Montague, then Chancellor of the Exchequer. He followed principally the plan proposed by Mr. Locke, and called to his assistance Mr. Newton, afterwards Sir Isaac Newton, whom he then made Warden of the Mint, and Dr. Halley. The kingdom was then divided chiefly into two great factions; so that from political motives Mr. Montague met with opposition in every measure he proposed. He lost, in the House of Commons, at first, many questions, essential to the success of his measures; but by bringing the same propositions repeatedly under the consideration of the House, he at last carried them, though with very small majorities.

The old hammered Coins, which had been most reduced, began at this time to be exchanged for such of the remaining Silver Coins as were more perfect, and less clipped, at a premium. The first measure therefore, which the Parliament adopted, was to pass an Act, forbidding the receiving or paying of any *broad Silver Money*, or Silver Money unclipped, of the Coin of this kingdom, for more than its nominal value in tale. But this measure produced another evil; for, in consequence of it, all the perfect and unclipped Silver Coins began

6th and 7th William III. ch. 17. sec. 2.

See Mr. Lowndes's Report, p. 114. See also Mr. Locke's Essay.

to be hoarded, so that they appeared no longer in circulation; and as the Parliament had not forbidden the exchange of the deficient or clipped Silver Coins for Guineas, or other Gold Coins, the former were then exchanged for the Gold Coin; and the Guinea, which had passed before generally for 21s. 6d., or 22s., began now to pass for 30s.; and it would have risen to a greater value, if the Officers of the Exchequer, and the Receivers of the public revenue, had not refused to receive it in payment, at a higher rate. To remedy this last evil, the Parliament passed two Acts, mentioned in a former part of this Letter, forbidding first the currency of Guineas at any higher rate than 26s. each; and afterwards, at any higher rate than 22s. each. They also passed an Act, suspending, for a limited time, the coining of Guineas; and as it was foreseen, that Guineas, either such as had been formerly remitted to foreign countries, or had been counterfeited abroad, would be imported in great quantities, the Parliament at the same time prohibited the importation of Guineas.

CHAP. 12.

7th and 8th William III. ch. 10, sec. 18.

7th and 8th William III. ch. 19, sec. 12.

7th and 8th William III. ch. 13.

To support the currency of the clipped and deficient Silver Coins, the Parliament enacted, that all taxes and debts due to the Crown, for excise, customs, &c. and the whole year's land-tax, might be paid to the collectors, at any time before the 4th May 1696, in the clipped Coins; and that all loans of Money, borrowed on the authority of Parliament, might also be paid in the clipped Coins, as if the same were good and lawful Money, unless otherwise specially directed. And in subsequent Acts the remainder of the clipped Coins was ordered to be

7th and 8th William III. ch. 1.

8th William III. ch. 2.

8th and 9th William III. ch. 6.

Chap. 12.

7th William III.
ch. 1. sec. 2.—
This clause of the Act is not printed in the common edition of the Statutes.

7th and 8th William III.
ch. 19. sec. 2.

received at the Mint, and by the Receivers of the public revenue for a limited time, by weight, but at a value exceeding the Mint price of Bullion.

To give additional credit to the new Silver Coins, as soon as they should be issued, the Parliament enacted, that the clipped Money "should be recoined by the Mill " and Press into current Money of this realm, to hold " such weight and fineness as are prescribed by the " present Indenture of the Mint, which weight and fine- " ness are declared to be, and shall remain to be, the " standard of, and for the lawful Silver Coin of this " realm."

Encouragements were at the same time given for bringing Plate to the Mint, and 6d. for every ounce of standard Silver so brought in was to be paid as a premium: and all persons keeping inns, or other public houses, were forbidden to have any Silver Plate in their houses, except spoons. It was further enacted, that no Bullion, either of Gold or Silver, in Ingots, or otherwise, should be exported, except upon proof before the Lord Mayor of London, that the same was not made of the Coins of this realm, or clippings thereof, or of Plate wrought within the kingdom. They permitted, however, Bullion, equal in value to 200,000*l.* sterling, to be exported by licence from the King, for the payment of his Majesty's forces in foreign countries.

As it was of great importance to bring the new Silver Money into currency as speedily as possible, the Recoinage was carried on not only at the Tower, but Mints were established for this purpose in different parts of the country, and persons of science were sent to these Mints, to superintend and control the operations there carried on.

This important business was very far advanced in the first two years; but it appears by accounts received from the Officers of the Mint, that four years were necessary for the completion of this Recoinage. The quantity of Silver Coins made on this occasion amounted in tale to 6,812,908*l*. 19*s*. 7*d*.; of which, 5,091,121*l*. 7*s*. 7*d*. was coined at the Tower, and 1,791,787*l*. 12*s*. was coined at the country Mints.

I have not been able to find, in any public office, an account of the whole charge and loss, which the public incurred by this Recoinage. The Officers of the Mint have indeed furnished an account of the charges for the making or fabrication of the new Money, or what may properly be called the Mint charges. They amounted to 179,431*l*. 6*s*.; but the losses sustained by the receipt of the principal part of the clipped and deficient Coins, at their nominal value, as well as the charge for premiums paid to induce persons to bring in the remainder, and to bring Plate and Bullion to be coined, are no where stated with any certainty. It is presumed however, that these charges and losses could not amount in the whole to less than 2,700,000*l*.*

* It appears, that the actual quantity of Silver Money either recoined or made of Plate, brought to the Mint, was 6,882,908*l*. 19*s*. 7*d*. If we suppose, that only two thirds of this sum, that is, 4,588,605*l*. 19*s*. 8¾*d*., were worn and clipped Coins, which were diminished nearly one half, and received at the Exchequer in payment of the public revenues, and of loans, at their nominal value, the loss to the public on this account

Great as this charge was, the losses which the Government, as well as the people of this kingdom, continued daily to suffer, till the Recoinage was completed, justified almost any expence, which might be incurred for their relief. To the great losses already stated, as occasioned by the defective state of the Silver Coin, it may be proper to add, that in every contract made by Government, or individuals, the deficiency of the Coin must have been taken into consideration, and the price of every article augmented, probably in a much greater proportion, than this deficiency would justify.

Mr. Locke, whose advice on this occasion was principally followed, as before observed, had considered the

---

would amount to 2,294,302*l*. 19*s*. 10½*d*. If again we suppose that the remaining third being 2,294,302*l*. 19*s*. 10½*d*., cost the public no more than 6*d*. per ounce, or about 10 per cent., this is a further loss to the public of 229,430*l*. Add to this the charges of coining, or Mint charges, amounting to 179,431*l*. 6*s*. These three sums make together 2,703,164*l*. 5*s*. 10½*d*. This is a very moderate estimate of the whole loss incurred by the public by this Recoinage. Mr. Lowndes, in his Report to the Lords of the Treasury, estimated the quantity of the worn and clipped Silver Money, then current, at 4,000,000*l*.; and the loss, which the public would incur by recoining it according to the old standard, at 2,000,000*l*. Anderson, in his History of Commerce, says, that the Recoinage cost near 3,000,000*l*. The common histories estimate it at 2,200,000*l*. It does not appear from the Journals, that the Parliament ever voted so large a sum, expressly for this purpose; but it is probable, that a considerable part of this loss shewed itself only in deficiencies of several branches of the revenue; and that the House of Commons, in making it good, did no more than vote sums to supply these deficiencies. It is extraordinary, however, that no account should have been made out at that time, of the actual loss occasioned by the Recoinage; or if any such account was made out, that it should not have been preserved in some of the public offices.

subject with that depth of thought, by which all his writings are distinguished; and he had treated of it in a philosophical and speculative view, with great ability; but he appears not to have adverted to many circumstances of a practical nature, necessarily connected with this subject; and it is probable that he was not well informed of the history of our Coins, which would have pointed out these circumstances to him. He asserted as a certain fact, "that Silver Coins made the " Money of Account, or Measure of Commerce, in " England and the neighbouring countries." How far this assertion is well founded, we shall have occasion to shew hereafter. He then laid it down as a principle which could not be controverted, that "an ounce " of Silver, whether in Pence, Groats, or Crown " Pieces, Stivers or Ducatoons, or in Bullion, is, and " always eternally will be, of equal value to any other " ounce of Silver, under what stamp or denomination " soever." Of this principle there can be no doubt: but from these two premises he drew the following conclusions:

First, That the high price of Silver Bullion at that time was to be ascribed to the defective state of the Silver Coins then in currency; and that whenever the Silver Coins were restored to their due weight, the price of Silver Bullion would fall, so as to be nearly the same as that, at which it was valued at the Mint. Secondly, that the Gold Coins, if their value in currency was not fixed by public authority, would pass in payment, with reference to the Silver Coins, *according to the current*

See Mr. Locke's Letter to a Member of Parliament in 1691.

CHAP. 12.   *rate;* that is, according to the relative value of Gold to Silver at the market.

If the conclusions resulting from the foregoing premises were universally true, and had operated on the present occasion to their full extent, it is certain, that as the Silver Coins then wanted nearly one half of their weight, the price of Silver in Bullion should have risen in the same proportion; that is, to about 10*s.* per ounce: and that the Guinea should have risen to nearly twice the value, at which it had hitherto passed in currency, that is, to about 44*s.*; but neither of these consequences happened. The price of Silver in Bullion rose to no more than 6*s.* 5*d.* per ounce; and the Guinea rose only to the value of 30*s.* It is true, that the further rise of the Guinea was prevented, by orders given to the Officers of the Exchequer, and to the Receivers of the public revenue, not to receive it in payment at a higher rate; and some time afterwards the value of the Guinea was still further limited, by the two Acts of Parliament, as before mentioned.

As the Silver Coin was so very defective, before the general Recoinage was undertaken, and as during this Recoinage there could have been very little of it in currency, it is certain, that the Silver Bullion, which was then purchased, must have been paid for principally in the Gold Coin. It was natural therefore to expect, that Silver Bullion would have taken its price in due proportion, with reference to the current value of the Gold Coin. But it is singular, that as the Gold Coin had not taken its value in a due proportion with reference to the deficient Silver Coins, so Silver Bullion did not take its price in a due proportion with reference to the current value of the Gold Coins. The Gold Coins, though they had risen $36\frac{4}{11}$ per cent. passed in currency at $46\frac{2}{3}$ per cent. less than their true value, compared with the deficient state of the Silver Coins; and Silver Bullion, though it had risen $24\frac{6}{31}$ per cent. was then sold at $9\frac{677}{847}$ per cent. less than its true value, compared with the current value of the Gold Coins.

Mr. Lowndes says, that the Guinea then passed at 30s., *with the almost unanimous consent and agreement of the common people;* and he adds, that there was *no other visible reason* for this extraordinary rise in the value of the Gold Coins above the price at which Silver Bullion then sold, except the *danger and vexation*, which the people had experienced from every Money transaction in the clipped and deficient Silver Coins.

Whatever may have been the causes of these strange incongruities in the value of the Gold and Silver Coins, and of the price of Bullion with reference to these Coins, as before stated, they serve at least to prove, that the events, which then happened, by no means corresponded with the conclusions, which, in Mr. Locke's opinion, resulted from the principles laid down by him, and on which he so much relied. They afford also strong reason to infer, that there are other causes, which may sometimes influence the value of Coins, while they are current only within the realm, as well as the price of the

CHAP. 12. precious metals in reference to them, besides the intrinsic value of the metal in such Coins.*

It may however be said, that those were times of confusion, and that no principles, however true, were likely in such times to produce their full effect. Let us see then what effect these principles produced, when the Recoinage was completed, and when all the clipped and deficient Silver Coins were driven out of circulation, and such only as were thought to be perfect were permitted to be current.

When the Recoinage of the Silver Coin was completed, the price of Silver Bullion did not even then fall, so as to be nearly † the same as the Mint price; and the Guinea, the value of which in currency had been reduced by an Act of Parliament to 22s., became current, without any interposition of public authority, at 21s. 6d.; but it

---

* There cannot be a stronger proof of the truth of this observation, than that which is afforded by the currency of the present deficient Silver Coins, which now circulate at their nominal value, and even sometimes bear a premium, though they are deficient, to the degree that will be stated hereafter.

† Whenever the balance of commerce is against this country, and there is a want of Bullion to be exported, Bullion will always sell at a small advance above the price at which it is valued at the Mint, in consequence of the laws prohibiting the exportation of Coin. This advance must always be sufficient to compensate the risk of melting down or exporting the Coin, and this compensation is generally estimated at about 1 per cent. And whenever the demand for Bullion to be exported is very great, the price of it will rise still higher, and it is probable that the value of the Coin would in such case rise in a like proportion, if that value was not limited by public authority. In such case however there will be always a greater temptation to melt down and export the Coin.

did not fall in so great a degree as it ought to have fallen, according to the relative value of Gold to Silver at the market. The consequence was, that the new Silver Coins were immediately melted down and exported; and though 6,882,908*l*. 19*s*. 7*d*. in tale had been lately coined, the most considerable part of this great sum, in the course of eighteen years, disappeared, and the public were deprived of the use of it; so that Sir Isaac Newton, in his Report of the 21st September 1717, says, "that if Silver Money should become a little "scarcer, people would in a little time refuse to make "payments in Silver, without a premium." Another consequence resulted from the same cause; very little Silver Bullion was brought to the Mint to be coined. From the year 1699, when the general Recoinage was completed, to the end of the year 1717, no more than 674,831*l*. 15*s*. 9¼*d*. in tale was coined; and of this sum 320,372*l*. 12*s*. were ancient Scottish Silver Coins, or foreign Coins permitted to be current in Scotland before the Union, which were recoined at Edinburgh into Coins of the English standard, by virtue of the Treaty of Union. Two other parts of this sum, that is 78,811*l*. 6*s*., coined in the year 1709, and 76,780*l*. 16*s*., coined in the year 1711, were principally made of Plate, brought to the Mint in consequence of special encouragements then given. From the Plate so brought in, 144,000*l*. was converted into Coin, and only 11,592*l*. 2*s*. was coined from Silver Bullion brought into the Mint in the usual course, during these two years: so that the natural or ordinary coinage of Silver,

Chap. 12.

Martin Folkes, Table of English Silver Coins. p. 131. Note.

during this period of eighteen years, amounted to no more than 210,459*l*. 3*s*. 9¼*d*.

The exportation of the Silver Coins was at that time occasioned by the high price of Silver Bullion at the market, and by the high rate, at which the Gold Coins continued to be current, compared with that of the Silver Coins. The high rate of the Gold Coins, to which the people then voluntarily submitted, can only be ascribed to the preference, which at that time began to be given to the use of Gold Coins in all payments, at least of considerable amount. It is evident, that during the late Recoinage the common people had become accustomed to the use of the Gold Coins; and the reason, which induced them still to prefer them, was perhaps the convenience of making large payments in Coins of that metal. This change, from what had been the case in the reign of Charles II. was probably owing to the great increase in the commerce of the country, and to an augmentation in the price of every commodity, so that payments in general required Coins made of the most valuable metal. The fact certainly is, that from this period the Gold Coins began to take the ascendency, and to become the more usual instrument of commerce and measure of property, in preference to the Silver Coins. In the reign of King William, when the Silver Coins were so very deficient, Mr. Locke had said, *It is no wonder, if the prices and value of things be confounded and uncertain, when the Measure itself is lost.* To restore this Measure the public had expended 2,700,000*l*. But notwithstanding so great an expence, this Measure of

Property, in the lapse of a very few years, was a second time lost, and had again no existence, unless it had passed into the Gold Coin.

In this state were the Coins of this kingdom in the year 1717, when the ministers of George I. alarmed at the great diminution of the Silver Coins, which had been made in such great quantities not twenty years before, took the subject into consideration. They applied to Sir Isaac Newton, then Master of the Mint, for his advice. The subject was referred to him, and he reported, "that " the principal cause of the exportation of the Silver Coin " was, that a Guinea, which then passed for 21s. 6d., was " generally worth no more than 20s. 8d., according to " the relative value of Gold to Silver at the market, " though its value occasionally varied, and it might be " worth something less, whenever there was a great " demand for the export of Silver, particularly to the " East Indies, and perhaps something more, whenever " a Plate fleet was just arrived from Spanish America." He then suggested, that 6d. *should be taken off from the value of the Guinea, in order to diminish the temptation to export and melt down the Silver Coin; acknowledging however that* 10d. *or* 12d. *ought to be taken from the Guinea, in order that Gold may bear the same proportion with the Silver Money in England, which it ought to do by the course of trade and exchange in Europe.* This proposal of the Master of the Mint may be considered as a second attempt to restore to the Silver Coin the quality of a measure. But it is evident, that Sir Isaac Newton, who was no less distinguished for modesty, candour, and

CHAP. 12.

caution, in every opinion which he advanced, than for the accuracy and strength of his understanding, and for the large and extensive view which he took of every subject that came under his consideration, offered this proposal only *as an experiment;* and he adds, that the effects of this measure *would shew hereafter, better than can appear at present, what further reduction would be most convenient for the public.* This great man appears to have been apprised of the fluctuation which frequently happens in the relative value of the two precious metals; and he was probably apprehensive, that if the rate, at which the Gold Coins were to pass, had then been reduced, in full proportion, compared with the value of the Silver Coins, there would be the greatest danger* that these Gold Coins, which were at that time almost the only instrument of commerce remaining in the kingdom, might in their turn be melted down and exported; and yet, if they were not lowered still further, the Silver Coins would, in a degree, be subject to the same evils as before.

In pursuance of the advice of Sir Isaac Newton, the Lords of the Privy Council recommended to His Majesty, King George I. to lower, by proclamation,† the value of the Guinea to 21s.; and the other Gold Coins in proportion.

---

* When the value of the Gold Coins is in exact proportion with that of the Silver Coins, the Gold Coins will certainly be exported before the Silver Coins, because the bulk of the Gold Coins is less than that of the Silver Coins, and consequently there is less risk, trouble, and charge, in exporting them.

† In all the Mint indentures from the 15th of Charles II. the Guinea had been called a Twenty Shilling Piece; and it was ordered to pass at that rate. But on this occasion a new indenture was made,

By this measure, which gave in effect the legal value of 21s. to a Piece originally intended to be current at 20s., the value of fine Gold, compared with that of fine Silver, was estimated, in the Coins of this country, as $15\tfrac{2859}{13640}$ to 1; and this last rise in the value of fine Gold compared with fine Silver was 5 per cent.; and the whole rise in the value of Gold from the 1st James I. that is, in a space of 115 years, was $39\tfrac{32}{67}$ per cent.; considerably more than one third.

But the Lords of the Privy Council, in executing this measure, did not conform to the principle adopted by Parliament, in the 7th and 8th of William III. of leaving the Guinea and other Gold Coins to be paid or received at any value under the rates by them limited. In the proclamation issued on this occasion, it was not simply said, that each Guinea *should not pass for more than* 21s., and the other Gold Coins in proportion; but it is expressly declared, *that the said respective Pieces of coined Gold shall be current at the rates and values then set upon them.* By this injunction, the Guinea and all the other Gold Coins became legal tender, at the rates therein declared. They could no longer vary in their value, according to the relative value of Gold to Silver, as they had varied since the year 1663.

But though the Guinea was then reduced to 21s., from 21s. 6d., it was still rated at a higher value than it ought to be, compared with the Silver Coins, by at least

dated 6th May 1718, in which this Piece of Gold Coin was called a Guinea, or a Twenty-one Shilling Piece; and it was ordered to pass for twenty-one Shillings Sterling.

4d., or 1 10/31 per cent. Experience has proved, that when Coins of two metals are made legal tender at given rates, those who have any payments to make, will prefer to discharge their debts or obligations, by paying in that Coin which is over-rated. From that period, therefore, all considerable payments have been made in the Gold Coin; and the Silver Coins have generally served only in making small payments, or in exchange for the fractional parts of the Gold Coins. It has before been observed, that, previous to this proclamation, the people were disposed to make their payments in the Gold Coins, in preference to those of Silver. This last measure tended to confirm what was before the disposition of the people, and gave the Gold Coins a complete ascendency in the currency of the kingdom; and the Silver Coins have since become a mere representative of the Gold Coins, for the purposes before stated. The greatest part of the good and weighty Silver Coins, which then remained, have since been melted down and exported. And it appears by the accounts presented by the Officers of the Mint, that from the year 1717 to the end of the last century, that is, in a period of eighty-three years, no more than 584,764l. 17s. 5½d.* in tale of Silver has been coined: and from the year 1760 to the end of the same century, that is, in a period of forty years, no more than 63,983l. 15s. 5d. in tale has been coined; and the Silver currency has gradually fallen into its present state of imperfection.

* A considerable part of this Silver Coin was made from the Silver brought into the kingdom by Lord Anson, taken in the Acapulco ship. Other parts were produced from Silver taken in other prizes.

CHAPTER XIII.

Of the alterations and debasements of the Coins by lowering the standard or fineness of the Metal.

I HAVE now completed the account of the alterations and debasements made in the Coins of the realm, under the two first heads; and will therefore proceed to treat of them under a third head, that is, by lowering the standard or fineness of the metal, of which the Coins were made; or, in other words, by diminishing the quantity of pure metal, and proportionally increasing the quantity of alloy. The reasons for treating this part of the subject under a separate head have already been assigned. The whole of these extraordinary transactions were indeed a convulsion in the monetary system, which never happened in this kingdom, except in the short period from the 34th Henry VIII. to the 6th Edward VI. But this mode of debasing Coins has been frequently practised in other countries, particularly in France, during the reigns of Philip de Valois, of his son John, who was some time a prisoner in England, of Charles VI. and of his son Charles VII. During a great part of the reign of these Sovereigns, the kingdom of France was distracted by internal factions, and by the invasions of the English under those great Monarchs Edward III. and Henry V.; and the French Kings before mentioned

98   OF THE ALTERATIONS AND DEBASEMENTS

CHAP. 13. were in great want of revenue to resist the wars, that were then successfully waged against them.

It is proper to begin by observing, that Henry VIII. in the 18th year of his reign, that is, in the year 1527, had ordered, that the Tower Pound should no longer be used in his Mints, and had adopted the Troy Pound in its stead. The only reason, that can be assigned for this change, is, that his Father, Henry VII. had, in the 11th and 12th years of his reign, by statutes enacted "for the "purpose of regulating weights and measures," introduced the Troy Pound into more general use, and made it the standard, by which all other weights were to be regulated; and Henry VIII. may perhaps have thought it right, on that account, to order, that the same sort of weight should be used in his Mint. This King, in his 34th year, that is, in the year 1543, began to debase the standard of the Silver put into his Coins, by reducing the old standard of 11 oz. 2 dwts. fine, and 18 dwts. alloy, to 10 oz. fine, and 2 oz. alloy. He at the same time reduced in a small degree the weight of his new Silver Coins, by putting into his Groats only 1 dwt. 16 grs. of Silver of the last mentioned standard, instead of 1 dwt. 18 grs. of Silver of the old standard, which had been the weight of them in his 18th year; and by these two different sorts of debasement he made the Pound of Silver of the old standard pass in tale for 2*l*. 13*s*. $3\frac{1}{4}\frac{11}{25}d.$, instead of 2*l*. 5*s*., at which it had passed in his 18th year; and the Pound in tale was thereby debased $7\frac{367}{999}$ per cent.

This King, in his 36th year, further debased the standard of the Silver put into his Coins, by reducing it to 6 oz. fine, and 6 oz. alloy; and he thereby made the Pound of Silver of the old standard pass in tale for 4*l*. 8*s*. $9\frac{1}{2}\frac{2}{5}d.$; and the Pound in tale was thereby further debased $16\frac{16}{999}$ per cent.

The same King, in his 37th year, again debased the standard of the Silver put into his Coins, by reducing it to 4 oz. fine, and 8 oz. alloy; and he thereby made the Pound of Silver of the old standard pass in tale for 6*l*. 13*s*. $2\frac{1}{4}\frac{3}{5}d.$; and the Pound in tale was thereby further debased $8\frac{8}{999}$ per cent. The Silver Coins of this Monarch continued in this state till his demise.

Edward VI. during the four first years of his reign, continued his Silver Coins upon the same footing, on which his Father had left them. But in his fifth year he debased the standard of the Silver put into his Coins, by reducing it to 3 oz. fine, and 9 oz. alloy; and he thereby made the Pound of Silver of the old standard pass in tale for 13*l*. 6*s*. $4\frac{3}{4}\frac{1}{5}d.$; and the Pound in tale was thereby further debased $8\frac{8}{999}$ per cent. As, during these debasements, the several Coins continued nearly of the same weight as they were before, the diminution of fine Silver was in a great degree compensated in weight, by a proportional quantity of alloy. It is proper also to observe, that Edward VI. in the 3d year of his reign, made Shillings of a better standard than his other Silver Coins, that is, of 6 oz. fine, and 6 oz. alloy. He is supposed also to have made a few Shillings of a still better standard, but he diminished the weight of such Shillings, so as to make their intrinsic value to be the

100   OF THE ALTERATIONS AND DEBASEMENTS

CHAP. 13.   same as that of his other Coins, of which the metal was more debased.

It has been already shewn, that Henry VIII. in the 18th year of his reign, had made an alteration in the standard of the Gold in some of his Gold Coins, by reducing it to 22 carats fine, and 2 carats alloy. In his 37th year he further reduced the standard of the Gold put into some of his Coins, to 20 carats fine, and 4 carats alloy.

Edward VI. in the 5th year of his reign, followed the example of his Father, by making his Gold Coins of 20 carats fine, and 4 carats alloy; but he afterwards reverted to the former standard of 22 carats fine, and 2 carats alloy, called the new standard, and made no more Gold Coins of an inferior standard.

Henry VIII. in the 36th year of his reign, reduced the weight of his 20s. Pieces of Gold of the new standard from 8 dwts. 8 grs. to 8 dwts.

Edward VI. in the 3d year of his reign, again reduced the weight of these 20s. Pieces of the new standard, by making them of 7 dwts. $1\frac{1}{4}$ grs. And in his 4th year he raised the nominal value of the Sovereigns of the old standard, which had for some time passed at 22s. 6d., to 24s.; and the other Gold Coins of this standard in due proportion. He continued however still to make his coins of the old standard of the same weight as they were before.

It is evident from what has been stated, that these two Monarchs, in the preceding debasements, observed no proportion in the nominal value of their Gold and

Silver Coins, compared with their intrinsic value. These last were more debased, and were rendered intrinsically much less valuable than those of Gold, compared with the nominal value, at which they were respectively made current. This great inequality will appear more clearly from the following table.

Fine Gold, compared with fine Silver, was estimated,
 In the 36th Hen. VIII. as $6\frac{9}{11}$ to 1.
 In the 37th Hen. VIII. as 5 to 1.
 In the 3d Edw. VI. as $5\frac{5}{33}$ to 1.
 In the 4th Edw. VI. as $4\frac{788}{033}$ to 1.
 In the 5th Edw. VI. as $2\frac{324}{033}$ to 1.

CHAPTER XIV.

Of profits made by exchanging Silver Coins for Gold Coins.

THE necessary consequence resulting from this disproportioned and very unequal value set on the Gold and Silver Coins, was, that enormous profits were made by exchanging Silver Coins for Gold Coins at their respective nominal values.

This profit was,

$$\left.\begin{array}{l}\text{In the 36th Hen. VIII... } 61\frac{1}{3} \\ \text{In the 37th Hen. VIII... } 120 \\ \text{In the 3d Edw. VI. ..... } 113\frac{9}{17} \\ \text{In the 4th Edw. VI. .... } 127\frac{121}{132} \\ \text{In the 5th Edw. VI. .... } 355\frac{545}{576}\end{array}\right\} \text{per cent.}$$

It followed that all the Gold Coins were in a short time either hoarded, melted, exported, or in some way or other driven out of circulation. King Edward VI. in his Journal, acknowledges, that Gold Coins were not freely exchanged for those of Silver without a premium; and Stowe, in his Survey of London, says, "that he had seen " twenty-one Shillings current given for one old Angel " to gild withal." It should be remembered, that ten Shillings was the highest nominal value, at which the

[margin: Stowe's Survey of London, vol. i. p. 88.]

Coin called an Angel was made current during this period. CHAP. 14.

So great was the confusion then introduced into the Coins of this country, that I have found it difficult to state and explain, with any degree of perspicuity, the several debasements and alterations made in them; nor is it easy to conceive, in what manner any exchanges or payments could at that time be made. The fact is, that all commerce was nearly at a stand. The farmers were unwilling to bring provisions to market; and when they offered them to sale, they did not know what price to set upon them. Merchants and tradesmen also greatly increased the price of every article, which they had to sell. The Government tried every method to keep up the value of the debased Coins then in circulation, and proclamations were issued for that purpose, which were not obeyed. To enforce obedience, Parliament passed a law already quoted, for inflicting penalties on those " who " should exchange any coined Gold or coined Silver at " a greater value than the same was, or should be, " declared by His Majesty's Proclamation to be current " for, within his dominions." Other Proclamations were issued, for obliging persons, under severe penalties, to bring their corn and provisions to market, and for setting prices on all the necessary articles of consumption. The Parliament passed laws for regulating the manner of buying and selling all sorts of beasts and cattle, as well as butter and cheese; and for limiting the prices at which all sorts of wine should be sold. There was an act also subjecting fuel to an assize, which, in order to exclude

5th and 6th Edward VI. ch. 19.

3d and 4th Edward VI. ch. 19.

3d and 4th Edward VI. ch. 21.

CHAP. 14.

7th Edward VI. ch. 7.
5th and 6th Edward VI. ch. 14.

from this trade such as were disposed to monopolize, forbad any person to buy fuel, "except such as burn it, " or retail the same." The law against regraters, forestallers, and engrossers, which has some time since been repealed, was passed on that occasion, and owed its origin to the obstructions, to which every species of internal traffic was at that time exposed. The farmers were disposed to export to foreign countries many of the most necessary articles of life, rather than bring them to the country markets to be sold and exchanged for the base Coin; and on this account the exportation of these articles was prohibited.

It was however at length discovered, that no effectual remedy could be applied to the evils then existing, but a total reformation of the Coins of the realm. This measure was undertaken in the last year of the reign of Edward VI. It is extraordinary, that the ministers of this Prince, who had hitherto committed such gross errors in debasing the Coins of the kingdom, should instantly adopt principles, which led to a system, not perfect indeed, but nearly as perfect as any, to which the other nations of Europe have hitherto attained in their Coins; and they carried on this reform with so much diligence and vigour, that, even before the death of this King, it was in part executed, to the general satisfaction of the public. Queen Mary suffered the Coins to remain in nearly the same state, in which her brother had left them: but Queen Elizabeth completed the plan of reform, which he had projected, and had begun to carry into execution.

CHAPTER XV.

Of the reformation in the Monetary System, begun in the reign of Edward VI. and finished in that of Queen Elizabeth.

HAVING thus presented to Your Majesty a short history of the great and extraordinary debasements made at that time in the Coins of the realm, it would be improper to omit some account of the principles adopted, and of the measures pursued, in bringing about this memorable reform; especially as the historians of those times, and the writers on Coins, have not given any satisfactory explanation of them. I shall also be thereby enabled to assign the causes, which have produced many of the defects now existing in our system of Silver Coins.

In conducting this reform, the ministers of Edward VI. first considered, what should be the standard of the Silver, of which the new Coins should be made. They determined not to make them of Silver of the old standard, that is, of 11 oz. 2 dwts. fine, and 18 dwts. alloy, but of the standard of 11 oz. 1 dwt. fine, and 19 dwts. alloy.

It is singular, that if they departed from the ancient standard, they should make so small an alteration; and if they made any, that they should not have brought it precisely to the same standard, of which some of the Gold

Chap. 15. Coins were then made; that is, the standard of what is called Crown Gold, and which is since become the only standard of the Gold in our Coins. The standard of the metals in these two sorts of Coin would, in such case, have been the same; and the quantity of alloy in each of them would have been in the same proportion, that is, one twelfth part; and such a regulation would have facilitated in future a comparison of the relative value of the two precious metals in our Coins.

The ministers of Edward VI. in the next place considered, what the weight of the Silver Coins should be in future. They probably thought it too violent a measure to return to the nominal Pound, or Pound in tale, as it was settled in the 18th of Henry VIII.; that is, before this Prince began to debase the standard of the Silver, of which his Coins were made, and when the Pound Troy of standard Silver was coined into 45 Shillings. They determined to take a middle course, and to coin the Troy Pound of Silver, of the standard before mentioned, into 60 Shillings by tale, and thereby to augment in nominal value, by one third, the Pound in tale. By adopting this rule they obtained the following advantage, that the Crown Piece weighed exactly an ounce Troy, the Half Crown Piece half an ounce, the Shilling 4 dwts. that is, one fifth of an ounce, or the sixtieth part of a Pound Troy; and the Sixpence 2 dwts. that is, one tenth of an ounce, or the hundred and twentieth part of a Pound Troy; all of which are aliquot parts of the Pound Troy; so that the people could thereby more easily understand what the weight of these

Coins ought to be, and on that account be the more induced to weigh them.

In carrying these principles into execution, the ministers of Edward VI. determined, in the first place, to endeavour to bring into circulation all the Gold Coins, which they understood to be hoarded in great quantities, and to make them the basis of their future proceedings. It should be remembered, that these Gold Coins had been debased in a very small degree, compared with the several debasements of the Silver Coins; and if brought into circulation, they would serve to supply, or at least in some degree diminish, the want of good Silver Coins, until the new Silver Coins could be made and issued. For the reason above mentioned, they advised the King to raise the Gold Coins of the old standard one third higher in value in tale, than that, at which they were made current in the 18th Henry VIII.; and for this purpose, to order by Proclamation, that the Sovereign, or Double Rial, which had been made current in the 18th Henry VIII. for 22s. 6d., should pass in future for 30s., and the other Gold Coins of the old standard in due proportion. The Gold Coins of the new standard were also raised nearly one third higher than that, at which they were made current in the 18th of Henry VIII. This measure produced the effect which was expected from it; the Gold Coins, which had been hoarded, were brought immediately again into circulation. These ministers then took measures for making and issuing, with the greatest expedition, new Silver Coins, at the rate of 60s. to the Pound Troy; that is, one third more

CHAP. 15. in nominal value, than that, at which they had passed in the 18th of Henry VIII. It appears therefore, that the principal object, which they had in view, was, to raise both the Gold and Silver Coins one third more in nominal value, than the rate or value, at which they had been current in the 18th of Henry VIII. In Gold Coins of the old standard, and in the Silver Coins, their design was exactly carried into execution; and in the Gold Coins of the new standard it was as nearly executed as existing circumstances would permit. The value of fine Gold, compared with that of fine Silver, was now therefore estimated, in Coins of the old standard, as $11\frac{193}{953}$ to 1; and in Coins of the new standard, as $11\frac{1}{20}$ to 1. The difference of these relative values of Gold to Silver, from those in the 18th of Henry VIII. is almost entirely to be attributed to the difference in fineness of the metal, of which the Silver Coins of the two periods were made.

The ministers of this King proceeded, in the last place, to decry the debased Silver Coins, that had been issued since the 34th of Henry VIII. They determined to do it by degrees, but with as little delay as possible. They adopted a plan for this purpose, not entirely consonant to the principles of justice. Having carefully examined into the intrinsic value of the several sorts of the debased Silver Coins then in currency, that is, of those of 9 oz. fine, of 6 oz. fine, and of 3 oz. fine, they found, that the whole taken together were worth intrinsically one half of their nominal value. By a proclamation they first decried them all one fourth of their former nominal value. And by another proclamation, issued very soon afterwards, they decried them another fourth, that is, upon the whole, to one half of their nominal value; being what they had estimated the whole, taken in a mass, to be intrinsically worth: but they made no distinction in their nominal value, though they were of different degrees of debasement.

Such were the measures pursued by Edward VI. in reforming the Coins of the realm. He died a short time afterwards. Queen Mary made no alteration, except that, in the first year of her reign, she reduced the standard of the Silver in her Coins to 11 oz. fine, and 1 oz. alloy, or eleven twelfths of fine metal, and one twelfth alloy, by which the Pound Sterling in tale was debased $\frac{160}{999}$ per cent. from what it had been made by her brother Edward VI. in the last year of his reign.

The debased Silver Coins continued to be current at the same nominal value, to which Edward VI. by his last Proclamation had reduced them, during all the reign of Queen Mary, and to the second of Elizabeth, while the new Silver Coins were making, and getting by degrees into circulation.

It appears by a proclamation of Queen Elizabeth, of the 29th September 1560, that as long as the debased Coins continued in circulation, they were the cause of great embarrassment, in all payments made within the realm, as well as in our exchanges with foreign countries. The people however made no complaints, but were satisfied with the measures that were taking for completing this reform. Terrified at the evils they had already suffered, they only apprehended some new project of debasement.

These apprehensions were not without foundation: Queen Elizabeth, at that time, had counsellors, who advised her to recur, for the sake of profit, to the same measures, which had been pursued by her Father and Brother, in debasing their Coins; but she rejected these counsels, by the advice of the Lord Treasurer Burleigh. In the 2d year of her reign she restored the standard of the Silver in her Coins, to 11 oz. 2 dwts. fine, and 18 dwts. alloy; that is, the standard of old Sterling; by which the Pound Sterling in tale was raised $\frac{329}{999}$ per cent. above what it had been made by Queen Mary, in the first year of her reign. In the next place, she further decried such of the debased Silver Coins remaining in circulation, as were of 9 oz. fine, and 6 oz. fine, not in the same manner, and in the gross, as in the 6th of Edward VI. but in different proportions, according to the different degrees of their debasement: and she ordered, that the third and worst sort of these debased Monies, which were only 3 oz. fine, should be no longer current. In order that the people might distinguish the different sorts left in currency, she caused different marks to be put upon them; and at the foot of her proclamation, issued for this purpose, there were engravings of the several sorts of these debased Monies, with the marks she had ordered to be put upon them. In a short time afterwards she issued another proclamation, ordering, that the two sorts of debased Money, so left in currency, should no longer pass in any payment whatever, but that they should be received at her Mint, and be exchanged for the new Silver Money, according to the value which she had lately set upon them by her proclamation. All this debased Money was thus at length driven out of circulation, and the reform was completed.

The joy expressed at the completion of this reform was very great. The Parliament and people, in their addresses to Queen Elizabeth, always mentioned the reformation of the Coin, after that of religion, as one of the principal merits of her reign; and it is recorded as such in the epitaph upon her tomb. Her historian, Camden, after having placed in a very strong light the evils, to which the people had been exposed, by the debasements made by Henry VIII. and Edward VI. commends very highly this last act of Queen Elizabeth, by which she at length drove out of circulation all the debased Coins. In language above his usual style, he calls it *magnum sane, et memorandum, quod neque Edwardus potuit, neque Maria ausa.* It must be acknowledged however, that the Queen was not entitled to all the merit in this business, which she herself exclusively assumed, and which historians and posterity have in general ascribed to her. The principles adopted by Edward VI. in the last year of his reign, comprehended the whole of this important measure, and were in general correctly conceived. Queen Elizabeth departed from some of these principles, and thereby rendered our system of Coins less perfect than he intended. The measures which Edward VI. pursued, were upon a larger scale, and more difficult to be executed, and

Camden's Elizabeth, p. 61.

CHAP. 15. therefore of a bolder character. King Edward, by one proclamation, brought into circulation all the Gold Coin that had been hoarded; and, by two subsequent proclamations, he in a very short space of time decried the whole of the Silver Coin then in currency, to half the nominal value, at which it had hitherto passed. Queen Elizabeth indeed, after an interval of seven years, further decried what remained of this debased Money, in a much smaller degree indeed, but upon better principles. It is evident, however, that she took this measure with a view of bringing these debased Coins to her Mint, without any loss to her revenue; and, for this purpose, she soon afterwards declared, that they should be no longer current. The principles, on which King Edward acted, laid the foundation for every future step in the proceeding; but it was his misfortune, that he did not live long enough to carry his plan fully into execution. It was the good fortune of Queen Elizabeth to ascend the throne, after sufficient time had been allowed for making and issuing a quantity of new Silver Coin, adequate to all the purposes of circulation: and she was thereby enabled to relieve the public, by taking out of currency all the debased Money, which still continued to embarrass commercial transactions; and to claim the merit of having brought this business to a conclusion.

Mr. Locke appears to have been of this opinion. See his answer to Mr. Lowndes.

It is at least doubtful whether this Queen acted wisely in altering the standard of the Silver in the Coins of the realm, as settled by Queen Mary at 11 oz. fine, and 1 oz. alloy; and in reverting to the standard of old Sterling, of 11 oz. 2 dwts. fine, and 18 dwts. alloy; for by this measure she again rendered the two metals, of which our Coins are made, of different and unequal standards; so that from thenceforth they became not of the same proportion or degree of fineness; and, for that reason, their relative values cannot now be so easily compared.

But Queen Elizabeth, in the subsequent years of her reign, pursued measures with respect to her Coins, which greatly diminish the merit, to which her former conduct had given her pretensions; for she authorised, by special commissions, small occasional deviations, from time to time, both in the weight of some of her Coins, and in the standard of the metals, contrary to the very terms of her Mint indentures. She made also, in the 43d year of her reign, Silver Coins, very much debased, for the use of her kingdom of Ireland;* and though this practice was in some degree justified by former precedents, it produced great embarrassments in the internal trade of that kingdom; and some merchants, who carried on commerce with it, were great sufferers thereby. The legality, however, of her proceedings in this respect, was sustained by a decision of her ministers of justice in that kingdom. And lastly, in the same year, that is her 43d, when her

margin notes: Sir Martin Folkes, Note, pp. 55 and 56, where he quotes a commission of the 29th Dec. 21st Elizabeth, and says, that he has seen others of the like import.

margin note: See the Case of mixed Monies in Sir John Davis's Reports.

---

* The Gold and Silver Coins of Great Britain and Ireland are now the same; and they have been so for a considerable period. The rate, however, at which these Coins are current in the two kingdoms, that is, the nominal value at which they pass as Money of account, is different; it is 8⅓ per cent. more in Ireland than in Great Britain. This difference was made by a proclamation of James II. dated 25 March 1689, when he returned to Ireland from France, after his abdication; and it has continued so ever since. See Simon's Irish Coins. p. 150.

CHAP. 15. honest Treasurer and faithful Minister Lord Burleigh was no more, she followed the example of her Father in the latter years of his reign, and of her Brother during the whole of his reign, except the last year, by debasing her Silver Coins. She then coined the Pound Troy of standard Silver into 62 Shillings, instead of 60, whereby the Pound Sterling was debased $1\frac{41}{273}$ per cent. from what it had continued to be since the 2d year of her reign; and by this measure she defeated one of the objects, which her Brother had in view, in the excellent plan, which he projected in the last year of his reign, and thereby acted contrary to a principle, wisely adopted by him, of making all the Silver Coins of known weights, and aliquot parts of the Pound Troy; and to this imperfection the Silver Coins of this kingdom have ever since been subject.

CHAPTER XVI.

Of apparent motives for the alterations and debasements made in the Coins at successive periods.

I SHALL conclude this history of the alterations and debasements made in the Coins of the realm, at successive periods, by giving a short account of the motives, which appear to have influenced the Ministers, by whose advice they were made, and the Sovereigns, by whose commands they were executed.

These motives were, first, a desire of augmenting the royal revenue. Secondly, principles of mistaken policy.

Augmentation of revenue was expected from the additional profits, which would in such case arise, from the right of Seigneurage. This Seigneurage was a certain portion or allowance of all the Gold and Silver brought to the Mint to be converted into Coin. It consisted of two parts. The first was such a portion as would be sufficient to defray the charges of coining the metals so brought to the Mint. This portion was called in the French Mints, *Brassage*, a term, which some writers derive from the two Latin words, *Brachiorum Labor*. The second portion was a profit which the Sovereign claimed, by virtue of his prerogative; and it is to this last, that the word Seigneurage most properly belongs. These were avowed profits; but in addition to these, some

Sovereigns occasionally derived profits from practices of a fraudulent nature. There is reason to suspect, as is before stated, that, by special orders, they sometimes authorised the principal Officers of their Mints to make their Coins either of less weight, or with more alloy, than was required by the terms of their Mint indentures; or they authorised a large remedy to be taken, (which remedy is nothing more than an allowance for errors in coining,) and did not require the Officers of the Mint to make their Coins as perfect as possible, but authorised or suffered them to coin just within the remedy; that is, they permitted them to take out of the Coins, either by diminishing the weight, or increasing the alloy, as much as the remedy would justify. These practices, however, were generally kept secret. This right or prerogative of Seigneurage was probably of Gothic institution; for the ancient Governments of Europe, prior to the invasion of the Goths, do not appear to have derived any profit from the making of their Coins. Some of them took indeed sufficient to defray the charge of the fabrication: but Le Blanc says, that the Roman Government did not take any allowance for it, and that it was defrayed out of the public revenue. After the invasion of the Goths, the profits of Seigneurage began to be taken by the Sovereigns of every state in Europe. Le Blanc has produced an ordinance of King Pepin, which shews, that this right of Seigneurage existed in France, as early as the year 755; he thinks it was of more ancient institution.

Mr. Necker, in his Treatise on the Administration of the French Finances, says, that the profits of Seigneurage

on the Coinage of Gold in France, at the time, when he CHAP. 16.
wrote, amounted to $1\frac{2}{3}$ per cent.; and on the Coinage of
Silver to $1\frac{7}{24}$ per cent. independent of what was retained
for Brassage, or the charge of Fabrication, which was
2 Livres per Marc for coining Gold, and $14\frac{1}{2}$ Sols per Ibid. vol. i. p. 20.
Marc for coining Silver; and that it produced a revenue
of about 500,000 Livres, or 20,833*l.* per annum. Mr.
Necker adds, "that the compensation for the expences of
"Coinage is found in the value given to the specie, and
"by that means falls on the people." From whence it
may be concluded, that the French Government gave a
nominal value to their Coins beyond the intrinsic value
of the metal that was in them, sufficient to compensate
the charge of Fabrication, and to pay to the Sovereign
the profits of Seigneurage, in the proportion before
stated. He observes however, that the profits derived
from Seigneurage were formerly more considerable. The
right of Seigneurage is still enjoyed by most of the
Sovereigns of Europe. There are no records, which
enable us to decide when this right first commenced in
this kingdom. It was extinguished by an Act passed in
the 18th Charles II. ch. 5. The profits derived from
Seigneurage were in former times so much considered as
a branch of the royal revenue, that they were occasion-
ally granted, in whole, or in part, to corporate bodies, See Le Blanc in
for their advantage, or for defraying certain charges various parts, and Du Cange,
expressed in the grant itself. They were sometimes under the words Seigneurage and
granted to individuals by way of pension. And when Monetagium.
the right of Seigneurage was extinguished in this king- See 18th
dom, by the before mentioned Act of Charles II. there Charles II. ch. 5. sec. 12.

CHAP. 16.

was a pension, payable out of the profits derived from it, granted for twenty-one years to Dame Barbara Villiers, by Letters Patent under the Great Seal, of two pence by tale out of every pound weight Troy of Silver Coins made at the English Mint: and the Legislature, from a principle of justice, ordered the payment of it to be continued out of the Coinage duties, imposed by that Act.

When the Sovereign was in great want of revenue, it was usual for him to increase the portion or allowance, which he took of the precious metals brought to his Mint. The profits derived from this source were of course various. An account of those received by the Kings of this realm, from the 28th Edward III. to the 15th Charles II. may be seen in the tables inserted at the end of Snelling's Views of the Gold and Silver Coin, taken, as he alleges, from a manuscript treatise in his possession. An account of those received by the Kings of France may be extracted from the tables at the end of Le Blanc's Traité Historique des Monnoyes de France. It appears from these accounts, that the profits so taken were sometimes enormous: they were particularly so in this country, during the latter end of the reign of Henry VIII. and the first five years of Edward VI. The historian Camden, in his observations on these transactions, imputes the debasements made by these two Monarchs in their Coins to a desire of augmenting their revenue; and Edward VI. in his Journal, expressly acknowledges, that such was the motive of his government for pursuing these measures. On these occasions the

Camden's Elizabeth, p. 61, 62.

merchant sometimes received, in return for his Bullion, a smaller number or portion of Coins; and the Coin itself was not diminished or debased. This was the more usual practice in the English Mint; but this manner of taking the Seigneurage, by which the merchant received fewer Coins in tale than the number that might have been made from the quantity of Bullion which he furnished, must have had the effect of discouraging the bringing of Bullion to the Mint. At other times this profit was taken out of the Coin itself, by diminishing its weight, which operated as a small debasement. But the far greatest profits were derived from this right of Seigneurage, when the Sovereign made a general debasement of all his Coins; for the ancient Coins then in circulation being of a greater intrinsic value than the new Coins of the same denomination debased, the holders of these ancient Coins brought them in general to the Mint to be recoined, for they obtained some profit thereby; so that by a general debasement of his Coins the King received his profits of Seigneurage from nearly all the Coins of the same description, then current in his dominions. It was, on this account, more usual to practise these debasements on the Silver Coins, than on those made of Gold; for the profits of Seigneurage on the Recoinage of the former were much greater than they would have been on that of the latter. As the old Coins were brought in voluntarily, it was not thought necessary, on these occasions, to issue a proclamation for calling them in; nor have I found any proclamation for that purpose. These debasements were certainly

CHAP. 16.

See Le Blanc, p. 158.

See Du Cange, article Monetagium.

high acts of injustice; they injured all those who derived their income from any subsisting grant or lease; they diminished the property of all creditors; they exposed the poor man, who could not accurately estimate the diminished value of the new Coins, to be imposed on in his purchases, by those who understood the business better than himself; they introduced confusion into all markets, and caused a sudden check and obstruction to traffic and commerce of every description; and they frequently produced discontents, and sometimes a tendency to insurrection. And though the Sovereign might obtain some temporary profit from these debasements, their natural effect was to diminish all the ancient revenues of the Crown; and it became on that account necessary to augment former taxes, or to impose new ones, to make the royal revenue equal to what it was before.

It appears, from the historians of France and of other foreign countries, that the people so severely felt the effects of these debasements, that they voluntarily paid a tax to the Sovereign, to induce him not to exercise his right in this respect; and this tax was called *Monetagium*. Le Blanc states many instances of this nature, and adds, that Charles VII. of France, when he had driven the English out of his kingdom, and determined to restore his Coins from the great state of debasement, to which he had been forced to reduce them, consented to reserve only so much of his profits of Seigneurage, as was necessary to pay his officers for the Fabrication of the new Coins; but that his subjects gave him in return the

Tailles and Aides; and he observes, "*que l'imposition* "*fixe des Tailles et des Aydes fut substituée à la place* " *d'un ancien tribut, infiniment plus incommode, que* " *n'étoient alors ces deux nouvelles impositions.*" In the Duchy of Normandy, when it was governed by the English Monarchs, there was a tax on hearths, paid every three years, called Monetagium; in return for which, the Sovereign of that Duchy engaged not to debase his Coins. Sir Matthew Hale, in his History of the Common Law, acknowledges, that our Kings of the Norman race had introduced this tax or custom into England; but that Henry I. in the first year of his reign, was induced to renounce his right to it; and it does not appear that any claim of this sort has ever since been revived.

<small>CHAP. 16.

Le Blanc, p. 92.

Hale's History of the Common Law, p. 116.
Matthew Paris, p. 38. col. 2.</small>

The principles of mistaken policy, being the second motive, which induced the Kings of this realm to debase their Coins, were of two sorts. First, an idea, entertained by these Kings and their ministers, that the Coins, though debased, and containing less pure metal than before, would continue to pass, according to their respective denominations, for the same nominal value; and that they should not only augment their own revenues, but that the value of the income of their subjects would not be thereby impaired. They idly supposed, that the new Coins, after such debasement, would be taken in payment, without any attention to the quantity of pure metal that was in them, and that the prices of commodities would not be augmented, in consequence of any debasements in the Coins, with

CHAP. 16.

margin note: Rolls of Parliament, vol. iii. p. 658.

which they were purchased. The folly of such an idea, in the extent to which it was carried, has been so fully exposed, not only by those who have written on this subject, but by the experience, which every attempt of this kind has afforded, that any discussion on this point appears to be unnecessary; and we need only refer to facts already stated, in the preceding history of the alterations and debasements made in the Coins of this realm, and to the consequences resulting from them.

The second motive was an idea, that they should thereby prevent the national Coins from being exported, and that they should be better able to retain them within the kingdom. It appears by the Rolls of Parliament, that in the 13th year of Henry IV. the scarcity of Money at that time was assigned as a reason by the Lords and Commons for requesting that King to debase his Coins, and he debased them accordingly: but the Parliament seems even then to have entertained a doubt of the wisdom of this measure; for the Lords and Commons at the same time expressed a desire, " that " the King would not continue to follow this advice, if " at the end of two years he should find by experience, " that it was not for the benefit of his kingdom."

I have already stated the strange maxim of James I. expressed in the preamble of a proclamation issued by him, in the 12th year of his reign, where he says, " that " the treasure of Gold and Silver brought into the realm " should be considered as an immoveable and perpetual " stock, which should never go forth again;" and an account has also been given of the many futile attempts made by that King, and his Son and Successor Charles I. to enforce the observance of this rule. It must likewise be admitted, that in former times persons of some eminence have entertained and supported the idea, that, by diminishing the intrinsic value of our Coins, they were more likely to be retained within the realm. This idea has been wholly exploded, since the principles of commerce and of foreign exchanges have been well understood. Mr. Locke, and many other writers, have clearly demonstrated, that the Coins of any country can only be retained within it, when the general balance of commerce or payments is not unfavourable; and that they will necessarily be exported, when the value of the whole of the merchandize imported exceeds the value of the whole of the merchandize exported, in order to pay the deficiency. If indeed the goods so imported are only an unusual quantity of stock, intended for re-exportation, and not to be used or consumed in the country, it is certain, that, upon the sale and re-exportation of such stock, the Coins will in due proportion again return, or a quantity of Bullion sufficient to replace them. These principles are indeed self-evident.

It will however certainly happen, that when Coins made of two different metals are current at the same time in a country, and the value of the metal, of which one of them is made, is under-rated at the Mint, compared with the price, at which it is sold at the market, the Coins of the metal so under-rated at the Mint will be exported; and, in return, a quantity of that metal, which is over-rated at the Mint, will be imported, in order to be converted into Coins. But this is a mere traffic in Coins, and it is not probable, that this traffic, though it produces a loss to the public, and is in that respect highly detrimental, will occasion much diminution in the mass or quantity of Coins circulating in any country, as long as the balance of commerce, or of payments to foreign countries, is not unfavourable. This traffic will in general only diminish the quantity of Coins made of one metal, and proportionally increase that of the other.

Upon a full view of this important subject, in which it has been necessary occasionally to censure some of the Sovereigns of this kingdom, for their conduct with respect to their Coins, I think myself bound in justice to observe, that the Government of England has in general committed fewer errors in regulating their Coins, than that of any other country of Europe. The debasements of the Coins of this kingdom have been less frequent, and in a less degree. In France, the Livre, or Pound in tale, contained originally a Pound of Silver in weight, as in England. By successive debasements made by the French government, the Livre in tale is now reduced to about a 74th part of what it was, when the Pound in tale and the Pound in weight were the same. In Scotland, where the Pound in tale originally contained also a Pound of Silver in weight, and continued in this state till the year 1296, the Scottish Pound in tale had been by successive debasements, before the union of the two kingdoms, reduced to a 36th part of its original value. In many parts of Germany, the Florin, which is still the integer or Money of account of those countries, was originally a Gold Coin, of the value of about 10 Shillings of our present Money. It is now become a Silver Coin, of the value of only 20d.; and its present value therefore is only equal to a 6th part of what it was formerly. In Spain, the Maravedi, which was in its origin a Moorish Coin,* and is still the Money of account of that kingdom, was in ancient times most frequently made of Gold. Le Blanc observes, that in 1220 the Maravedi weighed 84 grains of Gold, equal in value to about 14 Shillings of our present Money; but he adds, that the weight of it was soon afterwards very much diminished. This Maravedi, though its value is not quite the same in the different provinces of Spain, is now become a small Copper Coin, equal in general only to $\frac{43}{272}$ of an English Penny. In Portugal, the Re,† or Reis, which is still the Money of account in that kingdom, is become of no greater value than $\frac{27}{401}$ of an English Penny: it is so small, that, in estimating its value in other Coins, it is reckoned by thousands and hundreds. The Moeda, or Moidore, is equal to 4800 Reis; and this little Coin,

Chap. 16.

Le Blanc, p. 166.

---

* The name itself of this Coin is derived from an Arabic word, or rather from the name of certain Moors called Almoravides, who passed from Africa into Spain, and gave their name to the Money coined by them. This name has since been corrupted into Maravedi. There is another more fanciful derivation of the name of this Coin, which in Latin is called Marabitinus. It is said to mean "Maurorum spolia," because the Spaniards, in driving the Moors out of Spain, frequently obtained these Coins among the spoils taken by them. Botino, in Spanish, signifies booty, or spoils. See the Great Dictionnaire de Trevoux, article Maravedis.

† I have not been able to discover what was the original value of the Re.

Chap. 16.

called a Reis, has now in fact no existence but in name. Such has been the fate of all these Coins, and such is their present state of depreciation. In this Your Majesty's kingdom of England, where the Pound in tale and the Pound in weight were originally the same, and continued in that state till the 28th Edward I. that is, the year 1300, the Pound in tale has, by nine successive debasements, been reduced to not quite one third of its original value, the present value being to the original value as 32 to 93. It is evident therefore, that the Government of England has debased its Coins in a less degree than the governments of any of the countries before mentioned; and Le Blanc, in his excellent History of the Coins of France, thinks himself bound to render

Le Blanc, p. 266.

this tribute of justice to the English nation, "that the " subject of Coins has in general been understood in few " countries so well as in England."

I have now completed the account, which I proposed to lay before Your Majesty, of the several alterations and debasements made in the Coins of this realm, during a period of nearly seven centuries and a half. This account has necessarily extended to a greater length than I could have wished. The intricacy of a subject, which has never yet been sufficiently explained or understood, must serve as my justification. Many useful inferences may however be drawn from these transactions. The errors committed by our ancestors, and the ill consequences resulting from them, will serve as instructions, by which we may be enabled to avoid the evils and embarrassments, to which they were exposed, and to establish a more perfect monetary system in future.

The various calculations, to which it has been necessary to resort, have been made, under my direction, by a Professor of great eminence in every branch of the Mathematics.* Calculations of a like nature may indeed be found in some of the books already written on Coin; but these books frequently contradict each other, and occasionally fall into error.

* The Professor mentioned in the text has furnished me with a paper, which shews, that Snelling has committed errors in most of the calculations he has made, or has been mistaken in the conclusions he has drawn from them.

CHAPTER XVII.

Of the principles of Coinage, and reasons for adopting or confirming them.

I WILL now revert to the principles of Coinage, briefly stated in an early part of this Letter.

First, I will endeavour to prove, that the Coins, which are to be the principal measure of property, ought to be made of one metal only.

Secondly, I will shew of what metal the Coins of this kingdom, which are to be the principal measure of property, ought to be made.

Thirdly, I will shew upon what principles the Coins of the other metals ought to be made; and I will endeavour to illustrate the whole by the facts related in the foregoing history of our Coins.

The first of these positions has been shortly treated of in an early part of this Letter; and I have observed, that Sir William Petty, Mr. Locke, and Mr. Harris, are decidedly of opinion, that the Coins, which are to be the principal measure of property, must be made of one metal only; and it has been assumed, that their opinion on this point is too well founded to be shaken. Lest however this assumption should be supposed to have been premature, I will here insert the passages themselves, which so fully justify it.

Sir William Petty observes, *that Money is understood to be the uniform measure of the value of all commodities;* and then adds, *that the proportion of value between pure Gold and fine Silver alters, as the earth and industry of men produce more of one than the other. That Gold has been worth but twelve times its own weight of Silver, but that of late it has been worth fourteen; so there can be but one of the two metals of Gold and Silver to be a fit matter for Money.* ^{Sir W. Petty's Political Anatomy of Ireland, ch. 10.}

Mr. Locke observes, *that two metals, as Gold and Silver, cannot be the measure of commerce both together in any country; because the measure of commerce must be perpetually the same, invariable, and keeping the same proportion of value in all its parts; but so only one metal does and can do to itself. An ounce of Silver is always of equal value to an ounce of Silver, and an ounce of Gold to an ounce of Gold; but Gold and Silver change their value one to another; and one may as well make a measure, namely a yard, whose parts lengthen and shrink, as a measure of trade, of materials, that have not always a settled unvariable value to one another. One metal therefore alone can be the Money of account and contract, and the measure of commerce in any country.* ^{See Mr. Locke's further considerations concerning raising the value of Money, vol. ii. p. 75, 76. fol. edit. 1759.}

Mr. Harris says, *that one only of these metals, that is, Gold or Silver, can be the Money or standard measure of commerce in any country; for the standard measure must be invariable, and keep the same proportion of value in all its parts. Such is Silver with respect to Silver, and Gold to Gold. But Silver and Gold with respect to one another are like other commodities, variable in their value,* ^{See Mr. Harris's Essay on Money and Coins, part i. ch. 2. sec. 7.}

K

CHAP. 17. *according as the plenty of either may be increased or diminished; and an ounce of Gold, that is worth a given quantity of Silver to-day, may be worth more or less Silver a while hence. It is therefore impossible, that both these metals can be a standard measure of the value of other things at the same time.*

In the earlier periods of our history, when Silver Coins only were current, and no Gold Coins were made at the English Mint, the Monarchs of this kingdom had no occasion to advert to this principle. But when Gold Coins began to be made in the reign of Henry III. the rate, at which they were to be current, was always fixed in the Mint indenture, and they became at that rate legal tender, and consequently the measure of property, as well as the Silver Coins, which were current at the same time with them.

The Sovereigns of this country endeavoured to regulate the rate, at which these Gold Coins should be current, according to the relative value, at which Gold and Silver Bullion, in each respective period, sold at the market. It will be seen in the foregoing history, that they sometimes committed great errors in this respect; and the evil consequences resulting from these errors have been stated; but in general our Monarchs were for a long time more correct than might have been expected.* There was indeed less difficulty in those times in preserving the relative value of the Gold and

* I always except the eight years that elapsed from the 34th of Henry VIII. to the 6th of Edward VI. which I have treated as an unusual convulsion in the monetary system.

Silver Coins, according to the price of these precious metals at the market, than at present: for before the discovery of the Mines of America, the relative value of Gold and Silver fluctuated in a less degree than in later times. It should also be observed, that Gold Coins then constituted but a small part of the currency of the kingdom; and the commerce of this country with foreign nations was much less extensive, than it has been in the two last centuries; so that the circulation of our Coins was confined in a great measure within the kingdom, where the authority of the Sovereign, in giving a nominal value to his Coins, has a greater influence, and is more readily and correctly obeyed. In those early times, the traffic in exchanges with foreign nations was not much practised, or well understood.

It is certain, that so late as the reign of Queen Elizabeth, at least in the earlier parts of it, there did not appear to be any great fluctuation in the value of the two precious metals, compared with each other. But men of knowledge and foresight became at that time sensible of the diminution of the value of Money in general, compared with other commodities; and they began on that account to be convinced, that Coins were not a correct measure of property, when the value of them was to be estimated at distant periods. It was for this reason, that, by the advice of Lord Treasurer Burleigh, and of Sir Thomas Smith, then Secretary of State, the method of estimating a portion of the rents of colleges by the value of corn, and not of Money, was first introduced, in order to maintain the revenues of these colleges, in a due proportion with the price or value of the necessaries of life in successive periods; so that such revenues might at all times be sufficient to answer the wise and laudable purposes for which they were intended. This method of estimating the value of land of such description in leases has since been called a corn rent; and it was established by an Act passed in the 18th year of Queen Elizabeth, in which it was enacted, "*that in all future leases for life, or for a term of years, made by the several colleges in Oxford or Cambridge, and by those of Winchester and Eton, one third part at least of the old rent should be reserved in corn, according to the value of good wheat and good corn, to be taken after the rate at which they should be sold at their respective markets, on the next market day before such rents should be due.* I have mentioned this fact in order to shew, that the great men of those times were not inattentive to the value of Money or Coins; but the evil, which they intended to correct, arose from the diminution of the value of Money in general, compared with commodities, as is before observed; for no mention is made in the chronicles or histories of that period, of any fluctuation at that time in the relative prices of the precious metals. The evils resulting from the fluctuations in the relative prices of these metals, do not appear to have shewn themselves in any great extent, or at least to have been the subject of general complaint, till the reign of James I.

At this last period these evils were felt in a most alarming degree. I have so fully stated, in a former part of this Letter, the extent of these evils, and the embarrassments, that were thereby introduced into all commercial transactions, that I will not trouble Your Majesty with a repetition of them. I will only observe, that in the first years of the reign of this Monarch, the complaints of the exportation of the Gold Coin, on account of the low value, at which Gold was then estimated at the English Mint, compared with the value, at which Silver was there estimated, were great and incessant. To remedy this evil, King James raised the value of Gold in his Coins, by successive proclamations; but he at last raised it beyond the due proportion; so that during the remainder of his reign, and the whole of the reign of Charles I. the Silver Coins were in their turn exported, and a very small quantity of these last remained in circulation. The complaints of the want of Silver Coins were then as great as the complaints of the want of Gold Coins had been before. During a short period, in the middle of the 17th century, the relative prices, at which the precious metals were estimated at the Mint in our Coins, appear to have been in a sort of equilibrium, or to have maintained a due proportion with the prices, at which they respectively sold at the market. But in the 15th year of the reign of Charles II. that is, in the year 1663, when a new estimate was made of the relative value of Gold to Silver at the English Mint, that of Gold was under-rated. Charles II. then indeed raised the value of Gold in his Coins, but not sufficiently; and all the Gold Coins then made would have been immediately exported, if the Government had obliged the people to receive them as legal tender, at the nominal value given to them in the Mint indenture: but Government suffered these Coins to take the value, which the people set upon them, according to the relative price of Gold and Silver at the market. In a subsequent period the Silver Coins became greatly defective in weight, so that it was necessary to call them in and recoin them. A general Coinage took place by the advice of Parliament, in the reign of King William III. After this Recoinage, the Gold Coins passed in payment at a higher value than that at which they were still rated in the Mint indenture, or than the relative value of Gold to Silver at that time would justify; not however by authority of Government, but by the general consent of the people. The consequence was, that the new Silver Coins began immediately to be melted down and exported, notwithstanding the very great charge which the public had incurred in recoining them. A very considerable part, in the course of not more than seventeen years, had disappeared, and there was found to be a want of them in circulation. The same deficiency in the number as well as weight of the Silver Coins has remained to the present day, to the great inconvenience of Your Majesty's people. From the beginning of the reign of James I. to the period of which I am now speaking, Gold and Silver Coins were alternately exported, for the reasons just stated, to the great detriment of the public, as often as individuals could profit thereby.

It is proper to observe, that James I. consulted Sir Francis Bacon, Sir Edward Coke, and many other eminent men who lived in those times; but they all appear to have been at a loss for a remedy to the evil, to which the country was then exposed. The Treatise of Sir William Petty, entitled, *The Political Anatomy of Ireland*, in which he delivered his opinion, that the Coins, which were to be the principal measure of property, could be made of one metal only, was among his posthumous Works, published in the year 1691; and as far as I am informed, this extraordinary man was one of the first who fully asserted and maintained this opinion, suggesting thereby the remedy so long sought for in vain. Mr. Locke and others followed him in supporting the same opinion; but this true principle, which solved the difficulty, has never yet been carried effectually into practice.

It is certain, however, that during the whole of this period, when our Coins were in so great a state of confusion, the commerce of the kingdom was progressively improving, and the balance of trade was almost always in favour of this country; so that these evils did not spring from a want of the precious metals, but from a continued conflict between the Coins made of different metals; and this circumstance introduced and promoted the practice of melting down and exporting one or other sort of Coin, whenever the metal, of which either of them was made, happened to be under-rated at the Mint, and a profit could be made thereby; a species of traffic, from which the public cannot derive the smallest advantage, but must always be a sufferer; a traffic, carried on by a class of men, who are constantly preying upon the public, and who sometimes defraud individuals, by collecting the most valuable and weighty Coins, and returning into circulation those that are least valuable and most defective. The profits of such a traffic are not the result of public-spirited or laudable industry, and ought, on that account, to be discouraged as much as possible, by every wise government.

There is no circumstance that more clearly proves and illustrates the truth of this principle, " That Coins, " which are to be the principal measure of property, can " be made of one metal only," than the practice, which has long prevailed in several commercial states and countries on the continent, of making foreign bills of exchange, and sometimes other bills, exceeding a certain amount, payable in what is usually called Bank-Money. These states are subject, no less than others, to the inconvenience of having their Coins of different metals, ill constructed with respect to their relative value, and of having them frequently very defective. But being generally of small extent of territory, they are exposed also to another and still greater inconvenience: from being surrounded by many other countries, there is a constant influx of the Coins of all the neighbouring states into them, particularly if their commercial transactions are of great extent; so that their general currency consists of a mixture of their own Coins, and of those of the neighbouring countries, however ill-regulated or defective they may be. If bills of exchange were therefore to be paid in this mixed and imperfect currency, the uncertainty of the value of any sum, for which these bills might be drawn, would not only produce great embarrassment in all mercantile dealings, but it would render the exchange always very much against such a state or country; for the merchants of all nations are induced, from motives of prudence, rather to undervalue the Coins of every state, with which they have any commercial intercourse. To provide against this evil, the governments of Venice, Genoa, Amsterdam, and Hamburgh, and some others, have introduced a system, well adapted for their purpose. They have formed banks of deposit. The regulations of these different banks are various; but the general principle, on which they are all founded, is as follows. The directors or managers of these banks give *recipisses*, receipts, or notes, in return for the Gold or Silver Bullion, or Coins considered as such, and sometimes for other objects of value, placed by individuals in their custody; or they give them credit in their books to the amount of the value thereof, with a right of transferring the same.

CHAP. 17.

Smith's Wealth of Nations, 8vo. vol. ii. p. 219.

These receipts, and this right of making transfers, in some countries called Bank-Money, are regulated by, and therefore represent, some one of the national Coins current in each of these states, exactly according to the standard of their respective Mints; and they are understood therefore to retain, on this account, a certain and undisputed value; and as they are substantially worth more than the defective Coins in currency, they often bear, in reference to them, a premium, or what is called an *Agio*: this *Agio* is occasionally increased or diminished, in proportion to the scarcity and demand for these receipts

Sir Jas. Stuart's Political Economy, vol. ii. ch. 86. 89.

or transfers. As it is required by the laws of these states, that foreign bills of exchange in general, and sometimes other bills of a certain amount, should be paid only in this Bank-Money, it has gradually become the fixed standard or measure, according to which great mercantile payments are principally made. The inferior branches of traffic within those countries are left to be carried on in the Coins which are commonly current, whatever may be their intrinsic value.

But in extensive kingdoms, which are at the same time greatly commercial, such as Great Britain, no such establishment has ever existed. In such countries, where the business of commerce is not confined to one or a few cities or towns, but is spread over a large extent of territory, in every part of which trade and manufactures are in great activity, it would hardly be possible to carry such a system into execution. One bank of this description would not be sufficient, and great inconveniences might result from the establishment of many in different parts of the kingdom. It is expressly said by the writers on these banks of deposit, that one of the objects for establishing them was, to fix the residence of rich merchants in the places where such banks were situated. In Great Britain such an establishment is even less necessary than in any other country. The situation of Great Britain, as an island, preserves it in a great degree from the influx of foreign Coins, particularly of the smaller denominations: if any of a larger denomination are imported, (and great numbers of Portugal Gold Coins were imported in the reign of

Your royal Grandfather,) they are none of them legal tender, except by the authority of Your Majesty. And if such Coins sometimes pass in currency, (as has happened in the case before mentioned,) it is the voluntary act of the person who receives them, and at his risk. As a system of the nature before described has never subsisted in Great Britain, and could not be introduced into it with advantage, the Coins of the kingdom are necessarily the principal measure of all property, and the instruments of commerce; or, in other words, they are the only* legal tender in payment of all sums, whatever their amount may be, both to natives and foreigners; and from thence results the necessity, in this country, of having Coins made of one metal only, which should serve as an invariable measure for the purposes above mentioned; and for the same reason these Coins should be kept in the greatest possible perfection.

From the view I have thus given of this part of the argument, it appears, not only from the clearest deduction of reason, and by the concurrent opinion of the most eminent writers, but by the evidence, which long experience in this kingdom has afforded, to be a certain and incontrovertible principle, that Coins, which are to be the principal measure of property, can be made but of one metal only. The Coins made of other metals

---

* I do not think it necessary here to advert to the Acts for suspending payment in Cash at the Bank of England, though these Acts have made Notes of the Bank of England legal tender in certain cases; for these Acts are in force for a limited time only, and are no part of the permanent monetary system of the kingdom.

may be useful, and even necessary; but they must take their value, and pass in currency, according to the rate or value given to them by the Sovereign, with reference to that sort of Coin, which is the principal measure of property, that is, of the standard Coins.

As it is clear, that the Coins, which are to be the principal measure of property, can only be made of one metal, I will now proceed to the second head, and will endeavour to prove of what metal the Coins of this kingdom, which are to be the principal measure of property, ought to be made. This is a very controverted point, and more difficult than any of which I have to treat. It was the opinion of Mr. Locke, *that Silver Coins make the Money of account, or measure of commerce, all through the world;* and he adds, *he was sure they were so in England and the neighbouring countries.* He also asserts, *that Gold is not the Money of the world, or measure of commerce, nor fit to be so; yet it may and ought to be coined, to ascertain its weight and fineness.* Mr. Harris, in his Essay on Coins, concurs with Mr. Locke in this opinion. He says, *that in these parts of the world, Silver is, and for time immemorial hath been, the Money standard; and that it is the fittest material for a standard.* In another part of his Essay he asserts, *that all other metals, Gold as well as lead, are but commodities rateable by Silver.* He supports his opinion by the authority of many great and eminent men, whose writings and speeches on this subject he quotes in his Essay. Sir William Petty, who had certainly great abilities, and was more a man of business, and of the

See Mr. Locke's further considerations concerning raising the value of Money, p. 75. 76.

See Mr. Harris's Essay on Money and Coins, part 1. ch. 2. sec. 7.

world, than either Mr. Locke or Mr. Harris, in that part of his Political Anatomy of Ireland, where he treats of Money, says, *that Money is understood to be the uniform measure and rule for the value of all commodities; that one of the two precious metals is only a fit matter for Money; and, as matters now stand, Silver is the matter of Money.* But he expresses a doubt, *whether, in that sense, there be any such Money or rule in the world.* So that he confirms the principle, but doubts whether the governments of the world have ever conformed to it. Sir William Petty judged rightly. It is certain, that the governments of Europe have not in general paid attention to this rule; nor is it surprising, that persons, wholly occupied in official business, should not have had leisure to study or understand a subject, which is in its nature so abstruse and complicated.

<small>Sir W. Petty's Political Anatomy of Ireland, ch. 10.</small>

In treating this part of the subject, as far as it relates to the Coins of this realm, I will consider it in two views.

First, As a question of law.

Secondly, As a question of fact; that is, with reference to the practice and opinions of the people.

It will be fortunate, if this principal measure of property shall be found within these realms to be in Coins of one metal only; for I am of opinion, that, wherever it so exists, it is best that there it should remain; and that the true principle being thus ascertained, all change should be avoided if possible: for this measure of property, like every other measure, should continue to be always the same. But if this measure of property should now in a certain degree be found to reside and exist in Coins made of different metals, the Coins should in such case be so regulated, that as little change as possible be made; that is, no more than what is absolutely necessary to make our monetary system, according to the principles before stated, as perfect as the nature of the subject will admit; or at least to diminish the evils, to which it has hitherto been exposed.

I must now refer to what I have said, in an early part of this Letter, concerning the high prerogative, which the Kings of this realm have enjoyed and exercised for time immemorial, of giving to the Coins current within the realm their denominated value. Sir Matthew Hale has expressly delivered it as his opinion, *that the legitimation of Money, and the giving it its denominative value, is justly reckoned inter jura Majestatis; and in England, it is one special part of the King's prerogative.* And in treating afterwards of the " denominated or extrinsic value " of Coins, he immediately adds, *that it is, and of right ought to be, given by the King, as his unquestionable prerogative.* What is called by Sir M. Hale "denominated or extrinsic" value, is the rate or value, at which Coins are made legal tender; that is, the rate or value, at which they are to be paid or received in all bargains and contracts: and Coins, so far as they are made legal tender, are by law the measure of property.

I have stated in a former part of this Letter other authorities, in confirmation of this doctrine; and it is not necessary here to repeat them.

[margin: Hale's Pleas of the Crown, ch. 17.]

From the accession of William I. to the 41st of Henry III. Coins of Silver were the only Coins made in the Mints of this kingdom, as far at least as has hitherto been discovered. During that period therefore, Silver Coins were the only legal measure of property, except it be supposed, that foreign Gold Coins, such as Byzants and Florins, which might be occasionally current in this kingdom, were made, by royal proclamation, or other sufficient authority, legal tender, at a certain denominated value. Of this fact, however, no certain information has yet been obtained. From the 41st of Henry III. when Gold Coins began to be coined in the Mints of this kingdom, and the Coins so made of Gold were ordered to be current at a certain nominal value, it must be admitted, that these Gold Coins became legal tender no less than the Silver Coins, and consequently that they were from thenceforth, equally with the Silver Coins, the legal measure of property. And from this last period, Gold and Silver Coins continued to be the legal measure of property through all their various changes and debasements, at the rate or value, which the Sovereigns successively set upon them, till the 15th of Charles II. when the Guinea, which was then first coined, and the other Gold Coins then circulating with it, were permitted to take their value according to the relative value of Gold to Silver at the market. It may be said, and with truth, that by the rule of law, the Guinea, according to the Mint indenture, ought at that time to have been current at 20 Shillings, and the other Gold Coins in proportion; but the people, in their pay-

CHAP. 17.

Stat. 14.
Geo. III. c. 42.

Stat. 16.
Geo. III. c. 54.

Stat. 18.
Geo. III. c. 45.

Stat. 38.
Geo. III. c. 59.

ments, never conformed to this rule, and the Government never enforced the observance of it. This last practice continued to prevail till the 3d of George I. that is, till the year 1717, when the rate or value of the Guinea in currency was fixed at 21 Shillings by proclamation. It was then evident, that Government meant to enforce this regulation; and the Guinea, and the other Gold Coins in proportion, became from thenceforth at that rate legal tender. Subsequent to this period the Gold and Silver Coins were equally legal tender, or the measure of property, in all payments whatsoever, till the 14th year of Your Majesty's reign (1774), when, by a Bill, which passed the two Houses, and received Your royal assent, it was enacted, *that no tender in payment of Money made in the Silver Coin of this realm, of any sum exceeding the sum of 25l., at any one time, shall be reputed in law, or allowed to be, legal tender, within Great Britain or Ireland, for more than according to its value by weight, after the rate of 5s. 2d. for each ounce of Silver.* This regulation with respect to the Silver Coins, which was made in consequence of a general Recoinage of the defective Gold Coins, was intended by the Legislature as an experiment; accordingly, the Act was made to continue to the 1st of May 1776. The same regulation was continued by an Act, passed in the 16th year of Your Majesty's reign, for two years longer. It was further continued by an Act passed in the 18th year of Your Majesty's reign, to the 1st of May 1783, when, by neglect, it was suffered to expire. But the same regulation was revived by an Act passed in the year

1798, and is now in force. During the whole time that this regulation has subsisted, no objection has been made to it.

Copper Coins,* or, as they were originally called, Copper Tokens, were first made by royal authority in the 11th year of James I. that is, 1613. Coins of this metal were introduced into our monetary system to prevent the currency of private Tokens, made chiefly of Lead, of which there were at that time very great quantities in circulation. The practice of making Tokens of Lead first began in the latter end of the reign of Queen Elizabeth, who would never suffer Tokens of any kind to be made by royal authority. King James, when

^{CHAP. 17.}

Cotton's Pieces, 8vo. 1672. p. 199, 200. See Proclamation dated 19 May, 1613, and other Proclamations in the same reign.

---

* Though the Kings of this realm, while they were in possession of parts of France, occasionally coined Money of Billion at their Mints,* in the territories they possessed in that kingdom, for the use of their subjects there, it does not appear that any Billion Money was ever coined at the King's Mints in England, unless the very debased Silver Money, coined at the end of the reign of Henry VIII. and through a great part of the reign of Edward VI. ought to be called Money of Billion, rather than Silver Money. There were also coined during the reign of Edward VI. Pence, Halfpence, and Farthings, of a baser standard than even the other Silver Monies then current, at some of the King's Mints, particularly at the Mints of Canterbury and York.† Queen Elizabeth also, in the 43d year of her reign, coined Monies for the use of her kingdom of Ireland, which were called mixed Monies, and declared to be lawful and current Money in that kingdom, of a baser standard than Sterling.‡ I have sometimes thought that, from this period, the Coins circulating in Ireland began to be estimated as of less value, according to their respective denominations, than those circulating in England; but I know of no authority for this conjecture.

* See Le Blanc, p. 244, 245.
† Martin Folkes, p. 48. Stowe's Chronicle, p. 606.
‡ Sir John Davies's Report on the Case of mixed Monies.

CHAP. 17.

See Proclamation, 16 Aug. 1672.

he authorized* the making of these Copper Farthings or Tokens, prohibited by proclamation the use or currency of all private Tokens. But he did not oblige his subjects to take the Copper Farthings or Tokens made by his authority, otherwise than "with their own good liking;" and he expressly says in his proclamation, that he did not intend to make them "Monies or Coins." These Copper Tokens continued to be current, subject to the rule before mentioned, to the year 1672, when Copper Halfpence, which were then first coined at the royal Mint,† were ordered to pass in all payments under the value of a Sixpence; and from that time all the Copper Coins made at the royal Mint have been ordered to be current upon the terms last stated. But in 1797, when Copper Twopences and Pence were first made by royal authority, it was ordered by Your Majesty's proclamation of the 26th of July of that year, that no person should be obliged to take them in any one payment that shall exceed the value of one Shilling. And since by Your

* The right of making these Copper Tokens was given to individuals by patent, who sometimes made a very great profit thereby; for the intrinsic value of these tokens was in no degree equal to their nominal value. The Patentees pledged themselves however to take them back for something less than their nominal value; but it is not probable that they were ever returned to them in any great quantities.

† In the republic of Athens Copper Coins were the last introduced into circulation, as well as in England; though it was natural to suppose, that they would have been made use of in that republic in its less affluent state, and before its commerce had been carried to so great an extent. The succession of Coins made of different metals in Athens was first Silver, then Gold, and afterwards Copper; just as it has been in England. See Voyage du Jeune Anacharsis, Edition 4, in 4to. vol. iv. p. 357. and the authors referred to therein.

Majesty's proclamation of Dec. 4, 1799, it was ordered, that no person should be obliged to take the Copper Halfpence and Farthings, authorized in like manner to be made by Your Majesty, in any one payment that shall exceed the value of Sixpence.

From the foregoing short statement it is evident, first, that from the time when Gold Coins were first made in the Mints of this kingdom, these Gold Coins have been equally with the Silver Coins legal tender, and consequently the measure of property, according to the rate or value, which the Sovereign thought fit to set upon them. I do not think it necessary here to repeat what I have stated already, that Gold Coins, during a subsequent period, took a value superior to that at which they were rated in the Mint indenture. This was by general consent, and, consequently, at the option of the person who received them in payment, and not by the authority of Government; so that this superior value was not in truth the legal value. Secondly, that the Silver Coins of this realm, considered as Coins, are now legal tender only in sums not exceeding 25*l*. Thirdly, that the Copper Halfpence and Farthings, made at the royal Mint, are legal tender only in sums that do not amount to Sixpence. That the Copper Twopences and Pence, lately authorized to be made by Your Majesty by a private Artist, are legal tender only in sums not exceeding twelve pence. And that the Copper Halfpence and Farthings, in like manner authorized to be made by Your Majesty, are legal tender in sums not exceeding Sixpence.

Such appears to be the law on this subject. I will in the next place consider the question of fact, with reference to the practice and opinions of the people; and it will be found that the fact, except in a few instances, has corresponded with the law as I have stated it.

I have already observed, that in very early times Silver Coins were weights, as well as Coins, or, in other words, that a Pound in tale of Silver Coins was equal to a Pound weight of standard Silver; and that a Silver Penny, which was probably the only Coin then in currency, was the 240th part of a Pound in weight, and was intended to contain exactly a Pennyweight of standard Silver; so that these Coins expressed and defined the precise quantity of Silver, which they were intended to represent. The reverse of the Penny was stamped with a cross through the middle of it; the people therefore broke this Penny in the part where the cross divided it, and then it passed as a *Maille*, or Halfpenny. And they sometimes broke the half of this Penny into two equal parts, and each of these passed for the fourth of a Penny, that is, a *Fourthing*, or Farthing. This practice continued till Silver Halfpence and Farthings were coined.

During this period, so correct were our ancestors in regulating their payments in the Coins then current, that rules were adopted to remedy any defect, either in weight or fineness, that might be found in them. When these Coins were deficient in weight, from wear, or any other cause, they practised a method of payment, which was called *Compensatio ad Pensum;* the Coins were in such case put into a scale, and taken by weight, without any regard to their number. At other times the deficiency in weight was compensated by an estimated proportion or allowance, in order to save the trouble of weighing them. This proportion or allowance was a 40th part, or six Pennies in each Pound, and this was called *Compensatio ad Scalam*. And when a suspicion was entertained, that any of these Coins were not made of standard Silver, either from errors committed by the Officers of the Mint, (which in those early times were not uncommon,) or from other causes, a method was practised of ascertaining the fineness of these Coins, by a certain mode of assaying them, called *Trial by Combustion*. It is certain, that all these rules were observed by the Sheriffs in receiving the King's rents, and by them and others in making payments into the Exchequer. And as the Kings of this realm had at that time great estates in every county of England, from which their principal revenue was derived, it is probable, that the same rules were generally known and practised in all payments whatsoever.

This system of Coins, simple in all its parts, continued to subsist to the 28th of Edward I. In that year this Monarch first debased the Silver Coins of the realm; and from that time a Pound in tale no longer contained in weight a Pound of standard Silver; so that the Coins then made did not contain so much Silver as their names implied; and in all the successive debasements made in our Coins, of which an account has already been given, the quantity of standard Silver, which the Pound in tale was understood to represent, was by degrees further diminished; and the Pound in tale gradually differed, or as it were diverged, in a still greater degree from the Pound in weight. The denomination therefore of a Pound in tale, and of the Coins representing all its parts, became from thenceforth merely arbitrary, dependant on the will of the Sovereign. The Coins of different denominations were indeed understood to contain and represent a certain weight or quantity of standard Silver; but they did not contain so much as their names implied. And the weight of these Silver Coins frequently did not correspond with any aliquot part of the Pound, according to the weights then in use, but was sometimes made up of the fractional parts even of a grain. The practice of weighing then began, on that account, to be abandoned; for the people in general could not know what the precise weight of each Coin should be. The Gold Coins however continued to be weighed, and it was required, that these Coins should be *whole and weight*; and new laws were passed, and new proclamations were issued, concerning the weight of Coins; and these laws and proclamations wisely conformed to the state of the Coins in each respective period. At length an allowance for *reasonable wear* was authorized, first, with respect to the Silver Coins, and afterwards, with respect to those made of Gold. When in process of time Silver Coins of greater value than Pennies and Halfpennies were made, names were given to them, which were also arbitrary, and had no reference to the quantity or weight of Silver, which they contained, or to the value, at which they were to pass in currency. Such were the Groat and Half Groat, the Crown and Half Crown. There were Gold Crowns and Half Crowns, as well as Silver Crowns and Half Crowns: and even the Shilling, though the name of an aliquot part of the Pound in tale, was soon after it was brought into circulation called no longer a Shilling, but a *Teston*, as has been already observed, and continued to be so called for a considerable period.

From the time when Gold Coins were introduced into currency, under the authority of the Sovereign, of a certain weight, and at a certain rate or value, the Pound Sterling in tale represented a certain quantity or weight of standard Gold, in like manner as it represented a certain quantity or weight of standard Silver. The nominal value of the Gold Coins was from time to time enhanced, or their weight diminished, in proportion as the Silver Coins were debased, by diminishing the weight of them. And these Gold Coins equally passed in payment at the rate or value, which the Sovereign thought fit to give them. And from that time the Gold and Silver Coins were in fact, as well as by law, equally the measure of property.

It is certain, that during all this period the Silver Coins were the more common currency of the country, because they were better adapted to the extent of our commercial transactions at that time. But great payments were even then frequently made in Gold Coins, at the rate or value before mentioned.

CHAP. 17.

It sometimes happened, however, that both Gold and Silver Coins were, by various causes, alternately driven, in a great degree, out of circulation; and one of them remained in currency, and became in fact the principal measure of property. In the latter end of the reign of Henry VIII. and during almost the whole reign of Edward VI. the Gold Coins were driven out of circulation, and were melted down, or hoarded, as before stated; and from the 2d of James I. to the 11th of that King, the Gold Coins were again driven out of circulation, by being melted down or exported. During the whole of those periods the Silver Coins were in fact almost the only measure of property. From the 11th of James I. to about the middle of the last century, the Silver Coins were in a like manner driven in a great degree out of circulation, by being melted down or exported; the Gold Coins then became in fact the principal measure of property; but smaller payments must still have been made in the Silver Coins, though probably in such of them as were very defective. The causes, which produced these changes, have been fully explained already; and instances have been produced, when the people, in consequence of these confusions,*

---

* In Scotland, where the changes in the value of Money were more frequent, and in a greater degree than in England, conditions were sometimes inserted in contracts, to prevent any losses by such change. Thus Gavin Dunbar, Bishop of Aberdeen, in a contract with William Sutherland, of Duffus, dated the 5th of August, 1529, stipulated, "that " if it should happen that the Money of Scotland, or of any other " kingdom, which passes in Scotland, be raised to a higher price than " it is now taken in payment for, by which the Reverend Father, his

stipulated, at the time they sold their commodities, in what sort of Coins they would be paid. All these facts clearly prove, that the measure of property was not in fact confined solely to the Silver Coins, and that the people occasionally adopted in practice Coins of one metal or the other, as the measure of property, according to existing circumstances.

From the year 1663, the Silver Coins became in fact the only principal measure of property, according to the rate or value, which the Sovereign had set upon them. At that time there was however a great quantity of Gold Coins in currency, and the rate or value, at which they were to pass, was determined by the Sovereign in the Mint indentures. Such was in truth their legal value, for the reasons already stated, but, by general consent, the value of them rose or fell, like that of every other commodity; and they did not pass in currency according to the rate or value authorized by the Mint indentures, but according to the estimated value of Gold with reference to that of Silver at the market. After the general Recoinage, in the reign of King William III. when the Silver Coins were restored to a state of perfection, these Gold Coins did not even then pass in currency according to the rate or value given them by

"heirs or assigns whatever, be made poorer, or in a worse condition,
"he the said William Sutherland should pay to the possessors, whoever
"they may be, of the annual rent therein reserved, for every Mark
"and 32 Pennies one ounce of pure Silver, which should be at least
"*Alewyne Penny fine*, (that is, eleven Pence fine,) or else its true value
"in the usual Money of the kingdom of Scotland." See Ruddiman's Introduction to Anderson's Thesaurus, 8vo. p. 148.

CHAP. 17.

the Mint indentures, or even according to their intrinsic value, with reference to the price of Gold to Silver at the market. The Guinea was then current for 21*s.* 6*d.*, which was about 10*d.* more than its intrinsic value, compared with the perfect Silver Coins, that had lately been issued, and the other Gold Coins in proportion. This nominal value exceeded the intrinsic value of these Gold Coins, by $4\frac{1}{31}$ per cent.; and at this rate they were paid and received in all contracts or bargains. It is impossible to suppose, that the people would have received the Gold Coins in payment at a greater rate than their intrinsic value, compared with the new and perfect Silver Coins, unless they had preferred these Gold Coins to those of Silver as the measure of property, either from considerations of convenience, or from some other motive. Whatever the motive may have been, the fact is certain. It is equally certain, that a great part of the perfect Silver Coins, which had been so lately issued in great plenty, in a short time disappeared, and were either melted down or exported. From all these facts it may fairly be inferred, that the Gold Coins were in fact preferred, and from that time became the measure of property, in the opinion and practice of the people.

In the year 1717, the rate or nominal value of the Gold Coins was fixed by proclamation, and the Mint indenture was altered, and made in this respect conformable to the proclamation: the Guinea was ordered to pass at 21*s.*, and the other Gold Coins in proportion; at this rate the several Gold Coins have continued to be current ever since; they became from thenceforth legal tender at this rate; and the receiver, who before had voluntarily taken them at a higher rate, could not object to take them at the rate which Government had then set upon them, though this rate or nominal value was still greater than their intrinsic value, compared with the perfect Silver Coins. Before this time great payments had frequently been made at the Exchequer in bags of Silver, in like manner as they are now made in some foreign countries; but from that period to the present time no considerable payment has been made, either at the Exchequer, or by individuals, in Silver Coins; the only use, in which they have been employed, is in payment of small sums, or in exchange for Gold Coins. These Silver Coins have become therefore subordinate and subservient to the Gold Coins, being reserved for small payments. And the Gold Coins are now become, in the practice and opinion of the people, the principal measure of property; and the Silver and Copper Coins are only so in the degree before described.

I have hitherto treated the very important point now under consideration simply as a question of law, or as a question of fact, and have adduced no other reasons but such as result from sources, that have immediate reference to law or history: but as many able writers have entertained sentiments very different from mine on this point, I think it necessary now to offer to Your Majesty, in confirmation of my opinion, other reasons, which appear to me to be incontrovertible.

On this occasion I am under the necessity of recalling to Your Majesty's attention some particulars stated in a

CHAP. 17.

See Mr. Lowndes's Report to the Lords of the Treasury of the 12 Sept. 1695.

former part of this Letter. It has been shewn, that when the Silver Coins were very defective, in the reign of King William, immediately preceding and during the general Recoinage, *great contentions daily arose in all fairs, markets, shops, and other places throughout the kingdom, to the disturbance of the public peace, in consequence of the defective state of the Silver Coins.* That trade in general *was on that account greatly lessened; that persons, before they concluded any bargains, were under the necessity of settling the price or value of the very Money they were to receive for their goods,* and that *they set a price upon their goods accordingly. That these practices had been one great cause of raising the price not only of all merchandizes, but of every article necessary for the sustenance of the people. That the receipt and collection of the public taxes, revenues, and debts were greatly retarded.* The cause of these evils was at that time evident. The Silver Coins, which were then the principal measure of property, were greatly deficient; every commodity then rose in its value in proportion to this deficiency; they all took their value in reference to the Silver Coins: but none of these evils have happened for many years past, in consequence of the existing defect of our Silver Coins. There is no reason to suppose that any commodity has on this account risen in its price or value. The cause that these evils do not now exist results from a change in the practice and opinion of the people, with reference to the principal measure of property. The Silver Coins are no longer the principal measure of property: all commodities now take their price or value in reference to the Gold Coins, that is, in reference to the quantity of Gold Coins, for which they could be exchanged; in like manner as they took their value in a former period, in reference to the Silver Coins. On this account the present deficiency of the Silver Coins, great as it is, is not taken into consideration, in paying the price of any commodity, to the extent in which they are legal tender. It is clear therefore, that the Gold Coins are now become, in the practice and opinion of the people, the principal measure of property.

A like conclusion may be drawn from the present state of our Gold Coins, and from the value at which they now pass in currency. The Mint indentures of Charles II. James II. William III. and Queen Anne, and even of a part of the reign of George I. to the year 1717, had determined, that the Guinea should pass at the rate or value of 20s., and the other Gold Coins in proportion; yet they did not pass at that, which was then their legal rate or value, but at a much higher rate or value: and in a part of the reign of King William the Guinea was current at even so high a value as 30s. This increased rate or value was not owing singly to a mistaken estimation at the Mint of the relative value of Gold to Silver, but the Gold Coins rose or fell, as the Silver Coins were less or more perfect. No such increase or variation in the value of the Gold Coin has taken place since the year 1717, when the rate or value of the Guinea was determined by proclamation, and the Mint indenture, to be 21s., and the other Gold Coins in proportion; though the Silver Coins now current have

CHAP. 17.

long been, and are still, at least as deficient as they were in the beginning of the reign of King William. The Guinea and the other Gold Coins have notwithstanding constantly passed, since 1717, at the rate or value given them by the Mint indentures.

The two foregoing arguments clearly prove the opinion of the people of Great Britain on this subject, in their interior commerce and domestic concerns. I will in the next place shew, what has been the opinion of foreign nations concerning it. At the time of the general Recoinage of the Silver Coins, in the reign of King William, the exchanges with all foreign countries rose or fell, according to the defect or perfection of our Silver Coins. It has already been stated, that at this period *the exchanges to the Low Countries were so very low, that the public lost about 4s. in the Pound on all Monies remitted there; that the exchange to Hamburgh and to the East Countries was still lower, and to all places in the Mediterranean it was even more to our disadvantage.* The most favourable, therefore, of our exchanges, was, during this period, 20 per cent. against this kingdom. All these facts are confirmed by the most eminent writers on exchanges. The reason that the exchanges were then so low is also evident. Foreigners at that time considered the Silver Coins of this realm, then very defective, as the principal measure of property, and consequently of foreign commerce, and they rated their exchanges accordingly. The same evil however has never existed since the year 1717, though our Silver Coins have, during all this interval, been very defective.

See Mr. Lowndes's Report to the Lords of the Treasury, 12 Sept. 1695.

But, on the other hand, our exchanges with foreign countries were very much influenced to our disadvantage, when our Gold Coins were defective; that is, previous to the reformation of our Gold Coins, in the year 1774: and this circumstance was one of the principal causes, which then induced the Government to reform the Gold Coins, by recoining them, at a great charge to the public. The conclusion, naturally resulting from these premises, is, that foreigners have, for a considerable period, no longer considered our Silver Coins as the principal measure of property, and consequently of foreign commerce; but they consider our Gold Coin as such, and thereby estimate their exchanges.

Lest these arguments should not be thought sufficient, I will proceed to another, which ought, in my judgment, to have its weight. For many years previous to the Recoinage of the Gold Coins in 1774, Gold Bullion advanced in its price, considerably above the rate or value, at which it was estimated at the British Mint. It was frequently at $3l.$ $18s.$ and $3l.$ $19s.$ per oz. and sometimes even above $4l.$ per oz. On an average of its price for sixteen years, from 1757 to 1773, it was $3l.$ $19s.$ $2\frac{3}{4}d.$ per oz. which is $1s.$ $4\frac{1}{4}d.$ per oz. or $1\frac{381}{869}$ per cent. above the Mint price. But immediately after the Recoinage of the Gold Coin, in the year 1774, by which that Coin was brought to its present state of perfection, Gold Bullion fell to something under the Mint price; and for 20 years previous to the year 1797, the Directors of the Bank of England have, as I am informed, paid for it, on an average, not more than $3l.$ $17s.$ $7\frac{3}{4}d.$, which is $2\frac{3}{4}d.$ per oz. or $\frac{550}{1865}$ per cent. under the Mint price. It is evident from these facts, that the price of Gold Bullion was affected by the state or condition of our Gold Coins, though the price of this Bullion had not, since the year 1717, been so affected by the defective state or condition of our Silver Coins; that is, it rose in its price when the Gold Coin was defective, and it again fell in its price when this Coin was brought to its present state of perfection. The deficient or perfect state of our Gold Coins has influenced the price even of Silver Bullion in like manner. The price of Silver Bullion rose or fell from the same cause, which affected the price of Gold Bullion. From 1757 inclusive, to 1773, when the Gold Coin was defective, the average price, which the Directors of the Bank paid for Silver Dollars, was $64\frac{5}{8}d.$ per oz. which is equal to $66\frac{5}{8}d.$ per oz. for standard Silver. But immediately after the Recoinage of the Gold Coin, by which it was restored to its present state of perfection, the price of these Dollars fell, so that on an average of 24 years, to the 31st of December 1797 inclusive, the Bank Directors, as I am informed, have paid for these Dollars $61\frac{1}{4}d.$ per oz. which is equal to $63\frac{1}{4}d.$ per oz. for standard Silver, and is less than the average price of Silver, for the 16 years previous to the Recoinage of the Gold Coins, by $3\frac{3}{8}d.$ per oz. or $5\frac{35}{533}$ per cent. It does not however appear, that the price either of Gold or Silver Bullion was ever affected immediately before or since the Recoinage of the Gold Coin, by the very defective state of our Silver Coins. From all which it is evident, that the value of Gold or Silver Bullion has, for 40 years at least, been estimated according to the state of our Gold Coin solely, and not according to that of Silver Coin. The price of both these metals rose when our Gold Coin was defective; it fell when our Gold Coin was brought to its present state of perfection; and it may therefore justly be inferred, that, in the opinion of the dealers in these precious metals, (who must be considered as the best judges on a subject of this nature,) the Gold Coin has in this respect become the principal measure of property, and consequently the instrument of commerce.

Thus it appears, that not only the people of Great Britain, but the merchants of foreign nations, who have any intercourse with us, and even those who deal in the precious metals, of which our Coins are made, concur in opinion, that the Gold Coins are now the principal measure of property in this kingdom.

Mr. Locke has said, *that Gold is not the Money of the world and measure of commerce*, NOR FIT TO BE SO. It is difficult to determine what Mr. Locke means, when he asserts, *that Gold is not fit to be the Money of the world*. Gold, as a metal, is equally homogeneous, equally divisible into exact portions or parts, and not more consumable, or more subject to decay, than Silver; Gold has some of these qualities even in a higher degree than Silver. Mr. Locke must mean therefore, that Gold is, on account of its value, *not fit to be the Money of the world, or the measure of property and commerce*. It cannot, I think, be doubted, that the metal, of which this principal measure of property is made, should correspond with the wealth and commerce of the country for which it is intended. Coins should be made of metals more or less valuable, in proportion to the wealth and commerce of the country, in which they are to be the measure of property.

In very poor countries Coins have been, and still are, principally made of Copper; and sometimes even of less valuable materials.

In countries advanced to a certain degree of commerce and opulence, Silver is the metal of which Coins are principally made.

In very rich countries, and especially in those where great and extensive commerce is carried on, Gold is the most proper metal, of which this principal measure of property, and this instrument of commerce, should be made: in such countries Gold will in practice become the principal measure of property, and the instrument of commerce, with the general consent of the people, not only without the support of law, but in spite of almost any law that may be enacted to the contrary; for the principal purchases and exchanges cannot there be made, with any convenience, in Coins of a less valuable metal. In this Your Majesty's kingdom, so great is its wealth, and so various and extensive is its commerce, that it is become inconvenient to carry on many of the principal branches of trade, or to make great payments, even in Coins of Gold, the most precious of metals: on this account a very extensive Paper currency has been called to its aid: but this Paper can never be considered as Coin, for it has no value in itself; it only obtains its value with reference to the Coins which it represents. Certain descriptions of this Paper currency have, however, from a thirst of gain, been carried by many, and from a love of speculation defended by others, to an extravagant, and, I think, to a dangerous, extent. Paper currency should only be employed, where payment in Coins becomes inconvenient.

In illustration of the truth of what I have advanced, that Gold is now the proper metal, of which the principal measure of property and instrument of commerce should be made, it may be observed, that the value of Silver in this kingdom, at the accession of William I. compared with the price of other articles, was nearly as great as that of Gold is at present: the Silver Coins were then, and for two hundred and fifty years subsequent to that period, the only Money in currency; and the largest Piece was a Silver Penny, equal in value to something less than 3*d.* of our present Money. The rents of the Crown, as well as of individuals, were at that time usually paid in kind: and it is natural to conclude, that there must then have been but a small quantity of these Silver Coins in circulation. Every article of commerce is also supposed to have increased in price, since the 1st of William I. at least fifteen times, in the opinion of those, whose estimate in this respect has been the lowest; that is, the Pound Sterling in tale has been reduced to about one third of what it was at the period before mentioned: and the price of every commodity, compared with the Pound Sterling in tale, has at least augmented in a quintuple proportion: a Pound of Gold, therefore, compared with the present price of commodities, is of about the same value as a Pound of Silver was in the eleventh century, compared with the price of commodities at that early period: and, in this view of the subject, the Gold Coin is now as well adapted to serve as the principal measure of property, or instrument of commerce, as the Silver Coin was at the accession of the Norman Prince to the throne of this kingdom.

So true is the principle, that Coins must bear a due proportion to the wealth and commerce of every country in which they are current, that in former times it was found necessary gradually to introduce into the currency of this kingdom, Silver Coins, of a greater weight and value, in proportion as the wealth and commerce of it advanced. Thus Pennies, Halfpennies, or Mailles, and Farthings, were at first the only Silver Coins in currency. Groats and Half Groats were afterwards introduced; and in subsequent periods, first Shillings, or Testoons,* and afterwards Crowns and Half Crowns were coined, and for the same reason brought into currency. In like manner, when the commerce of the kingdom had increased to a certain extent, Coins made of Gold were first struck at the English Mint, and introduced into

---

* It is singular, however, that Sixpences or Testers, (or, as they are sometimes called in the Mint indentures, Half Shillings,) were one of the last Coins introduced into the English series of Coins. They were first coined in the 6th of Edward VI. when he began to reform the Coins of the realm. Their places had hitherto been supplied by Silver Groats, Half Groats, and Pence: but when Copper Halfpence and Farthings were coined, these smaller Pieces of Silver Coin were no longer necessary, and therefore disappeared.

circulation. It was natural, that Gold Coins, as of less bulk, and of greater value, should be so introduced, and should become legal tender, equally with our Silver Coins; and, in proportion as our commerce continued to augment, that they should gradually take the place of the Silver Coins; and at length, when our trade had attained the very great degree of extent and splendour, at which it has arrived in the course of the last 50 years, that they should become the principal measure of property and instrument of commerce, and leave to the Silver Coins the function of being employed only in the smaller and inferior branches of it. Hence it is evident, that the history of the Coins of a country throws great light on its progress in wealth and commerce.

CHAPTER XVIII.

Variations of the value of Silver and Gold Bullion.

THERE is still further reason for preferring at present the Gold Coins to those made of Silver, as the principal measure of property and instrument of commerce in these Your Majesty's dominions. This measure ought certainly to be made of that metal, which varies least in its price or value at the market. It is difficult to conceive, that in a commercial light the price or value of any commodity can be estimated, but with reference to some other commodity, either Gold or Silver, or something else; and the price or value of the precious metals is generally estimated with reference to each other; that is, according to the plenty or scarcity, and the demand there may be for each of them. It is certain too, that the price or value of Gold Bullion, in the British market, has for many years varied less than the price or value of Silver Bullion. From an account I have seen of the price of Dollars for 41 years previous to the year 1797, it appears, that the price of Dollars, during that period, has varied $16\frac{28}{117}$ per cent. It is true, that, before the general Recoinage of the Gold Coin, the prices, both of Gold and Silver Bullion, advanced, in consequence of the then defective state of our Gold Coins, as has been observed already: the true variation therefore in the price of Silver will be more accurately taken, by giving an account of this variation, subsequent to the general Recoinage of our Gold Coin. It appears by the account last stated, that the price of Silver in Dollars has varied in twenty-two years, that is, from the end of the year 1774, to the 31st of December 1797, 11$\frac{13}{17}$ per cent. and even in the course of one year, that is, the year 1797, no less than 9$\frac{1}{6}$ per cent.

The variation in the price of Silver Bullion appears to have been still greater, by another account, with which I have been favoured by the late Mr. Garbett, an eminent merchant and manufacturer at Birmingham: it there appears, that the Silver purchased by him, as a refiner, with Bank Notes, varied, according to his calculation, in the course of ten years, to 1793, more than 19$\frac{1}{4}$ per cent. and in one year only, more than 13$\frac{1}{4}$ per cent.

From information, on which I can rely, it appears, that the Bank Directors have in general paid for Gold Bullion, during twenty years previous to the year 1797, not more than 3*l.* 17*s.* 6*d.* per ounce. But occasionally, when they have been in want of Gold, and particularly during the six months previous to March 1798, they have raised the price 4$\frac{1}{2}$*d.* per oz. to encourage the importation of it; so that they then paid for it 3*l.* 17*s.* 10$\frac{1}{2}$*d.* per oz. being the full Mint price. But, as stated in another place, the average price, which these Directors have paid for Gold, during the before-mentioned twenty years, was 3*l.* 17*s.* 7$\frac{3}{4}$*d.* per oz. or 2$\frac{3}{4}$*d.* per oz. less than the Mint price; so that the variation in the price of

Gold has not amounted, during the whole of this period, to ½ per cent. It appears, by the account before mentioned, received from Mr. Garbett, that during the forty years in which he has bought and sold Gold Bullion, as a refiner, the price of Gold purchased with Bank Notes has varied in London nearly 5½ per cent. It is true, that by the same account the price of Gold has varied in a greater degree at Paris, Amsterdam, and Hamburgh, but by no means in the same degree as Silver.

It is possible, that as the Bank Directors are the only purchasers in this kingdom of Gold, for the purpose of converting it into Coin, the rule they have laid down of paying in general but one certain price for it, may have had the effect of keeping the price of this metal more steady than it would otherwise have been, and of preventing a greater fluctuation in it: and this circumstance accounts for the greater variation there has been in the prices of Gold and Silver Bullion, in the purchases made by Mr. Garbett, than in those made by the Directors of the Bank of England. As Silver Bullion is employed in manufactures, and in making plate, in a much greater proportion than Gold Bullion, and as a considerable quantity of it is annually exported to the East Indies, and as this metal is, on all these accounts, more an article of commerce than Gold Bullion, it is possible, that these circumstances may have contributed to produce a greater fluctuation in the price of Silver.

But to whatever causes the difference in the variation of the prices of these precious metals is to be attributed, the fact, that Gold Bullion varies in this kingdom less in its price than Silver Bullion, as before stated, is incontrovertible, from the accounts, with which I have been furnished. It is equally certain, that the Bank Directors, who, being at the head of all circulation, are obliged to supply the quantity of Gold Coin essentially necessary for carrying on the commerce of the kingdom, have not generally, during the period to which these accounts refer, found any difficulty in procuring Gold Bullion at the before-mentioned prices. I am told, that it was offered to them at these prices, and that, except on extraordinary occasions, they were not obliged to seek it, or to send to foreign countries for it. It may fairly therefore be concluded, that the price, at which they obtain this precious metal, is nearly the average price of it in the market of this kingdom; and, as it varies less in its price than Silver Bullion, it is in this respect the most proper and convenient metal, of which a steady and uniform measure of property and instrument of commerce can be made.

CHAPTER XIX.

Precautions necessary for regulating the principles of Coinage.

FROM all that has hitherto been offered, many of the conclusions are obvious; several of them indeed have already been stated, in former parts of this Letter, where the reasons have been adduced in support of them. These conclusions, however, it is necessary now to repeat, in order to collect together, and bring into one view, every principle intended to be established as the foundation of a new system of Coins.

After full consideration of this extensive, abstruse, and intricate subject, I humbly offer to Your Majesty, as the result of my opinion,

First, That the Coins of this realm, which are to be the principal measure of property and instrument of commerce, should be made of one metal only.

Secondly, That in this kingdom the Gold Coins only have been for many years past, and are now, in the practice and opinion of the people, the principal measure of property and instrument of commerce. The Integer, or Pound Sterling, which, at the accession of William I. was a Pound weight of Silver, and which, by successive debasements made by the Monarchs of this realm, was reduced, in the 43d year of the reign of Queen Elizabeth, to the $\frac{29}{62}$ parts of a Pound Troy of standard Silver, is now become, by the course of events, and by the general consent of the people, the $\frac{20}{21}$ parts of a Guinea, or of 5 dwts. 9½ grs. of standard Gold. At as early a period as the year 1485, that is, the 1st of Henry VII. a Gold Coin, called a Sovereign, then first introduced into circulation, was intended to represent this Integer, or Pound Sterling. In every subsequent reign to that of James I. Gold Coins of the same name, and intended to represent this Integer, were made at the Mint of this kingdom; their weight was generally diminished in proportion as the Gold Coins were, during that period, debased. From the accession of James I. all the new Gold Coins introduced into circulation were also intended to represent this Integer, or Pound Sterling; such as the Unite, the Laurel, and the Guinea; for the Guinea was originally rated in the Mint indenture at One Pound Sterling. It has been shewn, that in a country like Great Britain, so distinguished for its affluence, and for the extent of its commercial connections, the Gold Coins are best adapted to be the principal measure of property: in this kingdom, therefore, the Gold Coin is now the principal measure of property and standard Coin, or as it were the sovereign archetype, by which the weight and value of all other Coins should be regulated. It is the measure of almost all contracts and bargains; and by it, as a measure, the price of all commodities bought and sold is adjusted and ascertained. For these reasons the Gold Coins should be made as perfect, and be kept as perfect, as possible.

CHAP. 19.

It is, and has long been, a dispute among the writers on Coins, whether the charge of fabricating Coins, and even a Seigneurage payable to the Sovereign, should not be taken out of our Coins, as is practised in most foreign countries; and many eminent men have differed on this point. I incline to think, that the charge of fabrication should not be taken from those Coins, which are the principal measure of property and instrument of commerce; and still less any profit derived from Seigneurage payable to the Sovereign.

Because this principal measure of property would not in such case be perfect.

Because the merchants of foreign nations, who have any commercial intercourse with this country, estimate the value of our Coins only according to the intrinsic value of the metal that is in them; so that the British merchant would, in such case, be forced to pay, in his exchanges, a compensation for any defect, which might be in these Coins; and he must necessarily either raise the price of all merchandize and manufactures sold to foreign nations in proportion, or submit to this loss.

Because no such charge of fabrication has been taken at the British Mint for nearly a century and a half past; and, if it were now to be taken, the weight of the new Gold Coins must be diminished, to pay for this fabrication.

And lastly, Because these new Gold Coins would either differ in weight from those now in currency, or, to prevent this evil, the whole of our present Gold Coins must be taken out of circulation, brought to the Mint, and be recoined.

If the system now recommended should be adopted, and the Gold Coins be made the principal measure of property and standard Coin, all the multiples of this measure of property will be in the Gold Coins; and all its parts, below the value of the smallest Piece of Gold Coin, will be in Coins made of other metals, that is, of Silver and Copper. This system is much more simple, than if the Silver Coins were to be made the principal measure of property; for, in such case, these Silver Coins would be placed, as it were, between the more valuable Coins of Gold, and the less valuable Coins of Copper; and many of its multiples, as well as many of its parts, must be made of a metal different from that, of which this standard Coin is made.

Thirdly, it is evident, that where the function of the Gold Coins, as a measure of property, ceases, there that of the Silver Coins should begin; and that where the function of the Silver Coins in this respect ceases, there that of Copper should begin: it is clear, therefore, that so far only these Silver and Copper Coins should be made legal tender, and no further, at least not in any great degree: and it follows, that the Coins both of Silver and Copper are subordinate, subservient, and merely representative Coins, and must take their value with reference to the Gold Coins, according to the rate, which the Sovereign sets upon each of them.

The charge of workmanship should be taken out of these inferior Coins, because there can be no doubt, that they will pass in payment at their nominal rate or value, provided that their intrinsic value in metal and workmanship is equal to such nominal rate or value: they will take their value according to the rate, at which they can be exchanged for the several denominations of Gold Coins, especially as they will be current only within the kingdom, where the authority of the Sovereign will be sufficient to support their currency; and as they will be legal tender only for small sums, it is not probable, that they will ever be employed in payments of our balances with foreign nations, except in sums for which they are made legal tender, or be included in the estimate of our foreign exchanges, or in the least degree affect them.

The charge of workmanship may be taken out of these Coins, because it would be highly improper to bring this charge on the public revenue, when in truth it will no longer be necessary. The charge, to which the nation is already exposed in coining Gold* Coins only at the public expence, is greater than is generally imagined. The charge incurred for coining alone, from the year 1777 to 1803, was 273,439*l.* 15*s.* 6*d.* There were also other incidental charges, incurred on account of the Mint, during the same period, which amounted to 215,002*l.* 3*s.* 3*d.* The charge of coining Silver would

* An account of the charge and expences at His Majesty's Mint from the year 1777 to 1803, inclusive.

Charge of Coining.	Amount of salaries.	Contingencies and incidents.	Buildings and repairs.	Total.
273,439*l.* 15*s.* 6*d.*	110,233*l.* 14*s.* 4*d.*	59,585*l.* 8*s.* 7*d.*	45,183*l.* 5*s.* 4*d.*	488,441*l.* 18*s.* 9*d.*

Very little Silver was coined during this period.

be still much greater; and indeed so great, that the public ought not to bear it, unless it can be shewn, that some great public advantage would be derived from it.

By taking the charge of workmanship out of these Silver Coins, they will be retained within the kingdom for the purposes of internal traffic, for which they are intended, in like manner as the Copper Coins are at present; for no foreign merchant will receive his balance in Coins of this description, in payment of any sum greater than that for which they are made legal tender, if there is not a want of a sufficient quantity of Gold Coins, as the intrinsic value of the Silver Coins will be less than their nominal value. And it is further certain, that, in such case, the nation will be no longer exposed to the evils arising from a conflict between Coins made of different metals, or to the iniquitous practice of exporting them, whenever a profit can be made thereby; or to that of melting them down, for the purpose of converting them into plate, which frequently happened in the course of the last century, whenever the price of either Gold or Silver Bullion at the market rose above the Mint price.

The value of the metal, of which these Silver Coins are to be made, should be estimated, not according to the actual price of such metal at any given time, but according to the average price, which such metal has born for a certain number of years past, or which it is likely to bear in future in the market. For as these Silver Coins are to represent those of Gold in small payments, they should be made to represent them, not in any one time, but for a continued space of time, as truly and as correctly as the fluctuating value of the two precious metals will permit. It has already been shewn, that when Coins are made of two different metals, and intended to be current according to their intrinsic value, it is impossible that the Sovereign should follow with sufficient accuracy the various fluctuations and changes, which in a short time happen in the relative prices of these metals at the market, and thereby regulate the nominal value, at which the different Coins, made of these metals, should at all times be current. Experience has proved, that every attempt for this purpose has been unsuccessful. It follows therefore, that the metal of those Coins, which are intended to represent those of Gold in small payments, should be estimated according to a fair average of what is likely to be its value in future at the market, with due attention to every circumstance, which is likely to influence the price of it, and to the rate, at which this metal is estimated in the Mints of foreign countries. Coins of this description ought to be so made, that they may truly represent, but not rival, that Coin, which is to be the standard Coin, or ever come into competition with it.

Mr. Locke's idea, that Coins made of any other metal than that of which the standard Coin is made, should be suffered to pass in currency according to the relative value of these metals at the market, is not conformable to practice, and is without example, except in what happened to our Gold Coins for a certain number of years after the 16th year of Charles II. during a part of which time our monetary system was in a state of confusion. How are those who reside in the country, or in many great commercial and manufacturing towns, to estimate the relative value of Gold to Silver, where no Gold or Silver Bullion is bought or sold? Such a proceeding is also contrary to law; for in effect it transfers the right of setting a rate or value on the Coins, from the Sovereign to individuals: Coins ought always to pass in tale according to the rate or value, which the Sovereign sets upon them in his Mint indentures. But Mr. Locke's idea of the manner of valuing Coins according to the relative prices of the metals, of which they are made, at the market, is, with respect to those of Silver and Copper, absolutely impracticable. How are the poorer classes in particular, who principally make use of these Coins, to know what the relative prices are? Such a system would introduce confusion into all our commercial transactions, and would afford an opportunity to the money-changer, or dealer in metals, to raise a fortune by practising the worst of frauds on ignorant individuals, who must, in this case, be the greatest part of Your Majesty's subjects.

If it should be objected, that the principles of Coinage, which I humbly offer for Your Majesty's consideration, are wholly new, I think they should not be rejected merely on that account, in case they should be found to be reasonable. But what I maintain is, that a system consonant to these principles actually exists in a certain degree at present, though it has not been formally adopted by Your Majesty's Government. The present

CHAP. 19. Silver Coins, such as they are, are subordinate and subservient to the Gold Coins; and in this quality only are current. In proposing these principles, it has been my earnest wish, that as few alterations as possible should be made in the system of Coins, which at present exists. I am fully sensible of the embarrassments and confusion in commercial transactions, which any such alteration will at all times produce; my principal object therefore has been to shew, what is the present practice, and to prove, that the system, which now prevails, ought, as nearly as possible, to be continued, as well as to remove the prejudices, which some men of abilities entertain against it. The plan which I propose is expressly calculated for this purpose. My opinion is, and I hope I shall be excused in repeating it, that the Gold Coins should continue to be the principal measure of property and instrument of commerce; that the Silver and Copper Coins should continue to be subservient to, and representative of, these Gold Coins, as they are at present. Influenced by the same desire of not making any unnecessary change, I am also of opinion, that there should be no alteration in the present names, or relative value or rate of the Coins of this realm, as they are now settled in the Mint indentures, and pass in currency. I am sensible, that if a system wholly new were now to be introduced, the weight, the size, and the denomination of our Coins might perhaps be changed to advantage, and better arranged for general convenience. But I am apprehensive that any such change would produce great embarrassments, at least among the inferior classes of

Your Majesty's subjects, in their ordinary traffic and dealings. In all concerns, which so nearly affect the interests of men, they are naturally attached to systems and to names, which have long prevailed, because they are better acquainted with them, and are, for that reason, less exposed to fraud and imposition. Your Majesty may have observed, in the short history which I have given of the Coins of this realm, with what difficulty the several Coins of a new denomination have, in successive periods, been introduced into currency: it required, in most instances, many years to reconcile the people to them, and to establish their general use. It is certainly, therefore, most advisable to continue all the present denominations of our Coins, and to make them pass at the same nominal value, at which they are respectively rated in the present Mint indentures.

I do not pretend, that a new system of Coinage, founded on the principles, which I have endeavoured to establish, will be in all respects perfect; for the nature of the subject does not admit of absolute perfection: I am sensible, that it will be liable to the first of the imperfections stated in an early part of this Letter; that is, that the metal, of which this standard Coin, or principal measure of property, is to be made, will vary in its value in successive periods, even with respect to itself: it has already been shewn, that this imperfection is so inherent in the subject, that it does not admit of a remedy: this variation may be occasioned either by a greater or less production of the Mines, from which one or other of these precious metals is obtained. It was

CHAP. 19.   owing to an unusual production of the Silver Mines in
South America, that the value of Silver decreased in so
rapid and great a degree, in the 17th century, and that
the relative value of Gold rose in proportion: or, this
variation may be occasioned by the effects resulting from
extraordinary revolutions in the political world, such as
have lately happened in France, and in the countries
subdued by its arms;* where the persons who govern
France have, under the pretence of making them free,
first plundered, and then enslaved, the people; and
where vast quantities of Silver Plate, hitherto employed
for holy purposes, or for private splendour, have been
melted down, and brought to the market; so that the
price of Silver in that country was for a short time considerably reduced: or, this variation may be occasioned
by great and memorable conquests, which sometimes
bring an unusual influx of one or other of the precious
metals into the conquering country; such as happened
in ancient times at Rome, where Gold, when it was
first coined, that is, during the second Punic war,
A. U. C. 546, was estimated, in reference to Silver,

See the Appen-
dix to this
Letter, and the
authorities
there quoted.

as high as $17\frac{1}{7}$ to 1: the relative value of Gold to

* The Plate of all the churches and monasteries, as well as of
individuals, chiefly of Silver, was melted soon after the beginning
of the French Revolution, and converted into Coin. It is asserted in
some of the French papers, that the quantity of Silver Coin, thus
introduced into circulation, reduced the price of Silver in so great a
degree, as to make the relative value of Gold compared to Silver as
17 to 1; but for this fact I do not answer. It is however asserted,
that for some reason or other the National Institute of France have
long had under consideration a new system of Coins, particularly with
the view of regulating the relative price of the two precious metals.

Silver fell by degrees afterwards, so as to be estimated as 10 to 1; but after Cæsar had conquered Gaul, he brought into Italy immense spoils, of Gold in particular, taken principally from the cities he destroyed, or the temples he plundered; Suetonius says, "urbes diruit, "sæpius ob prædam quam ob delictum;" this influx of Gold into Rome reduced the relative value of Gold to Silver so low as 7½ to 1. Such an event must have caused a sudden convulsion in the monetary system of the Roman republic; but these are extraordinary occurrences, against which it is impossible to provide; and any variation, occasioned by revolutions or conquests, is seldom of long duration. Thus in France, the Silver, obtained in the manner before described, soon disappeared, and the Government was obliged to introduce Assignats, or a certain species of paper currency, into circulation, to supply, in their internal traffic, the place of the Silver Coins, which had already left them, by the operation of a declining foreign commerce, or to pay their numerous armies employed in foreign countries; and these Assignats perished in their turn. In Rome, the relative value of Gold to Silver, in which so great a change had been produced by the conquests of Cæsar, gradually returned to its former proportion, which, in ancient times, in Greece, as well as in Rome, was generally as 10 to 1. In a business of this kind, all that human policy can effect is, to provide against ordinary contingencies: it is all that I presume to expect from the system, which I now present for Your royal approbation.

CHAPTER XX.

Objections stated and considered.

IT is easy to foresee some objections, that will be made to this system; and I think it right not to pass them wholly unnoticed.

It will be objected, in the first place, that, by the proposed alteration in the Silver Coins, those of Gold will occasionally be drawn out of the kingdom.

Though I may incur the charge of being tedious, I will venture to preface what I have to say in answer to this objection, by treating shortly of the exportation of Coins generally in payment of commercial balances with foreign countries.

Whenever the balance of trade with any particular country is against this kingdom, and no bills of exchange can be obtained to pay this balance through other countries in a circuitous manner; and no Bullion, or foreign Coins considered as such, can be procured for that purpose; the Coins of the kingdom must be sent out to pay that particular balance. The laws of the country are a fruitless barrier* in this respect; and

---

* Mr. Necker, who agrees with me on this point, assigns one extraordinary reason for it, viz. that, by permitting the exportation of Coins, you create the necessity of making new Coins, and thereby increase the profits, which the King derives from his Seigneurage. Mr. Necker

if they could be enforced, they would only tend to injure and diminish our foreign commerce: but these Coins will be replaced by foreign Coins or Bullion received from other countries, and convertible into British Coins, as long as the general balance of trade is in our favour; and, in such case, the stock of national Coins within the kingdom will not, for any length of time, be greatly diminished.

When the general balance of trade is against this kingdom, Bullion or foreign Coins will be exported in preference to British Coins, at least as long as the law, which prohibits the export of these Coins, shall be in force: for this law increases the risk, and consequently the charge of exporting such Coins, above that of exporting Bullion or foreign Coins.

In the case last stated, either Gold or Silver Bullion will be first exported, according to the demand there may be for either of them in the market, to which it is to be sent, and according to the price, which each of these sorts of Bullion, or foreign Coins, considered as such, may bear in that market, compared with the price of it in England: but if there is no reason, on that account, to prefer one sort of Bullion to the other, the Gold Bullion will generally be sent in the first place, because it can be exported at a less charge than Silver Bullion,

<small>See the Evidence of Walter Boyd, Esq. taken before the Secret Committee of the House of Lords, p. 107.</small>

---

estimates these profits at no more than 25,000*l.* a year from all the Mints in the French territories. This is certainly a small sum, and does not arise from a very creditable source. Mr. Necker dignifies these profits, as applied to the Coin exported, by calling them a tax on national exports. Vol. iii. 8vo. c. 4.

as it is of less bulk ; and afterwards the Silver Bullion will be sent, if a sufficient quantity, of Gold Bullion cannot be procured.

When there is a want of both Gold and Silver Bullion, or foreign Coins, to pay the balance of trade, the Coins of the kingdom, of one description or other,' will necessarily be exported, notwithstanding any law, which may prohibit their exportation. The Gold Coins will be generally exported in the first place, not only for the reason I have already stated; but because they can more easily be concealed, and the law, which prohibits the exportation of them, and the penalties inflicted on that account, be more easily evaded.

For almost a century there have been no British Coins, which could be sent in payment of balances due from this kingdom to foreign countries, except the Gold Coins; for, from the defective state of our Silver Coins, none existed in the kingdom, which could be employed for that purpose, but at a great loss to the exporter; and yet the commerce of the country has, through the whole of this period, continued to prosper; and Gold Bullion, as has been proved already, has generally been at a reasonable price.

I entertain doubts, whether, if British Coins of any description are to be sent out of the kingdom, it is not more advantageous to the public, that the Gold Coins should be exported rather than the Silver Coins. Those Coins will first be exported, that are not deficient in weight, of whatever metal they may be made. For if they are deficient in weight, the exporter must pay the difference between the intrinsic and nominal value of such defective Coins. If, to remedy this evil, and to preserve all our Coins in a due state of perfection, the charge of Coinage is to be paid by the public, the charge of coining Gold is much less than the charge of coining a quantity of Silver of equal value: the Silver Coins are also more essentially necessary for carrying on the interior commerce of the kingdom, and particularly the retail trade, than the Gold Coins; It is of more importance, therefore, that these should be retained within the kingdom. The Gold Coins also have a substitute, which the Silver Coins have not, at least in an equal degree; they may be represented by notes, or paper currency, which will answer the purpose of all great commercial transactions, even if a certain proportion of our Gold Coins should be exported, till the balance of trade turn again in our favour, and the Coins so exported shall thereby be replaced.

I will now proceed to reply directly to the objection I have last stated. I have shewn already, that, in payment of foreign balances, British Coins of one description or another must be exported, when there is not in the kingdom a sufficient quantity of Bullion, either Gold or Silver, for that purpose: that in such case the Gold Coins will first be exported, in preference to those of Silver, though the Coins of these two metals should, as far as relates to their intrinsic value, be in a perfect state of equality, because it is more profitable, more convenient, and more safe, to export the Gold Coins; and it is perhaps more for the advantage of the public, that the Gold Coins should be so exported. But if it is meant by this objection, that, even when the balance of trade is generally in our favour, any difference in the intrinsic value of these two sorts of Coins will introduce a mischievous traffic in the Coins made of these two metals; or, in other words, that the Silver Coins of less intrinsic value will be exchanged for those of Gold of more intrinsic value, merely for the purpose of exporting the latter; I beg it may be observed, that our Silver Coins have been for almost a century in a very defective state ; that the present Silver Coins are, on an average, at least one third less in weight and value, than those that will be made upon the plan I have proposed; and yet the evil, which is the ground of this objection, has never happened. I do not conceive that the absence of this evil is to be imputed to the want of a sufficient quantity of these Silver Coins; for our present Silver Coins are mere Counters, without any impression on the face or reverse, or any graining on the edges, or indeed any exterior mark, by which they can be distinguished as Coins; so that the counterfeiter could easily have fabricated or imitated Coins of this description, with very little risk, and in any quantity: and his profit must have been very great, if he could have practised the fraud before mentioned; and yet it is certain, that he has never thought it for his interest to engage in this sort of traffic. It is proper further to observe, that Silver Coins have been legal tender, in payment for any sum, equally with the Gold Coins, during the greatest part of the period before mentioned; for the

Act, which declared them not to be legal tender for any sum exceeding 25*l.* did not pass before 1774: but according to the plan I have proposed, the new Silver Coins will not be legal tender for any sum exceeding the nominal value of the largest piece of Gold Coin in currency: if therefore no traffic of this nature has been carried on when our Silver Coins were so much more deficient than they will be in future, and when they were legal tender to any amount, it is not likely that this sort of fraud will be practised with the new Silver Coins, which will be so much more valuable, indeed nearly equal in intrinsic value to the Gold Coins, and when they will be legal tender only for a much smaller sum, and when, from their external form and beauty, it will be so much more difficult to counterfeit them: it is evident, from the experience we have had, that the profits, which can be derived from this practice, are not equal to the trouble and danger in carrying it on; so that no person will engage in it: but if it should be thought necessary, for the purpose of preventing this evil, to employ any further guard or restriction, I will submit to Your Majesty, whether it may not be advisable, that the Legislature should vest in Your Majesty, or such others as may be authorized by Your royal licence, (these will probably always be the Directors of the Bank of England,) the sole right of carrying Silver to Your Mint to be coined: Your Majesty will thus have it in Your power to limit and regulate the quantity of Silver Coins, which may at any time be sent into circulation; but I beg to be understood, that I do not mean by this

CHAP. 20. restriction, (if it should be thought proper to adopt it,) that Silver Coins of every description should not be sent in great plenty into circulation: it is highly important, for the convenience of Your people, particularly those of the lower classes, that they should at all times be current in great plenty.

The second objection, which will probably be urged, is, that the Silver Coins proposed to be made may fall in their value below their nominal rate or value, and that the price of all commodities may rise in proportion; and as these Silver Coins are principally made use of in the retail trade, those of Your Majesty's subjects, who are the least affluent, may suffer by this measure.

I should feel the deepest regret if there was the least probability, that any measure proposed by me could, in the smallest degree, produce the consequences stated in this objection; I am also sure I should thereby act contrary to Your Majesty's benevolent intentions. When Your Majesty signified Your royal commands to me, as well as others of Your servants, to take this subject into consideration, I am certain, that the object, which You then had at heart, was to remove a great inconvenience, to which Your people had long been exposed; and, for this purpose, to form a plan of introducing into circulation new and better Silver Coins, in sufficient plenty, founded on principles of wisdom and justice: and I am confident, that I shall be able to assign reasons, which will convince Your Majesty and the public, that the evils stated in this objection are not likely to result from the system, which I have ventured to recommend to Your Majesty.

Those who urge this objection are led into error, by supposing, that these new Silver Coins will fall in their value, in like manner as the defective Silver Coins fell in their value, before the general Recoinage, in the reign of William III. and that the price of all commodities will rise in proportion: they do not advert to several circumstances, which make the cases wholly dissimilar.

In the reign of King William III. the Silver Coins were understood to be the principal measure of property: the Gold Coins at that time changed their value, like other commodities, that is, were current for more or less, in reference to the state of the Silver Coins, and the relative price of Gold to Silver at the market: all our exchanges with foreign countries were then regulated by the intrinsic value of our Silver Coins. The reverse is the case at present. The Gold Coins are become the principal measure of property and instrument of commerce; and our commercial balances with foreign nations are not only regulated by them, but paid in them, as has been fully proved already: the Gold Coins no longer take their value with reference to the Silver Coins; but these Silver Coins, as well as every other commodity, now take their value with reference to the Gold Coins, and they pass in currency according to the rate, at which they can be exchanged into the Gold Coins. The Gold Coins have in fact become, for almost a century, the mercantile Money of the kingdom. When the exchange with foreign nations is at any time against this kingdom,

CHAP. 20. any defect in those Coins, which are the principal measure of property, will then first shew itself by a rise in foreign exchanges to our disadvantage; and the merchant, to compensate the loss he sustains thereby, will naturally raise in due proportion the price of all his merchandize: this increase of price gradually extends itself to every commodity, and at last reaches even the most common necessaries of life: such is the progress, by which the price of all commodities is raised, in consequence of a defect in our Coins. But this rise is influenced by a defect in that sort of Coin only, which is the principal measure of property, and in which our balances to foreign countries are regulated and paid. The truth of these principles is fully illustrated by comparing what happened in the reign of King William III. with what has happened of late years. In the reign of King William III. when the Silver Coins were the principal measure of property, and were greatly defective, the price of all commodities rose in proportion; but since the Gold Coins are become the principal measure of property, though our Silver Coins are upon an average as defective, as they were before the general Recoinage, in the reign of King William III. the price of commodities, even when purchased with Silver Coins, has not risen on account of the defect of these Silver Coins: the present defective Silver Coins continue to be paid and received at their nominal value, and according to the rate, at which they can be exchanged for our Gold Coins; sometimes, when they are wanted for particular purposes, they are exchanged even at a premium above their nominal value.

The errors in this respect of all the late writers on Coins have proceeded from a perusal of the works of Mr. Locke, without observing, that the state of the Coins of the kingdom is wholly changed from what it was when he considered this subject: it is probable, that if this great man had lived to the present times, he would have been sensible of the change: he would have applied his principles to the facts as they now exist, and would have drawn his conclusions in conformity to them.

It is extraordinary, that any one should suppose, that the proposed new Silver Coins will not pass in currency at as high a nominal value as the very defective Silver Coins now in circulation; for they will exceed them in intrinsic value by at least one third; and though these new Silver Coins may contain a small proportion of Silver less than what is required by the present Mint indenture, yet the difference in weight will be very inconsiderable, probably not more than is occasioned by wearing in a very small space of time: their intrinsic value, consisting of metal and workmanship, will be equal to their nominal value, estimating the value of the Silver they contain at a fair average.

If any one can entertain the idea, that these Coins will be sent into circulation in so great numbers, that their value will be depreciated by their plenty, I certainly have no such apprehension. If however there should be the least possibility, that this consequence would follow, the remedy, which I have proposed at the close of my answer to the first objection, may be immediately applied to prevent this evil.

Thirdly, the last objection of which I shall take notice, is, that by declaring the Gold Coin to be at present the principal measure of property, an alteration will be made in all bargains, and in the terms of all covenants and contracts, which were concluded previous to the change which has taken place, and when the Silver Coins were understood to be the principal measure of property.

This objection might have some weight, if the change had happened of late years only; but it has already been shewn, that it has existed, and that all payments have been regulated in conformity to it, for almost a century. This objection might also have weight, if this change had been brought about by the authority of Government. It has been shewn, that it was brought about, not by the authority of Government, but by the course of events, with the acquiescence, and I may say the general consent of the people.

Some instances may be produced, from the histories of France and of Scotland, of regulations in the laws of both countries, which directed, that any payments made by virtue of contracts, concluded previous to any debasement in their Coins, should be according to the rate, at which the Coins were valued before such debasement; but in all these cases the debasements were made by the authority of Government, and for the profit of Government: no law or regulation of this sort can be found, as far as I am informed, in the history or records of this kingdom.

After the lapse of almost a century, it is not probable that there can be any great number of bargains, covenants, or contracts, now subsisting, which were concluded previous to the change that has taken place in the principal measure of property. If any such should now exist, it is certain, that all those, who for so long a period have received any payments by virtue of them, must have consented to take these payments in the Gold Coins of the realm, according to the rate, at which they have been current, and are now current; and by this acquiescence for so long a term, they may fairly be presumed to have sufficiently expressed their assent to the change that has happened in the manner of making such payments, that is in the measure of their property.

With respect to the public debt, it is certain, that the last mentioned argument, founded on an acquiescence in the mode of payment for so great a number of years, applies no less to the public than to the private creditor. It is proper further to observe, that much the greatest part of this debt has been contracted since the change in the measure of property has taken place; and in the year 1740, when the annuities payable on the greatest part of the public debt were reduced from 4 to 3 per cent. a fair option was given to the public creditors, whether they would accept of the proposal made for this reduction, or be paid their capital: at that time, therefore, a new contract must be understood to have been made with these creditors; and it could then have been made only in the Coins, which were at that time the principal measure of property, that is, the Gold Coins.

CHAPTER XXI.

Of the Gold Coins previous to the year 1774, and of those now in circulation.

HAVING now completed all that I meant to offer on the principles of Coinage, and on the new system, which, in my judgment, ought to be adopted; and having endeavoured to answer the objections, which may be made to it, I will proceed to apply these principles more in detail to the several sorts of Coin, whether made of Gold, Silver, or Copper, and I will shortly treat of each of them.

The Gold Coins are the first in rank, and by far the most valuable of those which are current in Your Majesty's dominions. It is impossible to estimate, with any degree of accuracy, what may be the present quantity of them in circulation; we have not sufficient data, on which to found any reasonable calculation. There was indeed a time, when these might, in a certain degree, have been obtained: I allude to the general Recoinage of the Gold Coin, which commenced in the year 1774.

A short time previous to this Recoinage, the Directors of the Bank had sent Ingots of Gold to the Mint, amounting in weight to 20,337 lbs. which produced in Coin 950,245*l*. These Coins however were reserved in the coffers of the Bank, and not delivered to the public till the general Recoinage was completed.

During this Recoinage the said Directors sent to the Mint Ingots of *foreign* Gold, amounting in weight to 62,033 lbs. which produced in Coin 2,898,491*l*.

In the course of the general Recoinage, the old and defective Gold Coins, that were brought to the Mint to be recoined, produced in Ingots 355,233 lbs. 1 oz. 8 dwts. 6 grs. and in new Coins 16,598,266*l*.

It was supposed, that at that time there remained in circulation within the kingdom, of old Guineas and Half Guineas of due weight, about 5,000,000*l*. in nominal value: this last sum is merely conjectural; but this conjecture, as I well remember, was founded on the judgment of persons the best informed on such subjects.

The total of the several sums before stated amounts to 25,447,002*l*. Such therefore is the value of the Gold Coins, which on good information were supposed to have been in circulation immediately after the general Recoinage.

From that time the Mint has been employed in coining a very great number of Guineas, and other Gold Coins, partly from Ingots of what is called foreign Gold, and partly from Gold Coins become deficient in weight, and on that account returned to the Mint. The nominal value of what has so been brought to the Mint to be coined, as I am informed, amounts to 36,290,201*l*. 3*s*. 3*d*., that is, 18,720,388*l*. 14*s*. 6*d*. in Ingots of foreign Gold, and 17,569,812*l*. 8*s*. 9*d*. in Gold

CHAP. 21. Coins, which became defective in weight during this period.

Notwithstanding the immense quantity of Gold Coins, which have so been made and issued from the Mint, I cannot venture to estimate the quantity of Gold Coins now in Your Majesty's dominions at more than thirty millions in nominal value, that is, 4,552,998*l.* more than were in circulation immediately after the general Recoinage. This is certainly nothing but a conjecture. I can assign but one reason for supposing, that the Gold Coins now in Your Majesty's dominions should exceed the quantity current within the kingdom at the period last mentioned, by so large a sum as 4,552,998*l.* ; which is, that the general commerce of the country has certainly greatly increased since the year 1777, when the Recoinage of the Gold Coin was completed. On the other hand I can assign reasons from which I should infer, that they must now be less in number and value. The number and value of the Bank Notes, which are at present in circulation, compared with those that were in circulation at the first of these periods, is certainly much increased : the number of country Banks that have been established, and the quantity of Paper currency, under various descriptions, which has been issued by them, is increased in a still greater degree. It has already been observed, that these Bank Notes,* and the paper currency of

---

* I have been informed, that the Cash paid by the London Bankers, compared with what they pay on an average daily in Bank Notes, does not amount in one instance to more than one in thirty ; in another to one in forty ; in a third to one in one hundred and forty ; and in a

country Bankers, particularly Notes for very small sums, certainly take the place of the Gold Coins, make the use of them less necessary, and therefore drive them out of circulation. The complaints from the country on this subject are universal.

In estimating the quantity of Gold Coins now within Your Majesty's dominions, it would be absurd to rely on mere conjecture. I think that I reason on better foundations, when I draw my conclusions from the account that has been given, on good authority, of the quantity of Gold Coins that were in circulation immediately after the general Recoinage; from the increased commerce of the country since that time; and also from known facts, namely, that the quantity of Bank Notes, and the quantity of paper currency issued by country Bankers, have since that period greatly increased. There can be no doubt that these two sorts of paper currency have driven a great proportion of the Gold Coins out of circulation: the Notes of country Bankers prevent even the circulation of Bank Notes in any quantity, except in the Metropolis, and a small distance from it; and this observation

---

fourth instance the disproportion is still much greater. The difference in the relative quantity of Guineas to Bank Notes in the daily payments of those Bankers, arises from a difference in the nature of the business, which they respectively carry on. In the country every one must have observed, in their respective neighbourhoods, how very small is the proportion of Guineas, or Cash of any kind, to the country Bankers Notes that circulate there. The quantity must vary in different parts, according to the number of country Bankers that have been established, and the value of the Notes sent by them into circulation.

proves, that there is a constant conflict between the Coins and Notes of every description, and even between the different sorts of these Notes themselves; so that they tend to exclude and to take the place of each other. The preceding mode of reasoning I prefer to loose estimates and vague speculations, and I leave it to Your Majesty, and such of Your subjects as may peruse this Letter, to determine, whether it is not probable that I have rather over-estimated the quantity of the Gold Coins now within Your European dominions, when I suppose it to amount to 30,000,000*l*. I have been the more particular in endeavouring to ascertain this point in a reasonable degree, and to shew, that the quantity of Gold Coins now in Your Majesty's dominions is not so great as some have supposed, because it will throw light on a subject of great importance, connected with the Coins of the realm, which must, I am persuaded, soon come under the consideration of the Legislature; I mean the paper currency of the kingdom.

It is natural to ask, what is become of the great number of Gold Coins, which remained in circulation immediately after the general Recoinage, and the still greater number that have been issued from Your Majesty's Mint since that time. I answer, that a considerable part has been returned to the Mint and recoined: these appear, by what I have already stated, to be no less than 17,569,812*l*. 8*s*. 9*d*. Another, and perhaps a still greater portion has been sent out of the kingdom, during the present and the two preceding wars, particularly the first of these wars, that is, the American, for the payment of Your Majesty's foreign garrisons, and Your Majesty's fleets and armies serving in foreign parts, and the various charges necessarily connected with them. In proof of this it is proper to observe, that our exchanges with foreign countries are generally in our favour in time of peace, but they are less constantly in our favour when we are engaged in war: and though a part of these Coins, so exported, may have returned to Great Britain in the course of trade, a much greater proportion is either still circulating in foreign countries, particularly those belonging to the United States, or has been melted and converted into Ingots, for the supply of foreign Mints, or has formed a part perhaps of those Ingots, which have been sold in the British market, for the supply of the British Mint.

I am aware, that Mr. Necker, in his Treatise on the Administration of the Finances of France, has estimated the quantity of Specie circulating in that kingdom at the time when he wrote his Treatise, as amounting to 2,200,000,000 Livres,* or 91,666,666*l.* This appears to be an enormous quantity, especially when it is considered, that the Coins circulating in France were principally made of Silver; it is more than three times the value of the Gold Coins now circulating in Your Majesty's European dominions, according to what I have supposed, and yet, in Your Majesty's dominions, internal trade and

* Wherever the mention of Livres occurs, or where English Money is to be converted into them, the reader will allow 24 to the Pound Sterling. This estimate is not perfectly correct, but is sufficiently so for the present purpose.

maritime commerce are much more active and extensive. Mons. de Calonne appears by his writings to have carried his estimate still further. I cannot say that I place any great confidence in the estimates of either of these Gentlemen. They were political combatants then at war with each other, and contending for the favour of their Sovereign, and of his people; and for this purpose, it was the business of each of them to over-rate the wealth, and consequently the Coins circulating in the French dominions, particularly during his own administration. Mr. Necker appears to have much under-rated the quantity of French Coins exported annually from that country, as well as the quantity driven out of circulation, and returned to the French Mints in order to be recoined. It is probable, that these last, particularly those made of Silver, must be more numerous in France than in other countries, as large sums were paid in the capital and great commercial towns in bags of Silver Coin, and not by tale; so that more attention must have been paid to the weight of them. But supposing the quantity of Coins circulating in France to have been, when Mr. Necker published his Treatise, as great as he has estimated them, it is not impossible to account for the different proportion of Coins circulating in Great Britain and France, if we compare the extent of territory, number of subjects, and the commerce in each of them: I need only observe, that before the French Revolution, payments in commercial transactions were almost wholly made in France in Coins, and very little in what we call paper currency: and, on the other hand, that in Your Majesty's

European dominions such payments are principally made in paper currency, or in inland bills of exchange, and a very small proportion in Coins. I cannot help observing, that the different state of the two countries in this respect is a decisive proof in how great a degree a paper currency tends to exclude the use of Coins.

CHAPTER XXII.

Of the art of Assaying, and the deficiency from standard fineness in different Reigns.

As a part of this Subject, it is proper that I should now proceed to treat shortly of the art of assaying, as practised at Your Majesty's Mint; of the alloy put into the metals of which the Coins are made; and of the weight of the Coins as issued from Your Majesty's Mint; and of their fashion.

The art of assaying, as practised at Your Majesty's Mint, is carried to a very high degree of perfection. This art has been improving from the reign of Charles II. to the present time. In the reign of Charles II. the defect in fineness of our Gold Coins is stated to have been $9s.\ 10\tfrac{2}{11}d.$ per cent. At present the metal of which our Gold Coins are made is declared to be perfect standard:* this perfection in the fineness of the Gold of which our Coins are made is greatly to be attributed to the skill of that excellent Officer of the public, the late Mr. Alchorne. In several experiments or trials of

See the Records of the Trials of the Pix.

---

* Previous to the Recoinage of the Gold Coin in 1774, experiments were made of the fineness of the Gold Coin issued in the reigns of our several Princes from Charles II. to the present time, by melting Guineas of each reign into Ingots of 15 lbs. each; and from the contrary ends of each Ingot assays were made, by which it appeared, that in former

the Pix made by the Goldsmiths' Company on twenty-eight millions of Gold Coin, sent into circulation, there has been recorded no deviation in fineness. By the Mint indentures, if the Gold Coin does not vary more than 40 grains in fineness or in weight in the Pound, or in both together, which is called the remedy, such Gold Coin is allowed to pass as standard; or, in other words, it is to be considered as perfect as the Officers of the Mint are under any legal obligation to coin it. I have already observed, that in the before-mentioned trial of the Pix by the Goldsmiths' Company, there was no deviation in fineness; and in the same trial there has not been recorded more than an error of 4 grains in weight. The Officers of the Mint therefore might have varied in weight or fineness 36 grains more in each Pound, or as much as 13s. 7¾d. per cent. without incurring any blame or penalty on that account, provided such error was not committed by design. It is clear from hence, that the remedy allowed in coining Gold, by our Mint indentures, is too great, and it produces this ill effect, as I am informed, that our Gold Coins are estimated in foreign Mints at less than their intrinsic value: some of these foreign Mints are said not to make

reigns the Gold Coins were worse than standard in the following proportions.

Charles II. 26 grs. Troy worse than standard, 9s. 10$\frac{2}{11}$d. per cent.
James II. 30 - - - - - 11s. 4$\frac{4}{11}$d. per cent.
William 13 - - - - - 4s. 11$\frac{1}{11}$d. per cent.
Anne 7 - - - - - 2s. 7$\frac{9}{11}$d. per cent.
George I. 6 - - - - - 2s. 3$\frac{4}{11}$d. per cent.
George II. 3 - - - - - 1s. 1$\frac{7}{11}$d. per cent.
George III. standard.

CHAP. 22.   any difference between the Gold Coins of former reigns, and those made during the reign of Your Majesty, though these last issue from Your Majesty's Mint in so superior a degree of accuracy, both with respect to weight and fineness.

The alloy put into these Gold Coins is in its quality as proper as can be devised: from the great quantity of Gold Coins, which have been returned through deficiency in weight to Your Majesty's Mint, since the general Recoinage, a suspicion had been entertained, that the nature of the alloy put into these Coins rendered them too hard and brittle, and subject to abrasion and speedy diminution, by friction. To ascertain this fact, Mr. Hatchett, an excellent chemist, was employed, under the inspection of that very eminent philosopher, Mr. Henry Cavendish, to make experiments, for the purpose of shewing how far this evil was produced by the nature of the alloy put into our Gold Coins; and whether it could not be remedied by making an alteration in the alloy. The Gentlemen before mentioned employed a considerable time in making experiments on the quality of different metals. They exerted great ability as well as industry to ascertain the point referred to them; and in a Report,* made by Mr. Hatchett, it appears to be the result of their opinion, that Gold Coins are not so likely to wear by abrasion

---

* See the substance of this very curious and elaborate Report, in the Transactions of the Royal Society for the year 1803. This Report is so much esteemed in France, that I understand it has been translated, by order of the French Government, into the French language, by the Comptroller of the Mint at Paris, with Notes by Guyton de Morveau.

and friction, if they are alloyed with Silver and Copper mixed; but that the difference between them and Coins alloyed with Copper alone, provided the Copper be very pure, is so little, that there is no sufficient reason for altering the present alloy in our Gold Coins, consisting alone of pure Copper.

With respect to the weight of the Gold Coins, as issued from Your Majesty's Mint, I have shewn how small the error of late has been, and that they are made by the Officers of Your Majesty's Mint as correct and perfect as can be expected.

The fashion or form of these Coins is certainly subject to some defect, which exposes them too much to be worn or diminished in common use by abrasion or friction. The nature of the milling or graining on the edges is supposed to be too rough, and other parts of the Coin are thought to have too many sharp points. In what manner and to what degree this defect can be removed, can best be determined by the Officers of Your Majesty's Treasury, after having consulted the Officers of Your Mint, and examined the most eminent artists, as well as the Directors of the Bank of England: I shall say therefore nothing further upon it. I shall also say nothing on the beauty of the Coins, which I think should rather be referred to Your Majesty's judgment.

CHAPTER XXIII.

Of the Silver Coins, and the deficiency of those in circulation at different periods.

I PROCEED now to treat of the Silver Coins, which are the second in rank, and next in value to those made of Gold. The quantity of legal Silver Coins now in currency is certainly far too small for the purposes of commerce, particularly of the retail trade, and for the convenience of Your people. Their deficiency in weight is at present even greater than before the general Recoinage of the Silver Coins in the reign of William III. It is impossible to form any estimate or reasonable conjecture of the nominal value of the legal Silver Coins now in circulation; I mean of such as have been coined in the Mints of this kingdom: it is possible however to ascertain the value which they cannot exceed. The nominal value of the Silver Coins which were coined at the general Recoinage in the reign of William III. and those which have been occasionally coined since that period, amounts to 8,076,092*l*. Of these the Crown Pieces, amounting in value to 1,553,047*l*., have, as I have already observed, wholly disappeared;

their value therefore must be deducted from the total above mentioned.*

I think I may fairly estimate, that one moiety of the Half Crown Pieces have in like manner disappeared; half of their value, being 1,164,785*l.*, must therefore be deducted, which leaves 1,164,785*l.*, being the value of the remainder.

What may be the nominal value of the legal Shillings and Sixpences, and Silver Coins of smaller denominations remaining in circulation, it would be idle to attempt to form a conjecture; their number has certainly very much diminished. I will venture to deduct one third, and the nominal value of those that remain will then be 2,795,650*l.*

The total value of all the legal Silver Coins now in circulation cannot, therefore, according to this estimate, exceed 3,960,435*l.* : it is probably very much less.

There are certainly many counterfeits in circulation, but fewer I believe than is generally imagined. It is not very difficult to discover them; and the Officers of the Mint can readily distinguish them from the legal Silver Coins, by the quality of the metal.

The present deficiency in weight of the legal Silver Coins, according to their several denominations, has been ascertained by the two following experiments; the one made in December 1787; the other, in July 1798, by the Officers of Your Majesty's Mint.

---

* For some time after the general Recoinage, in the reign of William III. there were many Crowns and Half Crowns of Charles II. and James II. in circulation; but these have wholly disappeared, and cannot now be found, except in the cabinets of the curious.

In 1787 it was found that

$12\frac{8}{10}$ Crowns	were requisite	$12\frac{4}{10}$ Crowns	As
27 Half Crowns	to make up a	$24\frac{8}{10}$ Half Crowns	issued
$78\frac{1}{10}$ Shillings	Pound Troy,	62 Shillings	from the
$194\frac{6}{10}$ Sixpences	instead of	124 Sixpences	Mint.

In 1798 it was found that

$12\frac{33}{40}$ Crowns	were requisite	$12\frac{16}{40}$ Crowns	As
$27\frac{21}{40}$ Half Crowns	to make up a	$24\frac{33}{40}$ Half Crowns	issued
$82\frac{9}{40}$ Shillings	Pound Troy,	62 Shillings	from the
$200\frac{37}{40}$ Sixpences	instead of	124 Sixpences	Mint.

And if we compare the deficiency in weight of these several denominations of Silver Coins, according to the last experiment, with what they ought to weigh by the Mint indenture, the deficiency will amount in the

Crowns to $3\frac{101}{313}$ per cent.
Half Crowns $9\frac{801}{1101}$ per cent.
Shillings $24\frac{1004}{3280}$ per cent.
Sixpences $38\frac{2284}{6034}$ per cent.

It is singular, that these several Silver Coins, particularly the Shillings and Sixpences, though in general they retain no remains of any impression, or any rough edges, which would make them subject to friction, appear to have diminished by use in the short interval of eleven years, according to the experiments above mentioned, in the following proportions.

Crowns $\frac{100}{313}$ per cent.
Half Crowns $1\frac{333}{367}$ per cent.
Shillings $5\frac{55}{328}$ per cent.
Sixpences $3\frac{1189}{6034}$ per cent.

From this last observation it is fair to conclude, that these Silver Coins have even continued to diminish in weight since the last experiment made in 1798, and will probably diminish in future: and yet, though so very defective, they are still current at their nominal value, and sometimes even a premium is given for them, as I have already observed.

What I have said, in treating of the Gold Coins, of the art of assaying, as practised at the Mint; of the quality of the alloy; and of the correct weight, at which they are issued from the Mint, applies equally to these Silver Coins, so that I need not here repeat it.*

Permit me, however, in this place to observe, that the new Silver Coins will surpass all the others in beauty; and will, in that view, be acceptable to Your Majesty's people. They are not only made of a metal which takes a fair and pleasing impression, but, being of a greater number of denominations than those of any other metal, their various sizes afford a larger scope to the engravers and artists, for the exercise of their respective talents in design and execution.

From the present deficiency of the legal Silver Coins, and from the nominal value of those supposed to remain in circulation, an estimate may be formed of the charge, which would be incurred in making any compensation to the holders of them, for such deficiency, in case they should be called in or cried down.

It would ill become me to offer to Your Majesty any advice—whether, in this case, any compensation should be made, or what should be the amount of the compen-

CHAP. 23.   sation. Your Majesty will of course decide on this question by the advice of Your Parliament. It will be sufficient if I lay before Your Majesty such precedents as I have collected, in order to enable Your Majesty and the Two Houses of Parliament to exercise a proper judgment on this point.

CHAPTER XXIV.

An account of several ways of calling in deficient Coins.

I BELIEVE it will be found, that in foreign countries no compensation was ever made for deficient Coins, that have been driven out of circulation, or have been called in to be recoined. At so late a period as the year 1749, when the Government of Holland recoined all their Ducats, and called them in for that purpose, they paid no more for them than their value by weight. From the history of this kingdom it appears, that when Henry V. called in the deficient Gold Coins, in the 9th year of his reign, he received them by weight; but, in order to relieve his subjects from the loss they suffered on this occasion, he gave up, for a certain time, the profits arising from Seigneurage. When Queen Elizabeth called in all the base and deficient Silver Coins, in the second year of her reign, she received them by weight, paying for the best of them very little more than they were worth when melted down; and for such of them as were most debased, the exact value of the standard Silver they contained; telling her subjects, *that in no realm any Prince had done the same, or ought to do.* She also gave up the profits arising from Seigneurage. The Parliament of England in 1647 called in the clipped

See 9th Hen. V. Stat. 1. cap. 11. sec. 3.

See Scobel, 1647. ch. 91.

CHAP. 24. Money, paying for it according to its weight,* at certain rates: they allowed however the old Monies, which were diminished only by wearing and wasting, to continue still in circulation. Charles II. at the Restoration called in all the Money coined during the Usurpation, receiving it by weight; he gave up, I believe, half the profits arising from Seigneurage: these profits were wholly taken away by Act of Parliament five years afterwards, when certain duties, called Coinage duties, were given him to defray the charge of coining. At the general Recoinage of the Silver Coins in the reign of William III. Mr. Locke was of opinion, that the old Silver Coins should have been received according to their intrinsic value by weight: the House of Commons, however, contrary to the opinion of Mr. Locke, consented to pay all the loss arising from the defects of the Silver Coins, and ordered the receivers of the public revenue to take the clipped Money in payment, " though of a coarser alloy than standard, the " same not evidently appearing to be Copper, or base " metal, or washed with Silver only." We are informed, " that this regulation operated as an encouragement to " the further clipping of the Coins, and gave the clippers " all the advantage they could desire, as they were now " sure of a market for their clipped Money, whatever the " defect of it might be; so that what had been hoarded, " and hitherto escaped the shears, now underwent the " same fate; and the historians, who give an account

* The allowance the Parliament made, on this occasion, for the clipped Money, appears to me to be extraordinary; they allowed only 4s. 10d. per oz. Troy in the country; and 4s. 11d. in London.

" of this transaction, think it not improbable, that more
" was clipped under this general license than had been
" before." I have never been able to obtain an account
of the charge incurred for compensating the deficiency
of these Silver Coins. This compensation, as well as the
charges of the Mint for recoining these deficient Coins,
was enormous:* the nation was in a state of distress,
and even confusion, and the people were ready to pay
any thing out of the public purse, in order to relieve
themselves from the difficulties to which their private
concerns were exposed. When the deficient Gold Coins
were called in, in the year 1774, to be recoined, their
deficiency was compensated to the holders, according to
a plan then settled, which will be found in the Books of
Your Majesty's Treasury. This plan was successfully
carried into execution without complaint or murmur;
and as it was better managed than that at the Recoinage
of the Silver Coins in the reign of King William, the
charge for compensating such deficiency, and for the

* As the Receivers of the public revenue and the Officers of the
Exchequer received these deficient Coins at their nominal value, in the
receipt of the taxes, a great part of the charge incurred on that account
shewed itself in deficiency of revenue, and the amount of it therefore
has never been ascertained. It appears by the Journals of the House
of Commons, that large sums were occasionally voted for the payment
of the charge incurred from the deficiency of the Coins, and the charge
of Recoinage : but I cannot find any account, which collects together
the whole of this charge, or distinguishes between the charges of
compensation and recoinage; and I believe that no such account
exists: some assertions, or rather conjectures, will be found in printed
books on the extent of these charges; but no official account, as far as
I am informed, was ever rendered of them.

CHAP. 24. Recoinage, was much less, though very great: an account of it will be found in the Journals of the House of Commons, or in the Papers presented to that House. When, in the year 1797, Your Majesty ordered new Copper Coins to be issued, in consequence of an Address of the House of Commons, no compensation was made either for the legal, or, as they are called, Tower Halfpence and Farthings, or for the Counterfeits that circulated together with them; and yet it was reasonable to conclude, that they would be driven out of circulation, and be rendered almost of no value; and they were in fact so driven out in some parts of the kingdom. I have no doubt, that if that measure had been pursued with celerity and vigour, all the Counterfeits at least would have wholly disappeared: the people, and in particular the poorest classes, who suffered most from this measure, rejected the old Copper Coins, and bore the loss sustained thereby without complaint or murmur.

It would be improper for me to suggest any plan for crying down or calling in the deficient Silver Coins now in currency, whether their deficiency is to be compensated or not. It will be the duty of the Officers of Your Majesty's Treasury to submit to Your Majesty their advice, on the manner of carrying this part of the business into execution; and the plan, whatever it may be, should not, for obvious reasons, be disclosed till the moment of execution. I have already shewn on what principles the new Silver Coins should be made, so that they may be current at the same time with the Gold Coins, and that there may be no longer a conflict between the Coins made of the two metals, and a traffic driven in the exchange of one for the other; an evil to which the public was occasionally exposed for more than two centuries.

I have also stated to what amount the Silver Coin should be made legal tender.

CHAPTER XXV.

Of Spanish Dollars now in circulation.

IN the course of the last year, Spanish Dollars to a considerable amount were sent into circulation, with new impressions struck upon the face and reverse of them. They were issued, with the consent of Government, by the Bank of England, who engaged to receive them back at the rate or value at which they were sent into circulation. This measure was adopted in conformity to what had been practised with respect to Copper Tokens, in the beginning of the 17th century. I have already observed, that Queen Elizabeth would not suffer any currency of this description to be issued; and James I. when he did issue them, would not suffer them to be called Coins, but *Tokens:* many of these Copper Tokens were sent into circulation in a subsequent period, by individuals, particularly during the confusions that prevailed in the course of the civil wars. The Dollars issued in the course of last year are certainly not Coins, though they have the impression of Your Majesty: for they are not current under Your royal authority, and no one is obliged to take them as legal tender in payment of any debt. They are merely Silver Tokens.

The justification of this measure rests singly on the absolute necessity there was for these Silver Tokens, to pay the seamen of the Royal Navy, and the artificers in the great docks of the kingdom, from the want of Coins of the lower denominations, which are necessary for that purpose: the blame, therefore, if any such is to be imputed, falls not on those who permitted these Dollars to be issued, but on those who neglected to supply Your Majesty's subjects with a sufficient quantity of legal Silver Coins, to be employed in those payments, for which these Dollars now pass. But not only Your Majesty's sailors and Your own artificers are in want of legal Silver Coins; the labourers in every part of the country, and the manufacturers in the great and populous towns of this kingdom, and all Your good people in every part of it, particularly the inferior classes, suffer equally from the want of them. On this occasion allow me to submit to Your Majesty a moral consideration, which will, I am persuaded, make a strong impression on You: the lower ranks are occasionally led into excesses from the want of a sufficient quantity of Coins of the smaller denominations; for when they receive their weekly wages, they are frequently compelled by their employers to attend for payment at ale-houses, and places of that description, where Coins, or a low sort of paper currency sometimes called Silver Notes, are provided for that purpose; and the poor are thereby too frequently tempted to spend, in the purchase of liquors, a part of what they have gained by their industry, which ought to have been reserved for the sober maintenance of themselves and families.

CHAPTER XXVI.

Of the Copper Coins, and the relative expence of coining Gold, Silver, and Copper.

I PROCEED in the last place to treat of the Copper Coins, which are the lowest in rank and least in value.

It is more difficult to form any judgment of the value of the Copper Coins now in circulation, than of those made of Gold or Silver: in the year 1787, the Officers of Your Majesty's Mint were of opinion, that the lawful Copper Coins issued from the Mint, and remaining then in circulation, were equal in weight to nearly 1500 tons, and in nominal value to 322,000*l.* Sterling: no Copper Coins have been issued, I believe, since that time, from Your Majesty's Mint. Mr. Boulton coined, by Your Majesty's order, 1815 tons of Copper into Twopenny Pieces, Penny Pieces, Halfpence, and Farthings, amounting in nominal value to 282,075*l.* 5*s.* 8½*d.** The principle adopted in making these Coins was, that the nominal value of each Piece should be equal to the value of the metal which it contained, and the price of the workmanship employed in making it: these new Coins therefore

---

* Twopenny Pieces   6,019*l.* 15*s.* 8*d.*
  Penny Pieces   183,177*l.* 18*s.* 6*d.*
  Halfpence   88,506*l.* 18*s.* 4*d.*
  Farthings   4,370*l.* 13*s.* 2*d.*

were of much more intrinsic value than any Coins of that metal, which had been hitherto issued. The Lords of the Committee on Coin were under two difficulties:— it was impossible, in their opinion, to make any compensation for the great number of the different sorts of Copper Coins, legal or counterfeit, then in circulation: the Counterfeits were certainly of very little intrinsic value, and frequently not made of Copper: yet the Committee were apprehensive that the perfection of these new Copper Coins would have the effect of driving instantly the old Copper Coins of every description out of circulation, and would produce a sudden deficiency of Copper Coins, which Mr. Boulton, with all his art and machinery, could not supply with sufficient expedition, and that there might in consequence be a great confusion among the lower ranks of people. To avoid this evil the Lords determined to begin by coining Twopenny and Penny Pieces, as they hoped thereby to contrive to keep the old Halfpence and Farthings still in circulation, till they could provide a sufficient quantity of Copper Coins of the lower denominations, to replace those which were still current: this measure had the effect of not driving the old Halfpence and Farthings wholly out of circulation at the moment they were issued: but Your Majesty's subjects evidently shewed a disposition to get rid of the old Copper Coins of most descriptions as fast as possible, and called aloud, particularly from the Northern parts of the kingdom, for a supply of Halfpence and Farthings made on the principle adopted by the Lords of the Committee. The Committee for Coin proceeded to gratify them, by the advice they offered to Your Majesty; and You were pleased to order that Halfpence and Farthings on the same principle should be coined as fast as possible: but the inferior Officers of the Mint contrived to raise objections, which suspended the execution of this measure; and about that time the declining state of my own health prevented me from giving further attention to this business. It is singular, that few of the new Copper Coins ever made their appearance, either in London or its neighbourhood, though to my knowledge great numbers were sent thither: I am told, that the people were desirous of retaining them in preference to the old Copper Coins, and even in preference to the defective Silver Coins; and that they have them still in their possession: there cannot be a stronger proof of the estimation in which these Copper Coins were held by the people, even in those parts where they were not found in common circulation. I have heard also that persons, who from the nature of their trade and occupation were in possession of great quantities of the old Copper Coins, discouraged, from interested motives, the circulation of these new ones; and when a suspension was put to any further issue; in the manner before stated, they were enabled to effect their purposes.

The Lords of the Committee were subject to another difficulty. Though they had taken the price of the Copper of which these Coins were made, on what they thought a fair and sufficient average, the price of this metal rose upon them beyond their expectation, so that it became even higher than the price at which they had estimated it in the Copper Coins. This difficulty, however, would have been easily removed; the price of the metal in Copper Coins is of less importance than in those made of Silver, and much less than in those made of Gold: it is I believe a certain maxim, that all articles, which come into general use and demand, and for which the demand is occasionally very uncertain, vary in their price more than any others, especially where the quantity produced does not depend singly on the industry or will of man, as is the case of all metals: thus Copper varies in its price more than Silver, and Silver varies in its price more than Gold, as has been shewn already. The value of the Copper put into these Coins is also a consideration of less importance in another view; the price of the workmanship in making Copper Coins, compared with the value of the metal, is at least ten times more than in making Silver Coins, and forty-three times more than in making Gold Coins. On all these accounts the value of the metal in making these Copper Coins should be estimated on a much larger and more liberal average than in making the Silver Coins, where the average should be taken with as much care and accuracy as possible: the Lords of the Committee erred therefore in this respect, but it was an error easy to be corrected.

I should not omit to observe, that it was the wish of the Lords of the Committee to have made the new Copper Coins serve the purposes of weights, as this circumstance would have been of great convenience to all Your Majesty's subjects concerned in the retail trade.

CHAP. 26.   They so far attained their object, that each Twopenny Piece, made and issued in consequence of their advice, was of the weight of two ounces Avoirdupoise, and each Penny Piece of the weight of one ounce Avoirdupoise. But from the rise in the price of Copper, as before stated, it was found impossible to conform to this principle in the Halfpence and Farthings, which were afterwards issued.

It is certain, that the quantity of counterfeit Copper Coins greatly exceeds the quantity of legal Copper Coins: the Officers of the Mint were of opinion, in the year 1787, that even then they exceeded the legal Copper Coins. Their number has certainly increased ever since; the quantity of these counterfeit Copper Coins is in truth beyond calculation; and yet I am told that many principal manufacturers are obliged to make Coins or Tokens of this description, to enable them to pay their workmen, and for the convenience of the poor employed by them: so great is the demand for good Copper Coins in almost every part of the kingdom.

Though I was originally of opinion, for the reason already stated, that it was advisable to begin by making Copper Coins of a large denomination, yet I have always thought, and still think, that it is of the greatest service to the indigent classes of Your Majesty's subjects, that Copper Coins of the lowest denominations should be made and issued in great plenty. In all the Eastern parts of the world, particularly in China,* where labour

---

* It is extraordinary, that though great quantities of Silver are annually sent from this country and other parts of Europe to China, and other great quantities are annually sent from Acapulco to China

is paid for at a low rate, and the necessaries of life are very cheap, the Coins are made of very low denominations: the price of labour and of provisions is certainly the cause that these Coins are made of so little value; but I am not certain that the smallness of Coins does not so far operate on the price of the necessaries of life, as in some degree to reduce it: small Coins certainly enable the poor man to purchase and pay for a smaller quantity of any article, when he is not in want of a greater; they contribute also to his comfort and convenience, by enabling him to divide his little property into minute portions; and thereby promote economy where it was most wanted.

I have now concluded all I had to offer on the principles of Coinage, and on the application of these principles to the Coins of different metals, which circulate in Your Majesty's kingdom. I may have been diffuse, and consequently tedious; but in treating of a subject so little understood I was desirous to omit no fact or argument, which might enable Your Majesty to judge of the plan proposed by me; and which might enable others to make corrections in this plan; or to propose a better, more deserving of Your Majesty's approbation, and more acceptable to Your people. With the same view, I have endeavoured to place the subject in a

---

and its neighbourhood, the price of Silver should be so high in that kingdom, and their Coins continue of such small denominations. It is in my judgment a certain proof of what has been asserted by all writers, and particularly by later ones, of the very great population of that kingdom.

CHAP. 26.

variety of lights; in truth, in all the lights that have occurred to me, and more perhaps than are necessary. I shall be perfectly satisfied, if, in consequence of my labours, Your subjects shall receive the relief of which they have long been so much in want, and which they have sufficiently shewn that they expect to obtain from Your Majesty's love of Your people, and from the attention of Your Government. There is indeed one merit, which recommends the plan I have proposed;— that it may easily be executed, and that it tends less than any other to disturb what is now in existence, and to which Your people have long been accustomed. Men of science and talents must certainly be employed in the conduct of a business of this nature: in the reign of King William III. Mr. Locke, Mr. Newton, afterwards Sir Isaac Newton, and Dr. Halley, persons of great eminence, were on this account brought into the service of the public. I allow that it is natural to hesitate, upon the first view of a business, which is in its various parts so complicated, and which concerns the interests of every man: but I am persuaded, that, with the aid of men of adequate talents, it will be found more difficult in prospect than in execution.

CHAPTER XXVII.

Considerations on the state of the Mint.

BEFORE I conclude what relates to the principles of Coinage, and the fabrication of Coins, it is proper that I should offer some considerations on the state of Your Majesty's Mint, which is as it were the manufactory where Coins are made; for no new Coinage on a large scale can be undertaken, till some alteration and reform has been made in it. The subsisting regulations for receiving Bullion of any description into Your Majesty's Mint; for transferring it from one department to another; for preserving it in security while it continues in the custody of the different Officers; and lastly, for returning it in the shape of Coins to those to whom it belongs, are wise, and require no alteration: these regulations are very ancient, and probably of Norman origin. Some old statutes made in the reigns of Edward .III.[*] and Henry V. refer to these regulations; but they do not appear to have introduced any new ones; they contain only strict injunctions for carrying into execution such as had long subsisted.

I have already observed, that the art of assaying, as practised by Mr. Alchorne, and I believe by his

[*] See 25th Edw. III. Stat. 5. ch. 10. and also 9th Henry V. Stat. 3. ch. 3. sec. 6.

CHAP. 27. successors, at Your Majesty's Mint, is in a state of perfection; probably more so than in most of the foreign Mints; that the nature of the alloy put into the Coins is such, that, all circumstances considered, it ought not to be changed; and that the several denominations of Coins, of whatever metal they are made, are issued from Your Majesty's Mint of due weight; even more correctly than the present Mint indenture requires. What I have thus said of the security of the precious metals, while they continue under the custody of Your Majesty's Officers; and of the great accuracy observed in converting them into Coins, is certainly no slight commendation: but the Mint is defective in other respects; I mean in the lower departments, that is, in the operative or mechanical parts: it is in want of that new and improved machinery, which has of late years been invented, and from which every branch of British manufactures has profited in so great a degree. Coins were originally struck with a hammer only: in the reigns of Queen Elizabeth and Charles I. Coins were occasionally made by what is now called the Mill and Screw; but this instrument was never introduced into constant practice at the English Mint, till the year 1662, when letters and grainings were first placed on the edges of the Coins. From that time to the present this mode of making Coins has continued to be practised in Your Majesty's Mint; but the new machinery now employed in the manufactory of every sort of metal, in which the mechanics of this country far surpass those of any other, has not in general been admitted into Your Majesty's

Mint. It is an acknowledged principle, that machines, which act with a given force, can work with more truth and accuracy than the arm of man, the force of which necessarily varies occasionally, from several causes: another practice has been invented; that of striking Coins in a steel collar, so as to make them perfectly round, and all precisely of the same diameter; an improvement, which certainly contributes at least to the beauty of the Coin: new modes of putting what is called the graining on the edges of Coins have also been invented; which at the same time that they protect the Coins from being filed, equally with the present mode, do not occasion those rough points or edges, which expose them to wear by abrasion or friction. For these, and many other valuable inventions, the public are indebted to the ingenuity of Mr. Boulton, of Soho, near Birmingham. It is singular, that though the manufacturers of England have greatly profited by these inventions, the Officers of Your Majesty's Mint have never, or at least not sufficiently, availed themselves of them: the Mints of foreign countries are in search of them; and their governments in more than one instance have employed Mr. Boulton, in erecting Mints on his new principles; and Parliament has authorized the same. One Government (I need not name it) has, as I have learned from good authority, sent persons at different times, under pretence of treating with Mr. Boulton, in the course of his business, to obtain by artifice the knowledge of his inventions, for the benefit of the countries under its sway.

CHAP. 27.

But it is not only in the fashion and beauty of the Coins, that Your Majesty's Mint would profit by adopting these new inventions; there are other considerations, which strongly recommend their introduction* into Your Majesty's Mint: the Coins of the realm will thereby be made with much more expedition, and with less charge to the public. By an account which I have seen, Mr. Boulton can coin at least ten times as many pieces, in a given time, as can be coined at the Mint by the method now practised; and though, as I have already observed, the security of the precious metals, while in the custody of the Officers of the Mint, is at present very great, it will certainly be increased when fewer persons are employed in the operation. If a new Silver Coinage should be undertaken, expedition† is certainly of great importance; and I could wish that the whole might be performed at one Mint in the Tower, rather than at several Mints in different parts of the kingdom, as practised in the reign of King William, and at other preceding periods: it is certainly more easy to find

* In introducing this new machinery, eminent engineers and artists should be consulted; so as to be very careful not to lose in accuracy and beauty what may be gained in expedition and cheapness.

† By an account I have seen, it will be easy to coin 60,000,000 of Shillings, or 3,000,000*l.* Sterling in a year, with the aid of the improved machinery, or even double, if the nature of the business should require it. According to the estimate I have made, it will not be proper to begin to replace the present defective Silver Coins by new and perfect Silver Coins, unless a quantity, equal in value to 3,000,000*l.* Sterling, can be at once issued, for the use of Great Britain, and 1,000,000*l.* for Ireland. For when Coins, particularly such as are beautiful, are first sent into circulation, the people are very much disposed to hoard them.

artists of proper talents and abilities, sufficient in number to occupy the respective departments in one Mint, than in many.

The charges of Your Majesty's Mint ought certainly to be reduced: the accounts I have already stated, though little else than Gold has for many years been coined, sufficiently enforce the propriety of some reduction. This charge may easily be diminished, if the new machinery is employed: in truth, a new Mint indenture, in which all these charges are specified and ascertained, will be absolutely necessary. I have no doubt, that on this occasion Your Majesty will treat the present Officers of Your Mint with the justice and liberality to which they are entitled. Considerable fortunes have occasionally been made by the Masters of Your Majesty's Mint in former times: one great man, who was an honour not only to his country, but to human nature; for the powers of the human understanding were never exerted by any one with so much energy and perspicuity, or carried to such an amazing extent, on subjects that almost surpass human comprehension—this great man being for many years at the head of the Mint, derived an ample fortune from this source, to which he was fully entitled. By representations and reports he frequently apprised the Officers of Your Majesty's Treasury of defects, which he observed in the Coins, and of frauds committed by introducing foreign Coins into circulation at improper valuations. I say nothing either of any of his predecessors, or of those who have succeeded him: it is not indeed necessary; for Your Majesty, by a wise regulation

CHAP. 27. established in 1799, has prevented any future excess in the profits arising from the office of Master of Your Mint, by converting these profits into a fixed salary, not more than an adequate reward for the discharge of the duties of this office, if properly executed. The profits of the inferior Officers of Your Majesty's Mint are a proper subject of consideration for the Commissioners of Your Majesty's Treasury, who, as well as Parliament, have a right to call for such accounts as may afford them sufficient information. I have in my possession some papers and accounts, derived from a good source, which I shall be ready to furnish, if it shall be thought necessary: the very mode of paying these inferior Officers is not, in my judgment, for persons of that description, in all respects proper. They sometimes gain extravagant profits; at other times they have no employment, and do not derive from their business adequate means of subsistence. From the nature of the business they have not constant employment, nor can they command it, as in other occupations. Such a situation tends to introduce habits of occasional idleness, and may ultimately lead to discontent or dissipation. The Mint of every country should be a sort of College composed of men of science in the superior departments; and in the inferior, of eminent artists and artisans in their respective branches of business.

CHAPTER XXVIII.

Of the necessity of regulations to prevent the diminution of the weight of Coins, and of the ancient office of King's Exchanger.

I AM now arrived at the last point, that has immediate reference to the Coins of the realm, of which I mean to treat. I have said, in an early part of this Letter, that if Your Majesty should be pleased to approve of the principles of Coinage therein proposed, and shall order Your Coins to be made in conformity thereto, it will be the duty of Your Majesty's Servants to recommend to You such regulations as shall remedy, as far as possible, the fourth and last imperfection, to which Coins are exposed; that is, the evils resulting from the wear or diminution of Coins made of either of the precious metals, by abrasion or friction, and sometimes by other causes. These evils affect the Gold Coins in a greater degree than those made of Silver, because a grain of Gold is above fifteen times the value of a grain of Silver: a smaller defect therefore in these Gold Coins is of more importance than in those made of Silver; and any fraud in this respect can be practised with more facility and profit.

In proof of this observation, I will lay before Your Majesty two cases, which I have taken from a Report of

CHAP. 28. Sir Isaac Newton in 1717. In the last year of the reign of King William, many Louis d'Ors of France, each of which, compared with our Coins, was then worth but 17s. 0¾d., were brought into England, and were current here for 17s. 6d. Sir Isaac Newton, then Master of the Mint, represented this circumstance to the Lords of the Treasury, and a Proclamation issued, ordering that these Louis d'Ors should be current only at 17s.; and thereupon they were immediately brought to the Mint as Bullion; and no less a sum than 1,400,000l. was coined out of the Bullion they produced. In this case the advantage of 5¼d. per Louis d'Or brought so great a number of them into the kingdom, and the loss of ¾d. per Louis d'Or at most drove them out of circulation. At another time, Moidores passed in the Western parts of England for 28s., and the country was full of them: the Officers of the Mint represented to the Lords of the Treasury, that these Moidores were intrinsically worth only 27s. 7d.; and their Lordships ordered that the public receivers should take them only for 27s. 6d. The gentlemen of the country immediately complained, that these Moidores had all disappeared; so that a profit of 5d. per Moidore brought them into the kingdom, and a loss of 1d. per Moidore sent them all out again. From these two cases it is evident, that they who traffic in Coins, and who are concerned either in remitting Money, or in melting the Coins, will trade on so very small a profit, that it is very difficult to prevent the evils arising from this sort of traffic entirely; all that can be done is to diminish the temptation as much as possible.

In a former part of this Letter I stated, that in very ancient times Coins passed by weight; and that when they became deficient, whatever the cause might be, a compensation was made for such defect, in two different ways; the one called *Compensatio ad Pensum*, the other *Compensatio ad Scalam:* these two modes of making compensations I need not again describe: they continued in practice nearly as long as the Pound in weight and the Pound in tale were the same, and as long as Coins passed according to the weight or value of the Silver which their names implied. It has already been stated, that Edward I. in the 28th year of his reign, first debased our Silver Coins. I suppose, that for some time before this debasement the Silver Coins, which were then current, had become very deficient in weight; for I find in the Statute De Moneta, it was ordained, " that he who receives or pays Money, shall receive and " pay the same by weight; and that the Viewer or " Warden of the Mint shall weigh the same; and in " case it be new Money, and the Pound weighs not " twenty Shillings; and in case of Money that is much " used, if the Pound wants Sixpence, it shall be re- " delivered to him who brought the same; but if it shall " want more, it shall be done as of the rest;" that is, recoined. In this Statute a difference is first made between old and new Coins, and the old Coins are allowed to pass, though diminished by reasonable wear, provided this diminution does not exceed Sixpence, or the fortieth part of the Pound in tale, which was then the same as a Pound in weight: at that time very few

CHAP. 28,

Stat. de Moneta Magnum, 20th Edw. I. Stat. 4.

CHAP. 28.

Gold Coins had been made at the English Mint, and consequently there were very few in circulation: this Statute, therefore, evidently relates only to the Silver Coins.

In the 5th year of the reign of Richard II. complaint was made by the Officers of the Mint, that Gold as well as Silver Money was clipped and exported; and these Officers being called before the Parliament, and asked their advice, answered severally, that there was no other remedy, but that all Money should be of one weight, and that such as is not of due weight be bought according to its value, and that Gold should pass only by weight. I do not find that any such order was then given.

See Rolls of Parliament, 5th Richard II.

Several years afterwards, in the 9th Henry V. a Statute was passed, which takes no notice of the Silver Coins, but establishes the following rule with respect to the Gold Coins; "that none of the King's liege "people shall receive any Money of English Gold in "payment, but by the King's weight thereupon or- "dained;" and having observed, that many of the Gold Coins at that time current were not of one weight or good allay, it orders them to be recoined. Before this time the Silver Coins had been frequently debased, and the Pound in tale differed considerably from the Pound in weight. By the omission therefore of any mention of the Silver Coins in this Statute it may be inferred, that the practice of weighing Silver Coins began at that time to be discontinued.

No further regulation was made with respect to the

weighing of any of the Coins of the realm, till the 19th of Henry VII. In a Statute of that year it is ordained, "that the Gold Coin, if whole and of weight, should be "current: but that all manner of Groats, Half Groats, "Pence of 2*d.*, being Silver, as well English Coin as "Coin of other lands, clipped, minished, or otherwise "impaired, *except reasonable wearing*, shall not go, nor "be in any wise current for payment within this realm, "but utterly to be refused and forsaken in payment "from henceforth." In this Statute, the undefined term of *reasonable wearing* appears to have been first introduced into the laws of this kingdom: and this regulation of reasonable wearing extended only to Silver Coins; and even of these only to the Groats, Half Groats, and Twopenny Pieces, and not to any Silver Coins of a lower denomination: the Silver Pence were to be current without any manner of refusal or contradiction, provided they were Silver, and had the print of the King's Coin, except only certain Pence having the print of a spear or mullet, which were to pass only for a Halfpenny. By the same Statute, "the Mayor, Sheriff, Bailiff, Constable, "or other chief Officer or Governor of any town or place "where payment shall be refused, contrary to the rules "established in this Statute, shall enforce such payment:" so that these Magistrates became the judges of what was reasonable wearing; and it results from thence, that the true standard weight of these Coins would become as precarious and uncertain as the opinions of these Magistrates. By the Statute before mentioned, to prevent clipping it was ordered, "that every Piece

CHAP. 28.

19th Hen. VII.
cap. 5.

CHAP. 28.

"of Silver Coin should have a circle about the outer part thereof, and every Piece of Gold Coin should have the whole scripture about every Piece of the said Coin, without lacking any part thereof, to the intent that his Majesty's subjects may hereafter have perfect knowledge by the said circle or scripture when the Coins were clipped or impaired." It is probable, that such confidence was placed in this new device or manner of coining, that no evil was apprehended from clipping in future.

On the 12th day of October, in the 29th year of the reign of Queen Elizabeth, a proclamation was issued, which first allowed Gold Coins to be current, though deficient by reasonable wearing ; and there is a table at the end of this proclamation, which states the *abatement*, as it is there called, in the weight of every Piece of Gold Coin respectively, below which they should not be current, or legal tender; in this proclamation, what is meant by reasonable wear is first defined, but only as it relates to the Gold Coins. In the 10th year of James I. another proclamation, and again in the 16th year of that Prince's reign a further proclamation, and lastly, in the 3d year of Charles I. still another proclamation was issued to the same effect: in all which proclamations there were clauses regulating the abatement or deficiency by wearing, below which any Piece of Gold Coin was no longer to be current, or legal tender.

In the 14th year of Charles II. that is the year 1662, the use of the mill and screw was finally established in the Mint of this kingdom, as has been before stated, and graining, by means of this instrument, was first placed on the edges of all our Coins; and there is reason to believe, that such confidence was then placed in this new device, that no evil was thenceforth apprehended from the clipping and wearing of our Coins.*

In the 9th and 11th years of William III. a clause was inserted in a Statute then passed, which authorized the cutting any Silver Monies, which shall be diminished otherwise than by reasonable wearing;† but leaves the point, in disputed cases, to be determined by the chief magistrate of the city or district. It says nothing of the weight of the Gold Coins.

Your Majesty, by Your royal proclamation of the 12th of April, in the 16th year of Your reign, ordered the Gold Coins to be current, though diminished by reasonable wearing; and this, as well as another proclamation afterwards issued, defined what the abatement or deficiency for reasonable wearing should be, that is to say, the Guinea might be deficient 1.4382 of a grain, that is, it must not weigh less than 5 dwts. 8 grs.; the Half Guinea might be deficient .7191 of a grain, that is,

---

* Mr. Lowndes, in his Treatise on Coins, asserts, that the practice of clipping had then never been exercised on the milled Money, and he thought it never could, "because of its thickness and edging, though "no further provision should be made against the same by law." We have learnt since Mr. Lowndes wrote this Treatise, that milled Money, made either of Gold or Silver, can be diminished by some art or other, with great facility and expedition. I have read somewhere, that these arts began to be practised about the end of the reign of King William.

† This Statute does not define what is to be understood by reasonable wearing.

CHAP. 28. it must not weigh less than 2 dwts. 16 grs.; the Quarter Guinea might be deficient .3595 of a grain, that is, it must not weigh less than 1 dwt. 8 grs. And Statute 14. of Your Majesty, ch. 70. sec. 7. enforces Your Majesty's authority in issuing proclamations for regulating the weight of Your Gold Coins, and appoints the Mayors, Bailiffs, or chief Officers of corporate Towns, and Your Majesty's Justices of the Peace in other parts of the kingdom, to be judges in any disputable case, whether Gold Coin of any denomination ought to pass in payment, and directs them and all other persons to cut, break, or deface every Piece of Gold Coin that shall be tendered to them, which is so deficient in weight, that according to Your Majesty's proclamation it should no longer be current.

There were certainly in very ancient times great difficulties in the exchange of Gold and Silver Coins, arising, as I believe, not from any uncertainty in the relative values of Gold and Silver, but from the small number of Gold Coins then in circulation, and the imperfect knowledge which the people had of them: to remedy this evil, some of Your royal Predecessors expressly established an office, and the person who held it was called the King's Exchanger.* This Officer appears not only to have exchanged the Coins of one metal made at the royal Mint for those made of another; but as the exportation of all the Coins of the realm was

* See Rymer's Fœdera, tom. v. p. 416. De cursu Monetæ auri proclamando.—tom. iv. p. 500. "Quod marinarii et piscatores &c."—and tom. 18. p. 896. 3d Charles I.—and Stat. 9 Edw. III. ch. 7.

prohibited, he furnished persons going out of the kingdom with foreign Coins, in exchange for English Coins; and he furnished merchants strangers coming into the kingdom with the English Coins, in exchange for foreign Coins: this Officer had his deputies in many of the out-ports and principal cities of the kingdom; a considerable profit was made by this practice, of which the King is said to have had his share. When Gold Coins were exchanged for Silver Coins, a Silver Penny of that time was taken for the exchange of each Gold Noble, being the largest Gold Coin then in currency, and in like proportion for smaller Gold Coins: and when Silver Coins were exchanged for Gold Coins, a Silver Penny of that time was given for each Noble received in exchange for them, and in like proportion for smaller Coins; and the exchanger is said to have gained thereby $1\frac{1}{4}$ per cent. When this Officer exchanged foreign Coins for English, or English for foreign, the exchange was regulated by a table, hung up in each of his offices. The last person that was appointed to the office of King's Exchanger, was the Earl of Holland, in the 3d year of Charles I. as mentioned before. The appointment of a person of so high rank, who was at the same time a favourite of his royal Master, is a decisive proof, that the office was of considerable profit, as well as of importance. I have thought it right to state the nature of this office, as it existed in ancient times, that Your Majesty might be fully informed of the practice which formerly prevailed in this respect, but certainly not as an example to be followed at present.

CHAP. 28. I have thus laid before Your Majesty all I have been able to collect in the Statutes and Records of Your kingdom, of the various regulations which have been made from time to time, according to which the Coins of the realm were to continue in currency, and be legal tender. It is certain that Coins have always been diminished either by wearing or fraudulent practices: there have at all times been laws in this kingdom for punishing those who have been guilty of frauds committed in impairing or diminishing the Coins of the realm: indeed, laws of this description have been made in all ages, and all countries; for the crimes against which they are directed have ever been considered as of a very heinous nature: these laws contribute in some degree to diminish the evil to which Coins are exposed; but they are far from being sufficiently efficacious to prevent it. From what I have stated, it appears I think clearly, that nothing can prevent this evil, whether arising from wearing or fraud, but the practice of weighing Coins; so that when they have lost a certain proportion of their weight, from whatever cause it may arise, they may no longer be legal tender: the rule established with respect to the Gold Coins, in Your royal proclamation of the 12th day of April, 1776, was adopted after much consideration: I thought it, at the time when it was made, the best that could be devised, and I continue still to be of the same opinion: I know of no objection to it, but that it brings a great charge on the public in recoining these deficient Coins, when they are returned to Your Majesty's Mint: the amount of this charge for the last 27 years, that is, from the time when the general Recoinage of the Gold Coin was completed, will be seen in the accounts stated in a preceding part of this Letter: this charge has certainly been much greater than was expected. It may indeed be said, that the people will always be negligent in weighing Coins: to this objection it appears to me a sufficient answer, that if they are negligent, it is their own fault, and they ought to suffer for it: it is certain, that in the year 1774, and for many years afterwards, the practice of weighing Coins prevailed universally, and without any complaint; but of late years, I am afraid, it has been very much discontinued: I understand, however, that the Officers of the Bank of England continue to discharge their duty, by weighing all the Gold Coins that are brought to them; but that private Bankers, and even those resident in London, are very negligent in this respect: they are highly to blame; for they disobey Your Majesty's orders, enforced by an Act of Parliament.* I fear also, that Government may in

* In the year 1774, when the public were alarmed at the great deficiency of the Gold Coin, the following regulations were established; " that all Guineas coined in the last two years, that is, from the 1st " of January, 1772, shall not want more than a grain and half in " weight : that all Guineas coined in the twelve preceding years, that " is, from the 12th of October, 1760, shall not want more than three " grains ; and that all Guineas coined in the 98 preceding years, that " is, from the year 1662, shall not want more than six grains." These regulations, though much more complicated and difficult in execution than that which is at present in force under the proclamation of the 12th day of April, 1776, were, at the time they were made, much approved, and generally acted upon.

CHAP. 23.

some measure have contributed to this neglect, by omitting to republish Your Majesty's proclamation, requiring the weighing of Coins, which should be done from time to time, in order to call the attention of Your Majesty's subjects to the regulations therein established: the receivers of the public revenue should receive the strongest injunctions never to neglect what is thus required of them in the discharge of their duty. I remember, that when this subject was under consideration, at the time of the general Recoinage of the Gold Coin, another method of weighing Coins was proposed, which I will state merely for consideration. With a view of keeping the new Gold Coins for a greater number of years in currency, and of preventing their being returned too frequently to the Mint, it was proposed, that the deficient Gold Coins should continue in currency, and be legal tender, on condition that Twopence should be allowed for every grain so deficient; for Twopence is nearly the value of a grain of Gold. By this rule the Guineas might be weighed in numbers, and even in bags, as is now practised in some foreign countries with the Silver Coins, of which their currency principally consists; and, as I am informed, with Gold Ducats in Holland: and it was suggested, that a table should be constructed to shew what the weight ought to be of any number of Gold Coins, from one to a thousand, which might be carried in every man's pocket-book. This method is certainly conformable to the ancient practice of weighing Silver Coins, called *Compensatio ad Pensum*, as described in a former part of this Letter; and it would certainly have the effect of preventing, in a great degree, the exportation of heavy Gold Coins, or the diminution of them by any art whatsoever; for no profit could then be derived from these practices: it was thought necessary, however, by those who approved this system of weighing, that there should be a minimum in the weight of single Pieces, below which they should not be allowed to be current, but be defaced, and returned to the Mint. This method would certainly save some part of the charge, which is incurred by-recoining the deficient Gold Coins.

With respect to the new Silver Coins proposed to be issued for the use of Your Majesty's subjects, it is not necessary that so strict a rule should be observed as is required with respect to the Gold Coins; for the value of Silver is at the least fifteen times less than that of Gold: it would also be very difficult to enforce the practice of weighing the Silver Coins, in the same degree as that of weighing the Gold Coins; for the Silver Coins are chiefly employed in the retail trade, and by the inferior and least informed classes of Your Majesty's subjects: and yet even in these new Silver Coins there must be a minimum, below which they should not be allowed to be current; for they will otherwise in a short time be reduced to the very defective state of our present Silver currency. I am of opinion, that the larger Silver Coins may be allowed to be current, though each of them should be deficient in weight one pennyweight; and the smaller Silver Coins might be continued in currency, though each of them should be deficient half a pennyweight, or

CHAP. 28. 12 grains. This deficiency in weight of the Silver Coins will be nearly equal in value to the deficiency allowed in the Gold Coins by Your Majesty's Proclamation of the 12th day of April, 1776.

I have now finished all I have to offer on the remedies to be applied to the fourth and last imperfection to which Coins are exposed; that is, the wearing or diminution of Coins made of either of the precious metals by abrasion or friction, and sometimes by other causes.

CHAPTER XXIX.

Of Paper currency, so far as Coins are affected by it.

I SHOULD stop here, but there is a subject of so great importance, and so nearly connected with the Coins of Your Majesty's realm, that I should not discharge my duty, if I left it wholly unnoticed; I mean what is now called Paper currency; which is carried to so great an extent, that it is become highly inconvenient to Your Majesty's subjects, and may prove in its consequences, if no remedy is applied, dangerous to the credit of the kingdom. It is certain, that the smaller Notes of the Bank of England, and those issued by country Bankers, have supplanted the Gold Coins, usurped their functions, and driven a great part of them out of circulation: in some parts of Great Britain, and especially in the southern parts of Ireland, small Notes have been issued to supply the place of Silver Coins, of which there is certainly a great deficiency.

I will first observe, that if this practice is suffered to continue, as at present, without any limitation, there can be neither use nor advantage in converting Bullion of either of the precious metals into Coins, except so far as it may serve for the convenience of Your Majesty's subjects in their most private concerns; that is, no greater quantity than many of the writers, who have

CHAP. 29. of late speculated on this subject, will allow to continue in currency: the Bullion, of which these Coins are made, had better be exported in its natural state, like any other unmanufactured commodity, for the use of which the trade of the country has no occasion. The Coins of Your Majesty, when carried into foreign countries, will only be valued as Bullion; and the precious metals, whether exported in Coins or in Bullion, will equally serve the purpose of a commercial capital; and it is useless and absurd to impose upon the public the expence of making Coins, merely for the purpose of sending them out of the kingdom.

It has been a common artifice, practised by those who have written on Paper currency, to confound Paper credit with Paper currency, and even the higher sorts of Paper currency with the inferior sorts, such as immediately interfere with the use of the Coins of the realm. Paper credit is not only highly convenient and beneficial, but is even absolutely necessary, in carrying on the trade of a great commercial kingdom. Paper currency is a very undefined term, as used by speculative writers.* To find arguments in its support; at least to the extent to which it is at present carried, they have been obliged to connect it with Paper credit; so that the principles, on which the use of Paper credit is truly founded, may be brought in support of a great emission of Paper

* Paper currency, strictly speaking, consists only of Bills, or Notes payable or convertible into Cash on demand by the person who issued the same, at the will of the holder. See Report of the Secret Committee of the House of Lords in 1797, p. 249.

currency: I do not mean to say, that even the higher orders of Paper currency may not be very convenient, in carrying on many branches of the trade of a country so wealthy as Great Britain: the sort of Paper currency to which I principally object, is that which interferes with the use of the Coins of the realm, more especially in the payment of labourers and artificers, of the sailor and soldier, and in the smaller branches of the retail trade of the kingdom.

CHAP. 29.

Many words are not necessary to point out the evils to which Your Majesty's subjects are exposed, by the practice which now prevails, of issuing the lower sort of Paper currency by country Bankers; the complaints on this head are universal. The Notes of these country Bankers have credit only within a certain extent or district: if a traveller passes from one district to another, he must provide himself with the Notes of other Bankers, which have credit within the district on which he is entering; and an inconvenience to which travellers have hitherto been subject, in passing from one small independent state on the continent to another, is experienced by those who travel through Your Majesty's dominions, in passing from one district to another; so that the circulating medium of the different parts of Your Majesty's dominions is various; an evil which I believe never existed before in one great united kingdom.

But I have not hitherto described the principal evils resulting from this Paper currency. It was natural to suppose, that the precious metals, being no longer wanted in the same degree, for the purpose of being converted into Coins, the price of them would fall in the British market: on the contrary, for a considerable time, Bullion, both of Gold and Silver, has not been generally sold, but at a price above the rate at which each of them is valued at Your Majesty's Mint. It would not be proper for me at present to assign the probable cause of this apparent contradiction: In such a state of things, whatever may be the cause, no Bullion, either of Gold or Silver, will be brought to Your Majesty's Mint to be coined; for it cannot be coined without a loss to the person who brings it; and if it were converted into Coins, the moment they were issued they would be thrown into the melting pot, and reconverted into Bullion, because it would be of more value in the shape of Bullion than in that of Coins. Till some remedy is applied to this evil, no new system of Coinage can be adopted, with any reasonable hope of success.

When the situation of the Bank of England was under the consideration of the two Houses of Parliament, in the year 1797, it was my opinion, and that of many others, that the extent to which Paper currency had then been carried, was the first and principal, though not the sole cause of the many difficulties, to which that corporate Body was then, and had of late years, from time to time, been exposed, in supplying the Cash occasionally necessary for the commerce of the kingdom; for the Bank of England being at the head of all circulation, and the great repository of unemployed

Cash, it necessarily happens, that whenever a sudden increased supply of Coins becomes indispensable, in consequence of private failures or general discredit, by which Notes of the before-mentioned description are driven out of circulation, the Bank of England can alone furnish the Coins which are required to make up this deficiency; and this corporate Body is thereby rendered responsible, not only for the value of its own Notes which it may issue, but, in a certain degree, for such as may be issued by every private Banker in the kingdom, let the substance, credit, or discretion of such a Banker be what it may: and if the price of both the precious metals in Bullion should then be above that at which they are rated at the Mint, the Bank of England have it not in their power to supply this deficiency, but at a great loss to its proprietors; and even if they were to submit to this loss, and issue new Coins in consequence, it would only be, as has been already observed, in order that they might be thrown into the melting pot and converted into Bullion; so that till some remedy is applied to this evil, the Bank of England cannot, I think, return to the first principles of its institution, under which it has so long and so greatly flourished, and reassume, without any restriction, its payments in Cash.

The state of the Paper currency of this country, in its manner and extent taken together, is, I believe, without example in the history of mankind. The trade or profession of banking has been exercised in all countries and in all ages: it existed in the republics

CHAP. 20. of Greece,* and in ancient Rome: there were in all these states men who received Money as a deposit, repaid it upon the drafts of those who had entrusted them with it, and derived their profits from having this Money in their custody; but it does not appear that they ever issued Notes, such as are now called Paper currency.

In the middle ages the traffic in Money was exercised solely by the Jews; for Christian men, as they were then called, from a mistaken principle of religion, would not engage in it: but the Jews, who interpreted the law of Moses in a different sense from the Christians, thought that they might lawfully carry it on with strangers; and to them every man was a stranger, who was not a Jew. The wealth of these Jews, and the extortions and cruelties to which they were exposed on this account, contrary to the principles of humanity and justice, are well known to every one.

When commerce was first revived in the republics of Italy, Banking companies and private Bankers appeared in numbers, and carried on the trade in money, and particularly in bills of exchange, to a very great extent. The origin and history of the Banks of Venice † and Genoa ‡ need not be here inserted: the

---

* For what relates to the Grecian republics see the Voyage du Jeune Anacharsis, ch. 55. and the Grecian authors referred to therein. For what relates to the Roman republic see the words Præscribere and Præscriptio, in Gesner's Thesaurus, and the passages of Cicero and other authors referred to by him.

† Called Banco del Giro.

‡ Called Banco de Saº Giorgio.

wealth* of these Banks was very great; and many of the principal families in Italy derive their origin and their ample fortunes from persons who once exercised the trade of banking. I cannot however discover from history, that either the Jews before mentioned, or the banking companies established in Italy, or any of the private Bankers, ever issued what is now called Paper currency: it is certain at least that they did not issue it in so great a degree as to drive the Coins out of the country; for it is asserted by historians of undoubted credit,† that Italy at that time had drawn to itself almost the whole of the Gold of Europe.

After the example of what had been thus practised in Italy, Banking companies were gradually established in many of the principal cities of Europe, particularly at Hamburgh, Nuremberg, and Amsterdam: many of these corporate Banks issued Paper currency for the payment of foreign, and sometimes inland, bills of exchange: but this privilege was always exercised under certain regulations and restrictions, sanctioned by the governments of these places, for the security of the individuals who trusted them, and for the preservation of public credit. It is singular, that it was found necessary to require, that the Notes of these

---

* The wealth of the Bank of St. George at Genoa in process of time became so great, that Machiavel says, there was reason to apprehend that it would become possessed of all the territories of that little state. See Historia Fiorentina, lib. 8.

† See Histoire de la Ligue de Cambray, liv. 5. Bodin, Réponse à Maletroit, p. 49. and Histoire de Louis XI. p. 708.

CHAP. 29.   Banks should be accepted and employed exclusively in certain payments: but the privilege thus given never included any payments for which a single piece of Coin, or, as I believe, any small number of them, was sufficient, so as to interfere with the retail trade of the country. The reasons for establishing this Paper currency have been fully explained in a former part of this Letter; and I have never heard that private Bankers issued Paper currency in any European country, to the extent in which it is now practised in the British dominions: if it has prevailed any where to excess, it has been in the united provinces of America.

The practice of issuing Paper currency within Your Majesty's dominions first began in Scotland:* it was natural that this device should originate in a country where there was a great want of Coins and capital: the evils it produced were felt so early as the year 1765, when a wise law was passed by the Legislature, to restrain and regulate it within that part of the united kingdom. This law did not extend to England, for the evil at that time had not been felt here: Your Majesty's English subjects however soon followed the example of their Northern brethren; and in the year 1775 the mischiefs arising from the issue of small Paper Notes were so severely felt, that a law was passed for regulating and restraining it: but it was afterwards found

5th Geo. III. ch. 49.

15th Geo. III. ch. 51.

* See some account of Mr. Law, and of the famous Project presented by him to the Parliament of Scotland before the Union, and afterwards to the Regent of France, in Smith's Wealth of Nations, vol. i. p. 478. and the Histoire du Systeme.

that this law did not remedy the evil, and a second law, still more restrictive, was passed in 1777. These measures were recommended to the Legislature by many of the most eminent of Your Majesty's subjects and servants, to whose consultations I, though unworthy, was at that time admitted: I remember too, that the restrictions then imposed on this practice were considered by many as not sufficient.—It was necessary however for a temporary purpose to enact a short suspension of these laws, in consequence of the difficulties, to which public credit was exposed, in the year 1797. At the same time, the Bank of England was discharged by the Legislature from the obligation of paying in Cash: but, contrary to expectation, these suspensions have been continued to the present day; and from that period the Bank of England have issued Notes for smaller sums, and to a greater extent, than they ever did before: and the number of private Bankers spread over every part of the country during that interval, has been more than doubled.*

It is true that there have been a few memorable instances, I believe but three, in which, under the authority of Government, Paper currency has been issued to an extravagant extent, in a neighbouring country. The first was while France was governed by

CHAP. 29.

17th Geo. III. ch. 30.

---

* It is stated in the summary of the Report of the Secret Committee of the House of Lords in 1797, that the number of country Bankers, which had in 1792 amounted to 280, had in 1797 been reduced to 230. It appears by the list of country Bankers now published, that they amount to 517.

CHAP. 29.

a Regency, in the beginning of the last century; the two others are of a later date: and each of these experiments has proved, in its results, dishonourable to the Government, and disastrous to the people. During the emission of this Paper currency, the Coins of that country were in a very great degree driven out of circulation; but they re-appeared in considerable quantities, as soon as this Paper currency was discredited and annihilated. It ought always to be kept in remembrance, that this Paper currency was issued to so great an excess, either by corporate bodies, under the authority and protection of Government, or directly by the Government itself, and not on the sole credit and responsibility of unauthorized individuals.

It is certain, that the principles, on which speculative writers would justify the emission of Paper currency in Your Majesty's dominions, would leave it almost without limitation. The ablest writer on this subject, Dr. Adam Smith, appears however sensible, that there must be some limitation. That adopted by him is, "that the " whole Paper currency of every kind, which can easily " circulate in any country, never can exceed the value " of the Gold and Silver, of which it supplies the place; " or which (the commerce being supposed the same) " would circulate there, if there was no Paper Money." From this passage it may be inferred, that even in this writer's opinion Paper currency may be issued to so great an extent, as to take the place of all the Gold and Silver Coins necessary for carrying on the commerce of the kingdom, though it cannot *easily* be carried to a

Vol. I. p. 448.

greater. But later writers pay no attention to the moderation, with which this master of political economy has supported his system: and as they are not satisfied with the opinion thus given, we may presume they mean, that Paper currency may be made to represent, according to the system of the well known Mr. Law, even immoveable property; that is, a portion at least of the lands and buildings of the kingdom, and as such sent into circulation. It seems to have been discovered of late years in this country, that, by a new sort of alchemy, Coins of Gold and Silver, and almost every other sort of property, may be converted into Paper; and that the precious metals had better be exported, to serve as capital, to foreign countries, where no such discovery has yet been made. But this new sort of fictitious capital, thus introduced within the kingdom, has contributed more than any other circumstance to what is called *over-trading;* that is, rash and inconsiderate speculations, and what is almost a necessary consequence, unworthy artifices to support the credit of adventurers already ruined, as well as other evils, which tend to corrupt the morals of the trading part of the community, and to shake the credit on which not only Paper currency, but the internal commerce of the kingdom is founded. In every commercial system, capital is certainly a necessary ingredient: but the prosperity of the British commerce depends not singly on capital; it depends still more on the good faith, honour, and punctuality of British merchants, for which they are so justly celebrated.

CHAP. 29.

Impressed as I am with the idea, that no system of Coinage can be adopted with the prospect of permanent advantage, till some regulations have been made for remedying the evils resulting from the present state of Paper currency, I have thought it right thus to lay before Your Majesty some account of the excess to which it has of late been carried within Your kingdoms. I am unwilling to enter into further discussion on a question so important, and so much agitated, because it is not a fit subject for a Letter to Your Majesty: nor will I treat of the remedies, which ought to be applied, because these cannot be administered by the authority of Your Majesty, as in the case of Coins; but they require the authority of the Two Houses of Parliament, in conjunction with that of Your Majesty. Certain I am, that in a kingdom like Great Britain, the most commercial, and for its extent the richest perhaps that ever existed in the world, every branch of circulating medium, of whatever it may consist, should be founded on solid, wise, and honest principles; and Coins in particular, which are the only true measure of property and instrument of commerce, and by which every other circulating medium must be regulated, should be made and kept as perfect as the nature of the subject will admit.

CHAPTER XXX.

Conclusion.

I HAVE now completed all I proposed to write on the Coins of the realm, and I have treated shortly of Paper currency, so far as the Coins are affected by it. It is not improbable, that a treatise on a subject so abstruse and intricate, and consequently so difficult to be understood, may be thrown aside by many, and perhaps treated with levity: I remember that such was the case when the Recoinage of the Gold Coin was undertaken, in the year 1774. It is possible, that even those, who are not without a desire of information, may object, that I have consumed too much labour on points that are not worthy of it—*In tenui labor.* To these my answer is, that they are little aware of how much importance to the commerce of the country is a good monetary system, founded on principles of wisdom and justice; and how much Coins, particularly those of a lower denomination, contribute to the convenience of the inferior orders of society. I am not ashamed, therefore, in my present state of retirement, to have employed my leisure hours on this subject; a subject which occupied the attention and talents of men of no less character than Sir William Petty and Mr. Locke.

CHAP. 80.

To Your Majesty, if any apology is necessary, I may venture to offer other pleas in my justification. When I was in Your Majesty's service in the year 1774, I first turned my thoughts to this subject, in discharge of my public duty. It was in obedience to Your Majesty's commands that I resumed the consideration of it, after a long interval, when You appointed me in 1797 one of the members of the Committee of Privy Council for Coin : and though a short time afterwards, by the pressure of disease, all thoughts of this nature were blotted from my recollection, I have experienced at length, by the favour of Providence, a partial recovery; and awakened as it were from the sleep of death, I have been induced a third time to take up the consideration of this subject, by the representations that were made to me by Your Majesty's late ministers, of the distressed state of the southern parts of Ireland, where almost all Coins have disappeared, where a most degraded system of Paper currency has taken place even of the Silver Coins, and where this Paper currency, from the quantity that has been issued, has fallen in its value, and consequently into a state of discredit, very embarrassing to the poorer ranks of Your Majesty's subjects in those parts.

The subject of which I have treated is of such a nature, that it certainly has no charms to attract the attention of any man ; it is therefore from a sense of duty alone, that I have been induced to complete, under all my infirmities, what I had before projected. Conscious of my own inability at all times to fathom a science, on which men of the most eminent talents have disagreed, I offer with the greatest deference what I have thus written, to Your Majesty's consideration. Certain I am, that it will be treated by Your Majesty with every proper degree of candour, and accepted with Your accustomed condescension.

There is one circumstance, which more than any other will serve as an apology for my presumption in addressing this Letter to Your Majesty. In revolving the history of the Coins of the realm, I find, that the greatest of Your royal Predecessors, those most renowned for their wisdom in the internal government of their dominions, as well as for their martial exploits, have been most distinguished for the care of their Coins, and for making and keeping them perfect. There have been since the Conquest three great reformations of the Coins of the realm; that is to say, in the reigns of King Edward I.,* of Queen Elizabeth, and of King William III. Historians speak with the highest honour of Edward I. for calling in the clipped and counterfeit Money; for settling the standard, and for the laws which he made to prevent the impairing and counterfeiting of the Coins in future: and these measures are always recited among the many memorable acts of spirited legislation and public justice, for which the reign of that Prince is so deservedly celebrated, by the ablest writers on English jurisprudence. He rendered these services to his country, while he was engaged in

* Henry V. called in and recoined the Gold Coin; but in his time Gold could make but a small part of the currency of the kingdom.

the conquest of Wales, and in his attempt to subdue the kingdom of Scotland.

Queen Elizabeth perfected the plan of the reformation of the Coins of the realm, which her brother had begun to execute in the last year of his reign. She completed this reform with wisdom and spirit, in the midst of great internal convulsions, arising from unhappy differences in religious opinions, which were fomented by the intrigues and influence of the Papal authority, then powerful in this kingdom. She completed it in defiance of the repeated attacks of a Sovereign, the most powerful at that time in Europe, Philip II. King of Spain, who was supposed to aim at universal monarchy.

In the reign of King William III. that great restorer of the true principles of pure religion and rational liberty, the reformation of the Silver Coins was undertaken, while that Prince was engaged in a foreign war, for the defence of the independence and liberties of Europe. This war required a constant exportation of our treasure: all the exchanges were on that account against this country; and they were rendered still more unfavourable by the very impaired state of our Silver Coins: public credit was at a very low ebb; great taxes were to be raised at the very moment when the medium, in which the people were required to pay them, was in an uncommon degree depreciated; and what was still more discouraging, the only remedy, which could be applied to these evils, required that a considerable part of the Coins, which yet remained, should at once be taken out of circulation. The work however was successfully accomplished; and though some errors were committed, and an enormous expence incurred, the writers of all parties now concur in paying to this undertaking the just tribute of applause.

In a situation similar in many respects to those of Queen Elizabeth and King William, a reformation of Your Majesty's Coins is now become necessary. Your Majesty is engaged like them in a war for the defence of the liberties and independence of mankind: You have to contend with a neighbouring State, always the rival, and too frequently the enemy, of Great Britain; whose territories are now very much extended, though it may be doubted whether its real power is augmented in proportion: the navy of France, which in the reign of King William was nearly equal to that of this kingdom, is now greatly diminished; and the fleets of Great Britain, even though sometimes by accident of inferior force, are now victorious in every clime, and on every ocean where those of the enemy venture to contend with them. The power of the enemy is however augmented by the influence, which he exercises over almost every government whose territories are unfortunately so situated as to be accessible to his arms. Queen Elizabeth and King William had allies, who came forward to their effectual assistance. At present most of the continental Sovereigns seem appalled at the great power, which has unexpectedly arisen against them; and, in a state of disunion among themselves, appear to crouch to the influence and authority of the Person who wields this power, and assumes the right of prescribing laws of war and peace to all who have any intercourse with him. Your Majesty contends alone, not only in defence of Your own dominions, but in support of the independence of civilized nations in every part of the world. Fortunately for Your Majesty, the commerce of this kingdom is now much more flourishing than in any preceding period: the state of Your revenues is prosperous; and great as the burthen may be to which Your subjects are exposed, they cheerfully bear it. At a period when a reformation of the Coins must be undertaken, it is also a most favourable circumstance, that those of one of the precious metals, which have for many years principally supported the circulation of the kingdom, are in a reasonable state of perfection. On the other hand, when King William undertook the reformation of the Silver Coins, the ministers of that Prince had this advantage, that they acted upon known and long established principles of Coinage; but Your Majesty is under the necessity of adopting new ones, contrary to those which have hitherto prevailed; and a new difficulty has occurred, arising from the quantity and variety of Paper currency, which has of late years been sent into circulation in every part of the united kingdom: this fictitious sort of money has been carried to such an excess, as to usurp in a great degree all the functions of the real Coins: and unless proper remedies are applied, so as to remove both these obstructions, it is not possible that any system of Coinage can be carried into execution with success, and with a prospect of permanent duration.

In taking leave of Your Majesty, as I must now do, it would be the highest gratification to my private feelings, were I to express what long experience has taught me of Your Royal virtues: I could dwell with pleasure both on the principles of public government, which have always actuated Your Majesty's mind, and on those private excellencies, by which You are no less distinguished than by Your exalted situation. You have afforded a striking example of steady attachment to the cause of religion and virtue, and of abhorrence of vice and immorality: but by no quality have You been more distinguished, than by an uniform and affectionate solicitude for the happiness of Your people; nor are Your people, Excellent Prince, insensible of the blessings, which they have derived from these virtues: their affection for the Person of their Sovereign, their attachment to his Government, and their anxiety for his welfare, have manifested themselves in a signal manner, on the most trying occasions: to such a King, a Treatise, which professes to confer a benefit on His subjects, and particularly the inferior classes of them, cannot fail to be acceptable: I augur therefore with confidence, that Your Majesty will not disapprove of my conduct in addressing this Letter to You.

It is with the most fervent wishes for the continuance of Your Majesty's life, and for the augmentation of Your prosperity and glory, and with the sincerest sentiments of attachment and gratitude, that I presume to subscribe myself,

SIRE,

Your Majesty's

faithful and dutiful

Subject and Servant

LIVERPOOL.

May 7th, 1805.

APPENDIX,

CONTAINING

AN ACCOUNT

OF

RELATIVE VALUES OF GOLD TO SILVER AMONG THE ANCIENT PERSIANS, GRECIANS, AND ROMANS.

APPENDIX.

It is intended in this Dissertation to take a view of the relative value of Gold to Silver in ancient times; a subject highly interesting, but at some periods embarrassed with much doubt and obscurity.

Persons accustomed to methodical enquiry in general, and not previously acquainted with the subject of that now proposed, might perhaps, without hesitation, form a plan for conducting their researches, and entertain sanguine hopes of being able to accomplish it as much to their satisfaction, as the nature of ancient history will permit: nor could the adoption of such ideas, under such circumstances, be termed extravagant. For the laws of nations afford clear and unquestionable proofs of the political and moral duties, which they observe; and in whatever instances the laws of ancient nations have been tolerably preserved, we might expect to meet with clear information concerning the mediums, through which their mercantile transactions were carried on. To these resources, therefore, such persons would resolve to turn their attention, and would expect from them particulars free from doubt, and considerably connected: but, upon carrying their design into execution, disappointment would soon succeed. An enquirer into the relative value of Gold to Silver, in ancient times, finds reason to lament his inability to obtain information at every stage of his pursuit. Few passages relating to it have come down to us ; and perhaps in some countries few regulations concerning it were ever made and recorded as laws. In very early stages of society, agreements, adjusted by local and temporary circumstances, were perpetuated without doubt for some time by oral information only; and those agreements, even when intercourse had increased, and arts and civilization had advanced, it might be thought in some instances unnecessary to record, upon the supposition that what must occur daily could neither be mistaken, nor slip from the remembrance of the community. It is also highly probable, that in ancient times, as well as in modern, it might appear to some who governed highly advantageous to have nothing precisely fixed concerning the precious metals, considered as the common measure of property. Uncertainty gave them an opportunity of making alterations in their relative values to one another, suitable to their own private interests; and if such alterations were carried into execution, it is not to be supposed that they would transmit a written account of them to posterity.

Nor is a scantiness of materials the only circumstance, which we have to lament in an enquiry into the relative value of Gold to Silver in ancient times. The few passages, which can be collected, are defective, as no statement is given in them of the alloy put into the

Coins of either metal.* That a neglect of such a statement may materially affect the proportion, will appear evident from what immediately follows. According to the regulations at present in force at the British Mint, a Pound weight of standard Gold is coined into 44½ Guineas; a Pound weight of standard Silver is coined into 62 Shillings; and a Guinea is current for 21 Shillings. These particulars enable us to calculate the relative value of Gold to Silver, if we neglect the alloy in the Coins; for 44½ Guineas are equivalent in value to 1869 Sixpences, and 62 Shillings being equal to 124 Sixpences, the value of Gold is to that of Silver as 1869 to 124, or as $15\frac{9}{124}$ to 1. This would accurately express the relative values of the two metals, if the quantity of alloy in a Pound weight of standard in each bore the same proportion to the whole; which is not the case. In a Pound weight of standard Gold, at the British Mint, one twelfth is alloy; in a Pound weight of standard Silver it is $\frac{3}{40}$; and the relative value of pure Gold to pure Silver, according to these regulations, and the established currency between Coins of the two metals, is as $15\frac{2859}{13460}$ to 1.

* It is impossible to trace the Coinage of Money to its origin, with any degree of certainty. Different authors attribute its commencement to different nations. Herodotus, (lib. i. 94.) who, on account of his high antiquity in profane history, is entitled to a superior degree of respect, attributes it to the Lydians.

For the impressions on the Coins of different nations, see Hostus de Re Nummaria, lib. i. cap. 8.

It is a general and well founded opinion, that there was very little alloy in the ancient Coins. Several have supposed, (see Arbuthnot, chap. vi.) that there was only a fiftieth part of alloy in the Gold Coins.

The deficiencies of ancient authors in not mentioning the quantity of alloy put into their Gold and Silver Coins, are not, however, of such magnitude, as to arrest inquiry into the relative values of the precious metals: deductions may be made from them, notwithstanding the omissions; and the results, it is probable, will be either accurate proportions of their values of pure Gold to pure Silver, or very near approximations. Full, connected, and certain information we cannot attain. We must therefore be content with what we can glean and connect, as by so doing we can arrive at such knowledge as will afford some satisfaction to rational curiosity, and such as may be productive of some utility.

Several passages in Scripture, and also in Josephus, afford certain proof, that Gold and Silver were highly esteemed among the Jews, and that they were employed as the medium of traffic. Abraham weighed to Ephron the Silver, which he had named in the audience of the sons of Heth, four hundred shekels of Silver, current Money with the merchant.* Joseph was sold by his brethren for twenty pieces of Silver;† and the chiefs of the nation, in order to rebuild their temple, gave after their ability unto the treasure of the work, three score and one thousand drams of Gold, and five thousand pound of Silver.‡ We meet with no precise statement, however, with respect to the rate at which the Jews valued Gold, when compared to Silver; nor

* Genesis xxiii. 16.   † Genesis xxxvii. 28.
‡ Ezra ii. 69.

is there good reason to suppose that they had any coined Money before the times of the Maccabees.* A belief that Silver was most generally their current Money is supported by a great number of passages; a circumstance, which must have tended to keep up the value of this metal: but there is no reason to doubt, that it was frequently depressed, when compared to Gold, by national prosperity. We learn from Josephus, that, in the time of Solomon, Silver was as plentiful as stones;† and in Scripture it is said to have been in such abundance, that it was held in no estimation.‡

From Herodotus, the father of profane history, we obtain much curious information concerning the riches of eastern princes, and one satisfactory statement concerning the relative value of Gold to Silver. A minute detail of the former, however, is foreign to the present design. His account of the presents of Gyges, Crœsus, and other Monarchs, to the temples they revered, and whose oracles they consulted, convinces us at once of their piety and wealth: but his statement of the revenues of Darius, the son of Hystaspes, is more assisting to the present enquiry, as he there proceeds upon the supposition, that the value of Gold was to that of Silver as 13 to 1.§ It clearly appears from the same account, that both metals were used as Money, when the demands upon Government rendered a Coinage necessary; ‖ and there is every reason to

---

* See Clarke on Coins, p. 244. † Antiq. lib. viii. cap. 2.
‡ 1 Kings x. 21. § Herod. lib. iii. 95.
‖ Herod. lib. iii. 96.

believe, that the Historian's opinion of their relative value was founded upon their currency in exchange under Darius.

These relative values of the precious metals are the most ancient of which we have certain information; and it is highly probable, that in the time of Herodotus * they were also established in Greece. We are unable to say how long the proportion of 13 to 1 had been observed previous to the period of which we are now speaking; but we have reason to suppose, that the value of Gold did not long continue to be so high in Greece; for Plato, who flourished about fifty years after Herodotus, asserts in his Hipparchus, that the value of Gold was to that of Silver as 12 to 1.†

Xenophon was contemporary with Plato, and in his account of the expedition of the younger Cyrus, against his brother Artaxerxes, he also furnishes us with particulars for ascertaining the relative value of the two precious metals. The crown of Persia was the object which Cyrus wished to obtain; and having for this purpose conducted an army through Asia Minor, he advanced to the banks of the Euphrates, and passed that river, to attack Artaxerxes. His hopes and his doubts concerning the event increased as the time of the battle appeared to draw near; and, according to

---

* Herodotus read his history in the council at Athens, in the year 445 before Christ.

† Platonis Opera, tom. ii. p. 231. edit. H. Steph. 1578. Some of the best critics think that the Hipparchus is not the production of Plato: but as they agree in believing it to be of his age, the above statement is not affected by the doubt as to the real author.

the superstition of the times, he had recourse to a soothsayer to quiet his apprehensions. Being told that the king would not fight within ten days, and being under a persuasion, that, if he did not fight within that time, he would not fight at all, Cyrus promised the soothsayer ten talents, if his prophecy proved true. On the eleventh day, after the prediction had been made,* Cyrus paid the soothsayer. three thousand Daricks,† Persian Gold Coins; and by so doing, according to Xenophon, he fulfilled his promise. In this transaction, therefore, the fair and usual relative value of Gold to Silver was probably adhered to.

But it does not afford certain and indisputable data for estimating the relative value of Gold to Silver, and therefore, as is usual in doubtful cases, different proportions have been deduced from it. The opinion most commonly received, for a considerable length of time, was, that the Darick weighed two drachms. According

* Κύρυ 'Ανάβασ. p. 70. edit. Hutchinson. Cantab. 1777.
† A Darick was equal to the Attick Aureus. See Suidas on the word, p. 510. vol. 1. Cambridge edition of 1705. Writers differ in their opinion concerning the origin of this Coin; but preponderating reasons incline us to believe, that it was first struck by Darius Hystaspes. Authors agree in praising the fineness of the Gold in the Daricks; and Herodotus says, (lib. iv. 166.) that Darius, wishing his memory to be famous for what Kings had not done before, struck Coins from Gold, rendered as pure as it possibly could be made.

We are informed by Plutarch, (tom. iii. p. 385. London edition of 1723.) that the impression upon those Persian Coins was an archer; and from this circumstance, Agesilaus said, that he had been driven out of Asia by the King, by means of a thousand archers. For so many Daricks being sent to Athens and Thebes, and divided among the popular orators, they were induced to make war upon Sparta.

to this supposition, as Silanus the soothsayer received a talent of Gold, there being 6000 drachms in a talent, and as Cyrus had promised to pay him ten talents of Silver, the value of Gold was estimated to be to that of Silver as 10 to 1.

There are good reasons, however, for doubting the accuracy of this proportion. Plato, as above mentioned, states the proportion of 12 to 1 as a fact, free from doubt, and generally known. The place, it is true, where Cyrus rewarded Silanus, was in the neighbourhood of Babylon; and this distance from Greece might account for some difference in the relative values of the two metals, in the two different countries. But so considerable a deviation from the proportion in Greece must have struck the observation of Xenophon; and having attracted his attention, we may suppose it would have been recorded with his usual accuracy.

We are informed by Herodotus,* that Darius the son of Hystaspes enjoined, that his subjects, who discharged the tribute imposed upon them in Silver, should pay by the weight of the Babylonian talent; and that such as discharged it in Gold, should pay by the Euboic talent. The Historian also adds, that the Babylonian talent was equal to seventy Euboic minæ. If this regulation continued to be observed, and to be implied in agreements under Artaxerxes, it follows, that Cyrus promised the soothsayer 700 minæ of Silver, and paid him 60 minæ of Gold as an equivalent; and

* Herod. lib. iii. 89.

upon this supposition the value of Gold was to that of Silver as 11⅔ to 1.

It is highly probable, that this was the true proportional value of Gold to Silver at that time in Persia.* An interval of about one hundred and twenty years had elapsed from the commencement of the reign of Darius; and we may readily believe, that his regulations, concerning the discharge of tribute in the two metals, were still continued, and, consistent with strict justice, that they had been extended to payments of every description. The diminution in the value of Gold, from that which it had in the time of Darius Hystaspes, may be attributed to the extensive armaments of Xerxes, connected with other circumstances, of which, at this distant period of time, we are unable to give a clear and satisfactory account.

That Gold was at a lower value in Persia than it was in Greece, at the time of which we have been speaking, ought not to raise our astonishment. Many circumstances might be adduced to prove, that this precious metal had been, and still was, in much greater

---

* In the Philosophical Transactions for the year 1771, there is "An " Inquiry into the value of the ancient Greek and Roman Money : by " Matthew Raper, Esq." In this Inquiry Mr. Raper considers the promise of Cyrus to Silanus, and the reward made in consequence of it ; and, by supposing the Babylonian talent to weigh 72 Euboic minæ, he concludes, that the value of Gold was to that of Silver as 12 to 1. By proceeding thus, Mr. Raper procures a coincidence with the relative value stated by Plato : but this coincidence is obtained by means of a conjecture contrary to the express statement of Herodotus, as mentioned above.

plenty in Asia than in Europe: and this consideration alone is sufficient to enforce a conviction, that the proportion of 12 to 1 might exist in Greece, and that of 11⅔ to 1 in Persia, at the same time.*

In times previous to that of which we have been speaking, the precious metals were scarce in Greece. Philip, King of Macedon,† is said to have been so poor in Gold, in the former part of his reign, that he had only a small cup of it, which he placed every night under his pillow: but it was not long before this enterprising Monarch rendered it abundant in his own kingdom, and contributed to make it comparatively plentiful in Greece. Being informed, that in ancient times Gold Mines had been worked in his own dominions,‡ he caused those near Mount Pangæus to be opened. The success of this measure exceeded his expectations, as he drew from these Mines annually more than a thousand talents.§

About the same time the Phocians robbed Delphi of

* The relative values of Gold to Silver, at the principal European Mints, differ at this time considerably from one another.

† Σπάνιος γὰρ ὄντως ἦν τὸ παλαιὸν παρὰ τοῖς ῞Ελλησιν ὁ μὲν χρυσὸς ᾗ πάνυ· ὁ δὲ ἄργυρος ὀλίγος ἦν ὁ ἐν τοῖς μετάλλοις. Διὸ ᾗ Φίλιππον τὸν τῦ μεγάλυ βασιλέως 'Αλεξάνδρυ πατέρα φησὶ Δῦρις ὁ Σάμιος, φιάλιον χρυσῦν κεκτημένον, ἀεὶ τῦτ' ἔχειν κείμενον ὑπὸ τῦ προκεφαλαίυ. Athenæi Deipnosoph. lib. vi. p. 231. edit. Lugduni 1612.

‡ Senecæ Natural. Quæst. lib. vi. cap. 15. Strab. lib. vii. p. 331.

§ Diodor. Sic. tom. ii. p. 88. With the metal obtained from these Mines Philip struck his Gold Coins, called Philippics; collected together strong forces of mercenaries, and allured many Greeks by his presents to betray their country. Diodor. Sic. ibid.

the golden offerings, which had been made from time to time to Apollo;* and by this plunder they obtained Gold to the amount of more than ten thousand talents.† These circumstances contributed to render Gold so plentiful in Greece, that according to Menander,‡ who was born about the year 341 before the Christian æra, its value was estimated to be to that of Silver as 10 to 1.

It has been supposed, that Alexander completed his conquests in Asia before Gold was at this low value in Greece, and that the diminution in value happened in consequence of the wealth procured from the Persian treasures by that successful warrior: § but a careful examination of the above-mentioned circumstances may well incline us to doubt the truth of this conjecture. The Mines began to be productive to Philip ‖ in the 358th, and Alexander set out on his expedition to Asia in the 334th, year before the Christian æra; and as during this interval of twenty-four years the annual income from them was 1000 talents, or 225,000*l.* Sterling,¶ the whole sum derived from them in this period was 5,400,000*l.* Delphi was plundered, in the

* Athenæi Deipnosoph. p. 231.
† Diodor. Sic. tom. ii. p. 126. The Historian adds, ἔνιοι δὲ τῶν συγγραφέων φασὶν ἐκ ἐλάττω γενέσθαι τὰ συληθέντα τῶν ἐν τοῖς Περσικοῖς θησαυροῖς ὑπ' Ἀλεξάνδρῃ κατακτηθέντων.
‡ See Julius Pollux, lib. ix. cap. 6. §. 76.
§ See the Philosophical Transactions for 1771, p. 518.
‖ The dates are according to Wesselingius's edition of Diodorus.
¶ In reducing the sums mentioned by Diodorus to English Money, I have followed the learned Abbé Barthelemy. See Tab. XI. of his Anacharsis.

year 357 before Christ, of Gold to the amount of 10,000 talents, or 2,250,000*l.* Consequently, to the Gold in Greece at the accession of Philip to the throne of Macedon, an addition had been made to the amount of 7,650,000*l.* Sterling, previous to the expedition of Alexander into Asia. This accumulation must have had a powerful tendency to depress the value of this precious metal; and as we read of no intermediate proportion between those stated by Plato and Menander, we may conclude, that Gold was to Silver as 10 to 1 in Greece, before any accession was made to its wealth by the conquests of Alexander.* His acquisitions from the Persian treasures were great;† but his liberality was proportionally extensive. The sum in the treasury at his death amounted to 50,000 talents,‡ equivalent to 11,250,000*l.* Sterling; but we are not informed how much of this was in Gold. This precious metal, without doubt, was rendered more plentiful in Greece by what flowed into it from Alexander's seizures in

---

* Positive testimony, as to the time when the proportion of 10 to 1 began, cannot be obtained from Menander, as it is uncertain when he wrote the passage in which it is stated, and to what period it alluded. He was born, as mentioned above, about the year 341, and died about the year 293, before Christ : he therefore survived Alexander 32 years. But it is to be remembered, that the passage now under consideration was put into the mouth of a character in one of his plays : and it is highly probable, that the time affixed to the action of this piece was some years previous to that at which it was written.

† Several passages in Quintus Curtius might be produced in proof of Alexander's great acquisitions of wealth in Asia, and also of his great liberality.

‡ Justin. lib. xiii. cap. 1.

Asia;* but the opinion of those seems to have been well founded, who limited the amount of the influx to about ten thousand talents,† equivalent to 2,250,000*l*. Sterling.

There is reason to suppose, that the value of Gold continued to be to that of Silver as 10 to 1 in Greece, during the space of 170 years after the death of Alexander: but, in order to shew that this conjecture is well founded, we must turn our attention to the relative values of the precious metals at the Roman Mint.

More than 176 years elapsed from the building of Rome, according to Pliny, before the inhabitants of that city used coined Money. Servius Tullius, their sixth King, introduced it;‡ and, consistent with the frugality and limited mercantile transactions of the people, it was of Brass. This continued to be the only current Money till the 485th year of Rome, or the 269th year before Christ, when Silver Coins were first struck in that city.§ For some time previous to this last mentioned period, several circumstances had been gradually contributing to render such an extension of the Coinage necessary. The soldiers no longer depended upon their own individual industry in peace for their subsistence in war;

---

* Athen. lib. vi. p. 231. † See Note †. p. 277.

‡ Plinii Natur. Histor. lib. xxxiii. 13. At the same time Pliny informs us, upon the authority of Timæus, an ancient historian, that, previous to the first Coinage of Money, the Romans used unstamped bars of Brass, or Copper, as a medium of exchange.

§ Plinii ibid. Argentum signatum est anno urbis 485, Q. Fabio consule, quinque annis ante primum bellum Punicum

during almost a century and a half they had received regular pay from the state, and in return they had made several very important additions to its territories. They had obliged Pyrrhus to quit Italy, and had reduced the Tarentines to submission: and by these and other successes they had much extended the Roman dominion. The consequence of this was an adequate increase of their military establishments, and a correspondent extension of Coinage for their support.

The mark impressed upon the first Silver Coins at Rome was a chariot and a pair of horses, or a chariot and four horses; and according to these impressions they were called Bigati or Quadrigati: but Denarii is the general expression by which they were denominated.

Sixty-two years after the first Coinage of Silver at Rome,* Gold Coins called Aurei were first struck at that place. One scruple of Gold was then equivalent to twenty sesterces; which made for a pound, (according to Pliny,) in the proportion of the sesterces of the time, 900 sesterces. This statement of Pliny's has given much trouble to writers on ancient Coins, and has caused much variation in their calculations of the relative value of Gold to Silver at that time.

The first difficulty which occurs, on entering upon such a calculation, is, to determine the number of denarii then in the pound; as different writers have

---

* Aureus nummus post annum LXII. percussus est, quam argenteus, ita ut scrupulum valeret sestertiis vicenis: quod effecit in libras, ratione sestertiorum, qui tunc erant, sestertios DCCCC. Plinii Natur. Histor. lib. xxxiii. 13.

entertained different opinions concerning this circumstance. A persuasion that there were seven denarii in the ounce, at the time now under consideration, is supported by the strongest testimonies, and has therefore the highest claim to our belief. The assertions of Celsus * and Scribonius Largus † are clear and express to this purpose; and Pliny himself, when speaking of the debasements of Money, by lessening the weight, says, that the just number of denarii in the pound was 84.‡ This being allowed, the value of a pound of Silver was 336 sesterces, there being four sesterces in every denarius; and there being 288 scruples in a pound, and one scruple of Gold being valued at 20 sesterces, the value of a pound of Gold was 5760 sesterces. The value of coined Gold was therefore to that of Silver as 5760 to 336, or as $17\frac{1}{7}$ to 1.

The passage in Pliny, however, upon which this calculation is founded, guards us against concluding that this was the relative value of Gold to Silver in Bullion. According to the latter part of the sentence, and the best interpretations of it, the republic gained 900 sesterces in a pound of Gold,§ at the rate at which this first Coinage passed. Consequently the value of a pound of Gold in Bullion was 4860 sesterces; and

* Sed et antea sciri volo, in uncia pondus denariorum septem esse. Lib. v. cap. 17.

† Æque enim in libra denarii octoginta quatuor apud nos, quot drachmæ apud Græcos incurrunt. P. 6. edit. Patavii, 1655.

‡ Plinii Natur. Histor. lib. xxxiii. 46.

§ See Harduin's edition of Pliny, tom. ii. p. 612. and Clarke on Coins, p. 385.

therefore Gold was to Silver as 4860 to 336, or as $14\frac{13}{28}$ to 1.*

Several reasons may be advanced for the high rate

---

* Other conclusions have been made concerning the relative values of the precious metals at Rome, when Gold was first coined there; but they are founded upon an imaginary correction of the passage in Pliny, already mentioned, from a persuasion, that as it now stands it is erroneous. See Clarke on Coins, p. 387.

Mr. Raper, in the Philosophical Transactions for 1771, proposed the following as the sense of the passage (in Note *. in p. 280) now under consideration.

" The Gold Money was coined sixty-two years after the Silver, and " the scruple passed for twenty sesterces, which, as the sesterce was " reckoned at that time, ($2\frac{1}{2}$ asses,) made the pound of Gold worth nine " hundred *Silver* denarii (of 16 asses each)." p. 490.

" If the scruple was valued at 20 sesterces," says Mr. Raper, "the " pound, instead of being worth 900, must have been worth 5760, such " sesterces : but if for *sestertios* DCCÇC, we read *denarios* DCCCC, the " account will be clear and intelligible. The words *ratione sestertiorum,* " *qui tunc erant*, imply, that the sesterce of that age was different from " the sesterce of Pliny's time : but the quarter of the Silver denarius, " or Nummus Sestertius, of 4 asses, was the same at both times ; " and we know of no other sesterce but the ancient one of $2\frac{1}{2}$ asses. " Twenty such sesterces make 50 asses, for the value of the scruple of " Gold ; which, multiplied by 288, (the number of scruples in the " Roman pound) give 14,400 asses for the value of the pound of " Gold. And reckoning 16 asses to the Silver denarius, (which it " passed for at the time of this Coinage,) 14,400 asses make just 900 " such denarii ; which is Pliny's number." p. 518.

" If the pound weight of Gold was worth 900 denarii, 84 of which " were coined out of the pound of Silver, the value of Gold to Silver " must have been in the proportion of 900 to 84, or as $10\frac{5}{7}$ to 1." p. 520.

This proposed correction is very ingenious ; but the writer of this Appendix thinks that it is open to two strong objections. Mr. Raper has not supported it by the reading in any one MS.; and, from the general disposition and condition of the Romans, it may well be supposed, that Gold had a much higher value among them at that time than in Greece.

at which the first Gold Coins passed at Rome. The metal was far from being plentiful in the city, and the Romans had exacted the tributes from the conquered nations in Silver, not in Gold.* The interval between the first Coinage of Silver and that of Gold had also been filled up with events highly important to the Romans: it comprehended the whole of the first Punic war; Sicily had been reduced to submission; the Romans had become powerful at sea, and the second Punic war had been almost brought to a successful conclusion.

Hannibal, it is true, had repeatedly defeated their armies with great slaughter: but these defeats, instead of repressing, roused the bravery and patriotism of the Romans to the highest degree of enthusiasm. Whatever might be their situation, they shewed a disposition to face every danger, and undergo every possible hardship, for the good and glory of their country; and therefore it is probable they received the Gold Coins at a high rate of exchange, not only for their novelty, but from a conviction, that by so doing they were advancing the objects, which they had most at heart.

The above-mentioned proportion in the relative value of Gold to Silver did not continue long at Rome. Soon after her first Coinage of Gold her arms became

* Equidem miror populum Romanum victis gentibus in tributo semper argentum imperitasse, non aurum : sicut Carthagini cum Hannibale victæ argenti pondo annua in quinquaginta annos, nihil auri. Plinii Natur. Histor. lib. xxxiii. 15.

victorious in every quarter of the old world; her conquests were rapid and extensive; she quickly became acquainted with the riches and customs of eastern nations; and with profound policy she adopted such as were suitable to her own views of acquisition. Accordingly we find in the conditions on which the Romans made peace with the Ætolians, about 189 years before the Christian æra, that they coincided with the Greeks in estimating the value of Gold to be to that of Silver as 10 to 1.* From this circumstance there is reason to believe, that during all the convulsions and vicissitudes, which Greece experienced from the time of Alexander the Great to the period last mentioned, the relative values of the precious metals continued the same in that country.

An extraordinary influx of either of the precious metals into any place or district, and a subsequent and extensive exchange of it for the other, must always lessen its value. We have a remarkable proof of this upon Cæsar's return to Rome, with the plunder which he had collected in Gaul. He had amassed Gold in that country, according to Suetonius, to such an amount, that it was sold for three thousand sesterces, or seven hundred and fifty denarii, a pound, throughout Italy and the provinces.†

---

* Pro argento si aurum dare mallent, darent convenit; dum pro argenteis decem aureus unus valeret. Livii lib. xxxviii. 11.

† Suetonius, speaking of Cæsar, says, In Gallia fana templaque Deûm donis referta expilavit: urbes diruit, sæpius ob prædam quam ob delictum: unde factum ut auro abundaret, ternisque millibus

But writers on the subject differ in their computations of the relative value of the precious metals from this statement; some supposing, that the pound mentioned by Suetonius was the pound in weight, others, that it was the pound in tale. Upon the hypothesis that the pound in weight was meant, the value of Gold was to that of Silver as 750 to 84, or as $8\tfrac{3}{14}$ to 1,* there being 84 denarii in the pound weight. There is more reason however to believe, that the pound in tale, or one hundred denarii to the pound, was that which Suetonius meant, as it was by this that the Romans computed the value of exchange in their currency. Admitting, therefore, that there was no departure at this time from their usual practice, the value of Gold was to that of Silver as 750 to 100, or as $7\tfrac{1}{2}$ to 1.†

This depressed value of Gold can only be considered as a transient convulsion in the relative estimations of the precious metals in Rome and its dependencies. The cause was inadequate to the production of any durable effect; and it is highly probable, that the Gold of Gaul, when it had passed into the currency of the empire, was insufficient to support an advancement in the value of Silver through such an extensive circulation.

The tendency of Cæsar's conquests in Gaul to

---

nummum in libras promercale per Italiam provinciasque divideret. Suetonius de Jul. Cæsar. cap. LIV. edit. Pitin.

* Arbuthnot adopts this proportion, as does also Mr. Raper, in the Philosophical Transactions for 1771.

† Hostus adopts this proportion; as does also Clarke in his Book on Coins.

depreciate the value of Gold in Rome, and its provinces, perhaps might induce some to believe, that Alexander's victories in Asia must have had a similar effect in Greece; and to a degree beyond that admitted in this Dissertation. But it is to be remarked, that Cæsar's principal object in Gaul was plunder, and that he and his army returned to Rome with the spoils of the conquered country. On the contrary, Alexander's principal object was foreign conquest, not plunder; he never returned home: and his armies remained in the countries, which he had subjected to his power.

We cannot say with confidence how long the last mentioned proportion between the two precious metals continued; but we find, that in the time of Claudius, about a century after Cæsar's return from Gaul, the value of Gold was considerably advanced: for under this Emperor's reign it was thought proper, according to Tacitus[*] and the younger Pliny,[†] to limit the fee of an advocate to ten thousand sesterces; and this legal fee is stated in the Digest[‡] at one hundred aurei. Now as 10,000 sesterces were equal to 2,500 denarii, it follows,

---

[*] Tacitus, speaking of the Emperor Claudius, and this regulation, says, capiendis pecuniis posuit modum, usque ad dena sestertia, quem egressi repetundarum tenerentur. Annalium lib. xi. cap. 7.

[†] Suberat edicto senatusconsultum hoc : Omnes, quicquid negotii haberent, jurare, priusquam agerent, jubebantur, nihil se ob advocationem cuiquam dedisse, promisisse, cavisse. His enim verbis, ac mille præterea, et vænire advocationes et emi vetabantur. Peractis tamen negotiis, permittebantur pecuniam duntaxat decem millium dare. C. Plinii Epist. lib. v. ep. 25.

[‡] Licita autem quantitas intelligitur pro singulis causis usque ad centum aureos. Lib. 1. tit. 13. §. 12.

that the value of Gold was to that of Silver as 2,500 to 200, or as 12½ to 1.

We can trace the duration of these relative values of the precious metals at Rome, with more certainty than any which we have before recorded. There is no reason to doubt of their continuance through Nero's reign, as we have positive proof of their existence in the time of Galba. For Tacitus informs us, that when Otho entertained the Emperor Galba at supper, he gave to each man of the cohort, which mounted guard that night, a hundred sesterces;* and Suetonius, speaking of the same thing, says, that he gave each man an aureus.† Hence it is evident, that in Galba's reign, twenty-five denarii were equivalent to one aureus; and admitting, as usual, that the aureus was double the denarius in weight, the value of Gold was to that of Silver as 12½ to 1.

It appears, that these relative values of the precious metals continued during the interval between Galba and Alexander Severus, a period of more than a century and a half; for Dion Cassius, the Historian, flourished under the reign of this last mentioned Emperor; and he says expressly, that an aureus was equal in value to

---

* Per speciem convivii, quoties Galba apud Othonem epularetur, cohorti excubias agenti, viritim centenos nummos divideret. Tacit. Histor. lib. i. c. 24.

† Suetonius also, speaking of Otho's proceedings to obtain the supreme authority, says, Nullo igitur officii aut ambitionis in quemquam genere omisso, quoties cœna principem acciperet, aureos excubanti cohorti viritim dividebat. Suetonius de Othone. c. 4.

25 denarii: * a statement which gives the relative value of Gold to Silver as 12½ to 1, as before.

Although we seek in vain to ascertain the further duration of this proportion, it is highly probable, that it continued some time after the reign of Alexander Severus, as the state of the empire justifies such a supposition. At what period it ceased we are unable to say; but under the reign of Constantine the Great we find, that the value of Gold was much diminished. In his time also we find that new names had been affixed both to the Gold and Silver Coins: the Aureus was now known by the name of Solidus, and the Denarius, by that of Milliarensis. According to one of the laws of this Emperor, six solidi, of four scruples each, weighed an ounce;† and, according to one of the Glosses upon the Basilica, a solidus was equal to fourteen milliarenses.‡ Hence four scruples, or one sixth of an ounce of Gold, was equivalent to $\frac{14}{8}$ ounces of Silver,

* Histor. Rom. p. 784. edit. Hamb. 1752. From the passage in Dion Cassius, here referred to, there is reason to believe, that the value of Gold was to that of Silver as 12½ to 1, in the time of Augustus. For the Historian having mentioned the presents received by that Emperor, after his palace had been burned down, says, I call that Coin an Aureus, which, according to the custom of the Romans, is equivalent to 25 denarii.

† Siquis solidos appendere voluerit auri cocti, sex solidos quaternorum scripulorum nostris vultibus figuratos adpendat pro singulis unciis. Cod. Theod. lib. xii. tit. 7. §. 1.

The old reading is *septem solidos* &c. but there is reason to believe *sex* to be the true. See Thesaur. Variar. Lectionum D. Guidi Panciroli, p. 91.

‡ Thesaurus Juris Romani, &c. cum Præfatione Everardi Ottonis; p. 1764. Lugduni Batav. 1725.

there being now 8 denarii in the ounce. It therefore follows, that one ounce of Gold was equivalent to $\frac{84}{8}$, or $10\frac{1}{2}$ ounces of Silver, and consequently, that the value of Gold was to that of Silver as $10\frac{1}{2}$ to 1.

The history of the times does not enable us to trace the continuance of these relative values, and to mark the precise period, at which they ceased. From the political alterations, which succeeded the reign of Constantine, we may reasonably conjecture, that they were not of long duration; especially as we find, that under Arcadius and Honorius, about sixty years after Constantine, the value of Gold was much increased. According to the Theodosian code, the number of solidi in the pound was 72,* as in the reign of Constantine; and by a law made by the two Emperors mentioned above, five solidi were equivalent to a pound of Silver.† Hence the solidus was four scruples, and therefore 20 scruples of Gold were equivalent to 288 scruples of Silver. Consequently the value of Gold was to that of Silver as 288 to 20, or as $14\frac{2}{5}$ to 1.

The variations in the estimation of Gold to Silver, here recorded, may be attributed to causes, which must ever have a similar influence in society. A failure of

* Illud cautionis adjicimus ut quotiescumque certa summa solidorum pro tituli quantitate debetur, et auri massa transmittitur, in septuaginta duos solidos libra feratur accepta. Cod. Theod. lib. xii. tit. 6. §. 13.

† Jubemus, ut pro argenti summa quam quis thesauris fuerat illaturus, inferendi auri accipiat facultatem : ita ut pro singulis libris argenti quinos solidos inferat. Cod. Justin. lib. x. tit. 76.

the Mines, or whatever tends to promote the circulation of the Coins of either metal more than the other, will enhance its value, and therefore the price of Gold, when compared with other metals, will be raised, in consequence of a scanty supply from the earth, extreme luxury, or extensive trade. Wherever the second of these prevails, Gold will be most esteemed by the rich for its real or imaginary utility. Ornaments of it will gratify their pride, and Coins of it will most conveniently purchase for them costly indulgences. In large commercial concerns this precious metal will also be most desired, as by means of its intervention extensive exchanges may be carried on with the greatest facility. A dread of public insecurity and political convulsions will also have the same tendency, as the timid, and indeed the prudent, will be induced thereby to conceal their Coin, which can be hid most conveniently, from a fond hope, that, when the commotions are over, their property will procure them, in happier days, the comforts and enjoyments of life.

As Silver Coins are most convenient for the payment of troops, war must have a tendency to raise the price of this metal. A turn of commerce, unfavourable to a country, will also affect the relative values of the precious metals, and will raise the price of that, which is preferred by those with whom the inhabitants trade.

These principles account for the foregoing variations. The unsuccessful exertions of Darius Hystaspes against Greece, and the vast armaments of his son Xerxes, directed with similar fortune against the same country, must have had a considerable influence upon the relative values of the precious metals. During the preparations of these, splendour and luxury must in some degree have given way to the hope of conquest, and the prospect of revenge; and, with such a disposition, a preference of Silver must have been adopted, as by means of Coins of this metal the power was to be preserved, by which the objects in view were most likely to be obtained. Silver was not only most convenient, but even necessary, for paying the bulk of the forces; and in order to procure a sufficiency of this metal for carrying on the wars, Gold was exchanged, without doubt, at a lower value than formerly. The same circumstances must have had a similar tendency in Greece; and this tendency must have been rendered still more strong by the victories, which the Grecians obtained over the Asiatic invaders. That the value of Gold, therefore, when compared to Silver, should have been as 13 to 1 in the time of Herodotus, and that it should have been reduced to be as 12 to 1 in the time of Plato, is fully accounted for by the influence of these events.

The causes of the next reduction of the value of Gold in Greece have been already stated. Previous to the end of the fourth century, before Christ, the golden offerings, which the Asiatic Monarchs had made to the temple of Delphi, had only contributed to the splendour of that place; but having been seized by the

Phocians, there is every reason to believe, that they were converted into Coin, and circulated through Greece. The Mines which Philip of Macedon opened, about the same time that Delphi was plundered, supplied him with this precious metal to a large amount; and what he derived from these fruitful sources he appears to have distributed among the Grecian states, with a degree of liberality, corresponding to the extent of his ambition. The additions to the current Money of Greece, from these events, must have born a considerable proportion to the whole circulating medium of the country; and their tendency to lessen the value of Gold must have been aided by the frugality and contempt of wealth, which then pervaded almost all the states of Greece. That this precious metal therefore in Greece should be as 10 to 1, when compared with Silver, in the time of Menander, may justly be attributed to these circumstances; and as the subsequent successes of Alexander the Great, in Persia, must have brought into circulation much Gold, which had been formerly hoarded up in the treasuries, or kept for splendour, there is reason to conclude, that it had the same relative value to Silver in this last mentioned country, after his conquests.

When Gold Coins were first struck at Rome, the virtue and patriotism of the people were in their full vigour. Individual ease and emolument were absorbed in the view of general welfare and public honour: the high value, therefore, at which the Gold Coins were received, is rather to be understood as implying a donation to the state, than to be considered as a fair estimation of the relative values of the precious metals.

Frequent and extensive successes in war rendered the continuation of such donations unnecessary, and induced the Romans in a short time to conform to the practice, which they found prevailing in Greece, of estimating the value of Gold to be to that of Silver as 10 to 1.

The next succeeding depreciation of Gold was when Cæsar returned to Rome, after his conquests and acquisitions in Gaul. To what has been already said on this reduced value of Gold, it may not be improper to add, that perhaps the sudden and extensive exchange of this precious metal was owing to a conviction in Cæsar's mind, that Silver, and Coins of lower value, were more necessary for carrying his ambitious designs into execution.

Of the advanced value of Gold in the time of Augustus, and its long continuance afterwards, the only apparent cause was general profligacy. Licentiousness of manners, prodigality and rapaciousness, were the general features of the Roman character from the time of this last mentioned Emperor till the reign of Constantine the Great. In this interval a few displayed eminent virtues and abilities; but they were unable to produce a lasting reform among the bulk of the people. This interval was also marked by frequent and violent political convulsions; and all these circumstances must have maintained a dread of public insecurity in the minds of those, who observed present occurrences, and provided for future. There is every reason to believe, that these were the general causes, which rendered the value of Gold to be to that of Silver as 12½ to 1, during a period of about three hundred years.

The victories of Constantine the Great, and a general confidence in the wisdom and vigour of his administration, removed for a while these public evils; and, together with the reliance on Government, Gold in such plenty returned into circulation, that its relative value to Silver became as 10½ to 1.

The empire, however, did not long enjoy this prosperity. Divided power and consequent rivalry, civil war and internal distrust, imbecility in Government, and invasions by powerful enemies, revived a dread of public insecurity, and enhanced the value of Gold, when compared to Silver, to be as 14⅔ to 1.

As there is reason to believe, that the first of the relative values, already mentioned, existed under the reign of Darius Hystaspes, and as the last were settled under the Emperors Arcadius and Honorius, the existence of the whole amounted to more than nine hundred years. Some of them, it is highly probable, prevailed throughout the whole extent of the Macedonian and Roman empires, and consequently regulated the commercial intercourse of a larger portion of the globe than any relative values, more ancient, of the precious metals, or any which succeeded them. From a review of the whole there is also reason to conclude, that the extreme relative values of Gold, when compared with Silver, neither enhanced by a dread of public insecurity and general luxury, or depressed by sudden and unusual preparations for war, were as 12 to 1, and as 10 to 1.

www.ingramcontent.com/pod-product-compliance
Lightning Source LLC
Chambersburg PA
CBHW022101230426
43672CB00008B/1242